RAW MATE

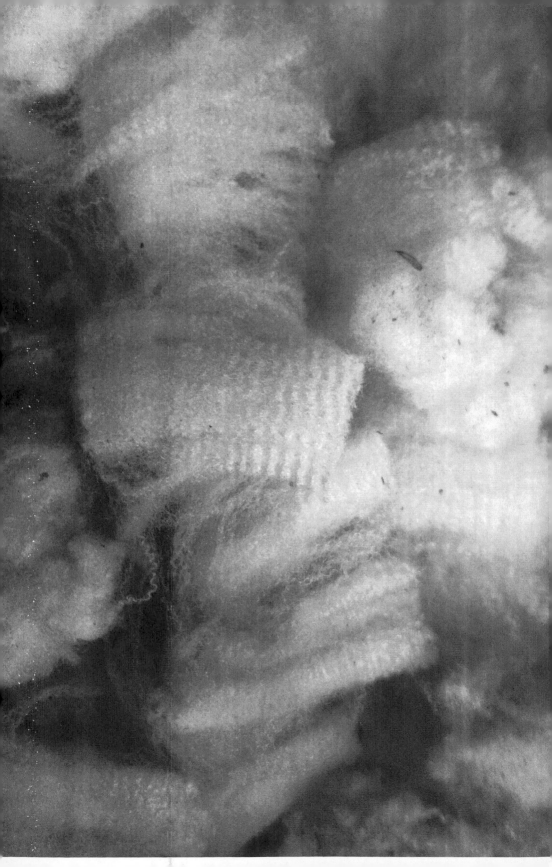

Raw Material

WORKING WOOL IN THE WEST

Stephany Wilkes

Oregon State University Press Corvallis

Library of Congress Cataloging-in-Publication Data

Names: Wilkes, Stephany, author.
Title: Raw material : working wool in the West / Stephany Wilkes.
Description: Corvallis : Oregon State University Press, 2018. | Includes bibliographical
    references and index.
Identifiers: LCCN 2018024381 (print) | LCCN 2018028907 (ebook) | ISBN
    9780870719523 (ebook) | ISBN 9780870719516 (original trade pbk. : alk. paper)
Subjects: LCSH: Wilkes, Stephany. | Sheep shearers (Persons)—West (U.S.)—
    Biography. | Sheep industry—West (U.S.) | Wool industry—West (U.S.)
Classification: LCC HD8039.S472 (ebook) | LCC HD8039.S472 U69 2018 (print) |
    DDC 636.3/145092 [B]—dc23
LC record available at https://lccn.loc.gov/2018024381

♾ This paper meets the requirements of ANSI/NISO Z39.48-1992
(Permanence of Paper).

Unless otherwise noted, all photos by author.

Oregon State University Press
121 The Valley Library
Corvallis OR 97331-4501
541-737-3166 • fax 541-737-3170
www.osupress.oregonstate.edu

for Ian
and
the people of this book

You can buy wool cheaper in Australia; let your forty acres of sheep grazing land go to waste. You can buy rice cheaper in some foreign clime; let your rice lands go to waste. You can buy woolen goods cheaper; burn your woolen factories, let your water-power run to waste, and cease to work your coal mines. God made a mistake when He gave you these gifts.

—William Lawrence, The American Wool Interest, in an address to the Farmers' National Congress at Chicago, November 11, 1887

You may start shearing for the money, but you end up shearing for the places it takes you and the people you meet.

—Mike McWilliam, champion sheep shearer and instructor

Contents

Author's Note

In the interest of privacy, two customers' names have been changed, and some names and identifying details have been omitted. In addition to my own sources (audio recordings, photos, journal entries, and field notes), I occasionally cite publicly available, complementary sources in the notes section, to provide interested readers with supplementary information.

Acknowledgments

This book is out in the world only because of the encouragement, nudging, and generosity of Ana Maria Spagna, who made it happen.

Mary Elizabeth Braun, Micki Reaman, Marty Brown, and Tom Booth at Oregon State University Press patiently shepherded this book, and me. Erin Kirk New designed its beautiful cover.

I have only followed what Rebecca Burgess had the courage to start. If she had not conducted her wardrobe experiment and held a wool symposium, not a single story in this book would have happened to me.

I am indebted to Jordan Reed, who shows me new ways of seeing and being in the world. His guidance, patience, and mentorship are the reasons I shear today. Robin Lynde has taught me most everything I know about sheep behavior and care, pasture management, lambing, hoof trimming, and everything else that transpires in and around a barn.

Sarah, Matt, Rebekah, Felicity, Chloe, and Gregory Gilbert bring light, levity, refreshing competence, and adventure to my life. All of my shearing classmates and customers (human and sheep alike) keep me excited about my work. I am only getting better at this, I promise.

I thank all of my teachers, past and present, but most especially Gary Vorderbruggen, Mike McWilliam, John Harper, Ian McKenzie, Robert Irwin, John Sanchez, Ron Cole, Jim Lewers, James T. Williams, Ryan Kieffer, Randy Helms, Trevor Hollenback, Judd Redden, Julia Scheeres, Anisse Gross, Joshua Mohr, Pam Houston, Ray and Barbara March, Elizabeth Bernstein, and Chelsea Lindman.

My fellow wool people have bestowed unwavering support and encouragement, most especially Hannah Bird, Carrie Butler, Bonnie Chase, Roy and Gynna Clemes, Lani Estill, Sally Fox, Carol Frechette, Cricket Frerking, Kate Hoag, Marie Hoff, Jaime Irwin, Alison Kent, Fran LeClerc, Joy and Jon Lee, Robin Lynde, Ralph McWilliams,

Krystle Moody, Mary Pettis-Sarley, Heather Podoll, Cara Randall, Kim Rodrigues, Lisa Waterman, and Allison Isaacs and Diane Dias at Imagiknit.

This manuscript benefited from the early reading and suggested changes of Lauren Back, Alice Cascorbi, Joanna Ellsworth, Jennifer Kelley, Robin Lynde, Rayne MacGeorge, Mary Noble-Tolla, Tadhg O'Higgins, Tom Pyun, and Lindsey Thordason. Author Clara Parkes explicitly connected the craft of shearing with fiber availability and, in so doing, lit the way to vocation.

I am grateful to the San Francisco Public Library, especially for the rare books room at the main branch, and to every person who digitized old city directories. Open Library enabled me to access books well over a hundred years old and, miraculously, instantly read them on my Kindle.

Mike Chaplin, Raymond Chow, Carlos Narváez, Wanda Leonard, and Bettina Schneider heal me from injury and make me physically stronger, to the extent I allow it.

Jeska Dzwigalski Kittenbrink and Rebecca Rudnicki have supported and encouraged me in all ways for over twenty years. Few people expressed genuine support in my decision to head for greener pastures and diminished income, and I will never forget those who did: Terri Shoemaker, Beatrice Thomas, D'Arcy Drollinger ("Be so big, I can't imagine you bigger"), Gary Riotto, Salvatore Manzi, Christina Harbridge, Patrick Higgs, Aram Price, Julia Turner, and every face in my dance family kept me on an often daunting path.

My trail angel, Janet Abra Sollod (1974–2017), and Jon Dudus (1977–2015) departed too soon. Better this book had been each of theirs.

My family is my greatest gift. Nicholas Filimon, Kathryn and Noel Kelly, Stephen Filimon and Vivian Caputo, and Stephany and the late Robert Luszczak have unconditionally loved and supported me in all endeavors, no matter what they may have thought about them. My brother, Nicholas, periodically asked, "When are you going to quit your job so you can shear more?" My mother, Kathryn Kelly, and my father, Stephen Filimon, have always encouraged me to find fulfilling work and live life on my terms. They provided ample, unstructured time for me to read, write, and play, free range and without hovering, and created a world in which I was able to think for long stretches and direct my own behavior.

Timothy and Leslie Wilkes feed me, house me, share their laundry room with stinky clothes and fleeces, and host a sullen, frustrated writer on their front porch. Michael Jon Watt shows me how to make it work.

And Ian, my life, finds the missing sheep in manuscripts, removes the "eons" that aren't, roustabouts, abides dags on the floor mat of the car, receives unfair blame for bruises bestowed by sheep, and patiently listens to more fiber and writing talk than anyone deserves. I am so glad you did not move to Chicago, for here we are. You are my greatest joy.

ONE

Emigrant

Two days ago, a former rodeo cowboy—a barrel of a man—said to me, "I tell you what, little sister. My first year, a man told me, 'I been to boot camp and shearin' school and shearin' school's harder.' And I think he's right."

Having had the shit kicked out of me by a sheep, I do too.

I rehashed the beating I had deserved for my inexperienced sheep handling. The ewe I'd pulled out of the pen after lunch seemed so much heavier than the sheep I'd sheared that morning, with a smooth, stretched-out, full belly, a sloshing, six-gallon ruminant system inside. Rotund. Breathing like a bull. Energetic.

As soon as I flipped the fighting, wheezing ewe onto her back, I could see what must be mastitis. Lambs had weaned recently. One side of her udder was swollen and hard, the tip of her teat engorged with white chunks that looked like dried cottage cheese: pus, congealed milk, or both. I wished I could administer an anti-inflammatory painkiller I did not have. Little wonder she fought so. I raised my left hand, shouted for someone to hand me a grease pen, and marked the sheep's forehead, a bright blue signal to the shepherd that this sheep had a problem to which he must attend.

Unfortunately—full or not, mastitis or not—this gal had to be sheared. In order to avoid nicking or cutting a sheep's teats and udder, shearers gently hold and roll the udder out of the way. This keeps the shearer fully aware of where both udder and hand are in relation to the sharp, motor-propelled shears. I preemptively winced at the thought of making this move, recalling what certain new-mother friends had told me about their own mastitis. I did not want to touch that udder. The sheep would, understandably, want to kill me. I had no choice.

While I dillydallied, trying to both avoid the inevitable and work up my courage to do it, the weight of the ewe's rumen pressed against her diaphragm, making her feel as if she were suffocating. I had trouble holding her up between my thighs. Laden with lanolin, she slid down. I grabbed her forelegs to pull her back up between my quads, the two of us looking a bit like trapeze artists who have just locked forearms. Sheep hate having their legs grabbed, but they're the only nonslippery thing *to* grab, a mistaken reflex only experience can correct. The sheep responded by bracing her back against the floor, rearing up, and bucking her back end and hips off the plywood floor like a bronco—as I held her forelegs, she folded herself in half, scooped both rear legs up, and reached them all the way back over her head, kicking them straight into my chest, sternum, chin, lip, and forehead, leaving scallop-shaped scrapes and cuts. Her hooves needed trimming.

And that was before I'd gotten anywhere near her infected udder. Nearly an hour later, the ewe stood in the sun, several pounds lighter for the wool she'd lost, reunited with her flock, and munching alfalfa from a feeder, by all appearances content. I felt like I'd been beaten around a boxing ring.

Ten minutes into the drive to my father-in-law's house, the sun sliding behind the western hills, I admit I have no business operating a motor vehicle. My arms cannot control the steering wheel at sixty-five miles an hour, slow even by right-lane standards on California Highway 101. My mouth actually waters at the first sight of a Coca-Cola billboard, which I didn't know was possible. I need sugar.

I cannot go into a restaurant. I reek of manure. My heavy, brown work pants are soaked with so much lanolin that I look like I'm wearing chaps. Stray bits of wool and straw are plastered to my arms and chest, shellacked in place by dried sweat. Bruises cover my forearms, neck, chest, and chin, and my bottom lip is thinly split.

Cloverdale is the next town. I exit and, like a mirage, Pick's Drive-In appears, its 1950s sign straight from a California road-trip dream. It has a counter and stools outside and a patch of grass. I don't have the strength to pull up the emergency brake and will just have to take my chances with an earthquake.

A look of concern passes over the perky, smiling face of the teenage girl at the counter. I sit on a stool and order a root beer float. "If I didn't know better I'd say you spent your day in a barn," she says. If this is a witty way of telling me I stink, well, that's a fact.

A few minutes later the root beer float slides across the counter, foamy, a vanilla butterfat iceberg melting into brown, dancing fizz. The domed plastic top has condensation I could lick. "On the house," she says. I hand the $5 bill already in my shaking right fist to her, managing a "tip, thanks" before turning around on the stool and weeping at her kindness. Back in my car, I sip at the root beer float through sobs and hand tremors so strong I almost spill it.

I snivel, snotty and self-pitying. Today is Wednesday, the third day of a five-day sheep-shearing school. Tomorrow morning, our class will be half the size it was today. I am not the only one who had a rough go of it.

It began innocently enough. I moved to California in early 2007 to take a chance on the man who would, happily, become my husband. I signed up for a beginning knitting class at a local yarn shop, hoping to make new friends and brush up on the knitting skills my grandmother had taught me twenty years earlier. I needed yarn for my class project and, though I didn't know much about yarn, I knew that I'd moved to one of the wool-producing states in the United States. California is second only to Texas, followed by Colorado, Wyoming, and Utah.[1]

I checked the yarn labels as I squished each delightfully cushy skein and my heart sank: every richly dyed hank was imported, primarily from Peru, Uruguay, China, Turkey, and sometimes England or Ireland. But the yarn shop occupied two large storefronts, and skeins were stacked to the ceiling in both. I figured I was just missing something, so I asked the clerk, "Where's your local yarn section?"

Her brow furrowed. "Oh! Hmm…I don't think we have any local yarn," she said. "Lamb's Pride is made in Nebraska, but I think that's the only US yarn we have." She reached into a shelving unit stuffed with yarn, from floor to ceiling, extracted two skeins of Lamb's Pride yarn, and held them out to me. I stared at the lone brand of domestically made yarn in just two weights, worsted and bulky. Lovely though it was, how could it be all there was?

Six countries (Australia, China, New Zealand, Argentina, South Africa, and Uruguay) account for approximately 55 percent of global wool output.[2] But according to the United States Department of Agriculture (USDA), 3.7 million US sheep still produced 27 million pounds of wool in 2013. In California alone, more than four hundred thousand wool-producing sheep provided 2.6 million pounds of wool. However, the big surprise, the statistic that stunned me—only .03 percent of California's wool is processed within the state. Most US-grown wool is exported, 65 percent to China and 35 percent to India. California, producer of nearly six thousand bales of wool annually (enough wool to fill twenty semitruck trailers every year[3]), remains a net importer of wool goods.[4]

This did not make sense to me. With sheep all over the American West, why wasn't any of their wool available as 100 percent California yarn and, subsequently, a sweater? Why did we "import" the wool we'd grown and exported? Local food was all the rage, especially in the San Francisco Bay Area, with its world-famous farmers markets and residents like Alice Waters, founder of Chez Panisse, and Michael Pollan, Mr. Omnivore's Dilemma himself. Everyone wanted to know their food and their farmer and felt obliged to cook things like nettles, sunchokes, and ramps, which are wild-harvested leeks. Didn't these same people care about where their clothes came from? Weren't synthetic fibers at least as off-putting as a factory-farmed hamburger?

I began my search with the recently released and popular *The Knitter's Book of Wool* to learn more about the domestic yarn landscape. Yarn, after all, is the foundation of all fabric. Spun and woven finely and tightly enough, the thinnest threads become fabric and, later, our clothing. In the first pages of her book, author Clara Parkes alludes to the same problem I'd noticed, but implies the tide is starting to turn:

> Just as the food world is moving away from large-scale monoculture toward locally produced artisanal products, the knitting world is embracing a return to the local and artisanal. Sheep farms, spinners, and large yarn companies alike are producing new yarns...that represent diverse kinds of fiber. The next time you discover a new skein of wool...I want you to have a good idea where it came from, how it's likely to behave, and what you should do with it.

Parkes's book increased my appreciation for wool, and though its purpose is not to explain why local yarn isn't already available, it does hint at some challenges, including a "severe shortage of shearers in the United States." Though it may seem obvious, I had not realized how fundamental shearing—the act of removing wool from sheep—is to the fiber-production process. I also felt concerned: Was a shortage of shearers one of the barriers to obtaining domestically produced yarn?

I will never understand why my next thought was, "This might be something I could help with." I had never seen a sheep shearing in real life, nor had I handled—or even petted—a sheep. I had no idea what was involved and, strangely, did not think to dig more deeply into why there were so few shearers to begin with. Curious, I searched online for "sheep shearing schools." Though there were hardly any in the United States and just one in California, that one happened to be a two-hour drive north of my San Francisco home. I signed up for email notifications about shearing school and soon received a reply from a woman named Linda.

> John forwarded me your request for information about shearing school. Our shearing school is held irregularly and generally in May. If we have enough interest, we contract with an instructor to lead the class. I maintain a list of interested people. Let me know if you would like me to include you on that list. Normally we decide in January or February whether or not to host a class. Hope this helps.

I archived the email and forgot about it. But I remained fascinated with the problem of local fiber. Additional online searches for yarn or fabric sourced, milled, and spun entirely in California led me to the 2011 Oakland Fiber & Textile Festival. Though small as fiber festivals go, it offered a beautiful selection of local fleeces and yarns.

I picked up a gorgeous blend of Black Welsh Mountain and Romney wool, made by California grower and spinner Gabrielle Menn, the very sort of yarn Parkes extols as having "crunch" in *The Knitter's Book of Wool*:

> There's an important distinction between crunch (picture a freshly baked loaf of whole-grain bread) and scratch (that same loaf of bread left sitting out on the kitchen counter for a few days). Crunchy yarns are healthy and

vibrant, with fibers that have persistence and personality. In a garment they stand their ground, keep you warm, and wear well.

I'd never met a crunchy yarn before, but I knew it immediately when I saw it, touched it, and smelled it. It was unlike any yarn encounter I'd ever had. Each label bore the face of the sheep from whom the wool had been sheared. Menn's wool wasn't dyed but was naturally a deep espresso brown: the ewe herself, not dye, made a color. The yarn smelled faintly sheepy, though not in a bad way, of clean soil, mild soap, lanolin, and damp grass. I kept catching myself sniffing it. This yarn was better and more special than the average, so why was there so little of it? Why had I found it only at this fair, not in that wonderful, big yarn shop?

Further sleuthing led me to the blog of Rebecca Burgess. Burgess had taken a personal search for local fiber and clothing to another level entirely. For one year, she committed to developing and wearing a wardrobe made entirely with dyes, fibers, and labor found within 150 miles of her Northern California home. Because there were no textile mills or clothing factories within that radius, Burgess had to team up with local farmers and fashion artisans to build her experimental wardrobe by hand. Her yearlong project proved to her (and to me) that, all over the United States, there are still enough "regionally grown fibers, natural dyes, and local talent to provide a most basic human necessity, and one that we've perhaps heedlessly outsourced: our clothes."[5]

Rebecca's homespun project was compelling. Over the next few years, I followed as it grew into a nonprofit organization called Fibershed, with a mission to "generate awareness and teach the necessary skills to build and sustain a thriving bioregional textile culture that functions hand-in-hand with principles of ecological balance, local economies, and regional organic agriculture." On a foggy day in November 2012, I attended the inaugural Fibershed Wool Symposium, held in the tiny coastal town of Point Reyes Station, California, ground zero for the farm-to-table food movement. Organic dairies abound, Joel Salatin of Polyface Farm is a popular speaker, and farmers read the *New Yorker* below posted signs declaring opposition to "smart" gas and electricity meters because they use wireless signals to transmit usage data. Residents of Marin County will not be persuaded or placated by the Federal Communications Commission and the World Health Organization.

I entered a beautiful old community center consisting of two large rooms with high vaulted ceilings, fat wooden beams, antique transom windows, and golden hardwood floors. Beyond the check-in desk, the room was busy with tanned, generously freckled women of all ages, adorned in hand-knit sweaters and fingerless gloves. They were chatting and smiling and drinking coffee. A few outsized men mingled, too, dressed in cowboy boots and button-down plaid shirts tucked behind polished belt buckles. Organic baked goods filled a buffet table. Along the edges of both rooms, a handful of local fiber vendors worked tables, selling gorgeous yarn, lambskin vests, woven wool blankets, and more. I stuck a name tag on and was handed a schedule for the day, a card with naturally dyed yarn samples attached to it, and a poster that read "Grow Your Clothes."

It felt like Christmas morning. I'd found my people. Or, at least, the sort of people I wanted to be.

The symposium began with a keynote speech by Rebecca Burgess herself, who reminded us that, for almost all of human history, wool was key to human survival: it provided clothing and thus warmth and protection, our most basic, physiological requirements. Sheep also supplied humans with food (meat and milk) and shelter materials.[6] Wool was felted (a combination of wool, heat, and agitation create felt fabric) to make the wall panels of yurts, woven into tapestries to keep out cold air, and used as rugs and building insulation, as it is today. Wool is efficient: warm even when wet, quick drying, renewable (providing at least one fleece per animal per year), compostable, and requiring no human hunting of dangerous wild game, with domesticated sheep living right beside us.

Wool as we know it today was developed over several thousand years of selective breeding by humans. Wild sheep have a stiff, hairy outer coat that covers a short, wooly undercoat that grows only in the winter. They shed the undercoat each spring, which could be either gathered or plucked from the animal, thereby creating the term "wool gathering."[7] Humans selectively bred this self-shedding out of sheep over the course of about ten thousand years.[8] We created sheep with wool that must be sheared off every six to twelve months.

As the day went on, I learned firsthand the many reasons why my yarn shop wasn't full of local yarn. A panel of small flock owners described problematic points in the domestic wool supply chain. Many small flocks do not produce wool in sufficient quantity to sell it commercially, which means a farmer pays for the care and feeding of the sheep, pays the shearer, and then either composts or gives away the unprocessed fleeces. Alternatively, a small flock owner can make a substantial investment to get into the fiber business, either by selling raw fleeces directly to hand spinners and felters, or by paying a mill to wash, dye, and spin the wool into finished products like yarn, or both.

As Burgess had discovered, few wool mills remain in California and the United States. Historically, there was never much large-scale, commercial wool processing in Northern California (compared with the number of mills in the Carolinas and on the East Coast), but there was some. In the late 1800s and early 1900s, much of the wool produced in California was shipped to mills in the San Francisco Bay Area or farther north along the Pacific Coast to the Humboldt Bay Woolen Mill, which operated from 1901 through World War II, or to mills in Oregon.

In the San Francisco History Collection of the San Francisco Public Library, I found a description of the Black Point Mill, which stood at the end of Fisherman's Wharf, where Ghirardelli Square stands today. In 1861, the *Daily Alta California* called it the first wool mill in California, implying that, by then, a sufficiently high number of western sheep produced enough wool to make the Black Point Mill a worthwhile business endeavor.

> This establishment, at Black Point, is the pioneer of woolen manufactories in this State, having been erected in the year 1859....In front of the main building, and situated just at the edge of the water, is the wash-house, to which every fleece after being assorted, from the finest Merino to the coarsest Mexican, is brought....After washing, the wool is spread in great vats, on the beach and on the hill, and dried, which process consumes some twenty-four hours.

The 1868 volume of the *San Francisco City Directory*, the Yellow Pages of its day, explicitly connected wool mills with American values of independence and pride: "Year by year the manufactures of these mills have increased in variety and fineness until at the present they produce fabrics that...rendered us independent of importations from abroad."

In the twenty-first century, we—or at least US corporations and federal policy makers—care less about remaining "independent of importations from abroad" than about taking advantage of low wages, higher profits, and a convenient lack of environmental and labor regulations overseas. Because of federal trade policies and agreements that favored the outsourcing of textile manufacturing, most US woolen mills were closed by the early 1990s, with just a handful—primarily on the East Coast and in the Carolinas—hanging on to the present day.

Today, a dearth of domestic wool mills means that small flock owners, if they want to be in the fiber business, must pay to ship wool long distances despite the fact that nearly half the weight of the fleece will be lost in skirting (removing vegetable matter, manure, and other contaminants) and scouring (a multistep washing process) at the mill. Sheep secrete lanolin, a waxy, heavy oil (and the reason a raw fleece is referred to as "in the grease"), which constitutes anywhere from 5 to 25 percent of the weight of freshly shorn wool.[9] Even at bulk freight rate, overland truck shipping costs more than the equivalent on a container ship. A fiber producer must consider these costs when figuring out how much to charge for a finished fiber product, and many of the small wool producers at the symposium said they cannot afford to sell their yarn wholesale to local yarn shops (at least, not at a price point the average knitter could afford)—another reason why my local yarn shop might not carry locally produced yarn.

The rarity of shearers and wool mills, and the cost of shipping and processing wool, however, are not the only challenges for small fiber businesses. Once it reaches one of the few remaining US mills, a producer's wool might wait in line for three to nine months. It's not unusual for twelve to twenty months to pass between a lamb's birth and a wool producer realizing income from its wool and the constant work of sheep husbandry, shepherding, feeding, lambing, hoof trimming, vaccinating, and more.

By late morning, I no longer wondered why there was so little local yarn. I marveled that there was any at all.

Not surprisingly, most small-scale wool producers cannot afford the thousands of dollars and long wait times required to have a small batch of wool processed in this manner. Later in the wool symposium, a panel of sheep shearers said as much. All four men on the panel described ranchers offering to give them fleeces for free or throwing wool away because it is cheaper to toss than it is to pay for shipping and mill costs.

Matt Gilbert, one of the shearers on the panel, had sheared sheep throughout Central and Northern California for nearly fifteen years, since he was thirteen years old. In that time, he had seen "an awful lot of wool get thrown away, and seen a lot of people who want local products made out of that wool. But there's no mill that can produce yarn out of the fine fibers that you would like to wear." As a knitter who wanted local yarn, I found these "wool as garbage" revelations somewhat nauseating. Gilbert said he wanted to start a mill because he strongly believes this needs to change, and that it's something we can change.

Of course, deciding what to do with the wool is only a problem if a small wool producer can find someone to shear it off in the first place. A woman in the audience asked the panel members, "Why aren't there more shearers?" It's not an easy life, they said. It's dirty, seasonal, unsteady work. Professional shearers who work on commercial shearing wagons must travel to different states, if not different countries, following the seasons in order to keep working. (Australia and New Zealand, big wool-production countries, have their winters when the United States has its summer and vice versa, so some shearers travel back and forth.) One shearer, John Sanchez, was more blunt: "Because there's easier ways to make a lot more money. I mean, 'backbreaking' is too light a word for it."

In spite of this statement, in spite of the fact that the men on the shearing panel looked like they'd walked out of a casting call for *True Grit*, I thought, "How hard could it be? I could learn to shear sheep at shearing school and travel to ranches. I don't need to buy land or shear one hundred head in a day. I can shear the small flocks nobody else wants to come out for."

I wasn't exactly thrilled with my day job or career path. After nearly twenty years of working in software development, I could recite a litany of sins committed by my employers: hedge funds that defrauded clients, shameless embezzlement, unpaid salaries, overt sexual harassment, hush money, and more. One of my employer's venture capitalist investors recently asked me out for beer during a board meeting, followed me to a bar where I was meeting my husband, and, on weekends, sent text messages asking me out on dates. I do not know how he got my personal mobile number, but he knows it does not matter that he puts these things in writing.

Maybe, I thought, if enough small flock owners needed a shearer, I could be freed from my desk to spend more time outside. A few months later, in the first week of February 2013, I received an email from the University of California Hopland Research and Extension Center. A shearing school would be held in May. A payment of a few hundred dollars had to be made to reserve a place in class. Decision time.

I hesitated. Knitting was one thing, but sheep? Livestock? *Live* livestock? I was from Detroit, Michigan, not Miles City, Montana. I had never been in 4-H or even attended a state fair. How could I feel drawn to this? I was a cliché, the burned-out city dweller wanting to get "back to the land" that I'd never even been on in the first place. Everything and everyone around me said that manual labor was a lost cause financially, a relic of times past, something best left to "undeveloped" nations, yet I was skeptical. Making nothing did not seem to have worked out very well for us.

I pulled out my credit card and registered for sheep-shearing school. It ran for five days just once a year, if that, so it was now or never. How badly did I want local yarn?

TWO

Greenhorn

At the threshold of the redwoods of Northern California, across a green-girded, two-lane bridge, the farming community of Hopland flanks two banks of the Russian River. Though named for the bitter hops that propelled its local economy from the 1870s to the mid-1950s, Hopland also lived on timber and sheep ranching. Sheep grazed land logged for old-growth coastal redwood, which enabled landowners to avoid paying taxes on standing timber. In the 1880 US Census, over three hundred thousand sheep outnumbered people in Mendocino County by twenty-eight to one.[1] Today, by contrast, fifteen thousand sheep call Mendocino County home, and I will soon meet a few hundred of them.

Hopland holds approximately eight hundred residents, the Solar Living Institute, the Hopland Band of Pomo Indians of the Hopland Rancheria (a reservation), and the Hopland Research and Extension Center (HREC), part of the University of California's Division of Agricultural and Natural Resources. Since 1951, the Extension Center has served as an experimental field station and produced volumes of research in animal science, watershed management, wildlife biology, and more. But its name and mission obscure its true charm and glory: more than fifty-three hundred acres of oak woodland, grassland, sage scrub, and streams in the high hills of Mendocino County, vistas of waist-high grass shining like silver, rolling down to the river.

I'd grinned at the wood, red-painted sign that read "Caution: Sheep on Road" when I arrived at 7:30 a.m., more in the mind-set of vacation than vocation. A pair of handmade shearing slippers lay on the passenger seat, sewn from two Goodwill sweaters felted in my washer and dryer. I made the slippers, little more than wool sacks that tie around the ankles, in response to one of the few hints relayed in advance of class: sheep shearers wear suede, leather, or felt slippers, not cowboy boots. Slick lanolin from the sheep's wool coats the plywood shearing floor: shearers in rubber and similarly hard-soled shoes can't get traction. Professional shearing slippers cost $55 plus shipping, a high investment for a five-day flirtation with agricultural labor. Mine cost $4 and less than two hours, all told.

I drive past a few small houses, kids' bicycles, mailboxes on posts, and reach multiple buildings. Unsure of where to go, I enter the one that most looks like it could hold classrooms. The chipper woman at the desk points behind me and says, "Oh, you're all down at the barn." Of course.

I am surprised to find that the Extension Center is more working ranch than school, with secure feed storage for alfalfa pellets, hay, and straw; a livestock quarantine facility; and a bunkhouse, along with a brand new, modern building with a kitchen, labs, and multiuse rooms. Six barns contain dozens of corrals and sheep shelters for seven of thirty-two fenced pastures, and mechanical, welding, and woodworking shops maintain and support the other facilities.

A chill, humid breeze promises late-season rain. I skid down a gentle slope, littered with acorns that roll underfoot, toward the ninety-six-hundred-square-foot main barn. Though I can't see any sheep, I can hear them, a loud, insistent chorus ceaselessly bleating "meeyaah" more than "bah." Their tone sounds somewhat accusatory. The barn's imposing sliding doors are open at each peaked end, and its roof overhangs sheep pens along both sides, providing shelter from rain and sun. Several dozen sheep eat beneath the eaves, their jaws grinding alfalfa and hay in wall-mounted wire feeders.

I enter the dark barn and pass a few pens with single ewes and their recently delivered twin lambs, happily stumbling and bleating about their mothers. Farther ahead, sheep ears, faces, and noses poke over the sides of pen walls. Five to seven sheep stand in one square pen after another, a grid of white wool. Their voices—some deep and hoarse, others more straightforward, and still others high-pitched whines—bounce from the metal barn roof, amplified and multiplied.

Assembled in the center of the barn, a handful of instructors and eighteen students sip coffee from travel mugs and hold heavy, three-ring binders that contain sheep-shearing manuals from the American Sheep Industry Association (ASI). The shearing floor is, quite literally, a plywood floor immediately adjacent to a wall of hinged, waist-high pen doors that swing open and shut, reminiscent of chutes around a rodeo ring or bullfighting arena. Whenever a sheep runs into or kicks at them, the pen doors bang open a little. Overhead, four mounted electric motors hang from wooden crossbeams. These motors power the shearing handpieces that hang from each of them, giving the rigs their name: "the drop." The handpieces look like oversized versions of the electric shaver and combs I use to cut my husband's hair, if somewhat more dangerous, since they lack the guards that prevent us from cutting ourselves.

John Harper, who earned a master's degree in range management from Arizona State and organizes the sheep-shearing program at the Extension Center, is a gentleman rancher, banjo player in a bluegrass band, grandfather of several, and modern-day western agrarian. Gregarious, with a broad smile and genuine enthusiasm for his work, he gives us all a warm welcome. John has short, wavy blond hair just beginning to gray and sports a meticulously maintained horseshoe-style mustache. He wears a pearl-snap cotton shirt with sleeves rolled to his elbows, faded blue jeans, and a tan leather belt with "John" stitched across the back.

After John's introductory remarks, another instructor, Gary Vorderbruggen, announces that Mike McWilliam, champion shearer, will demonstrate by shearing two sheep. Broad-shouldered, firmly planted with his feet hip-width apart, Mike radiates stability. Most of the time, he tilts his chin slightly upward, as if deep in thought or attempting to better see from beneath his baseball cap brim. Wire-rimmed glasses rest on his soft, round face, and he wears the only clothes I will ever see him in: khaki work pants and a heavyweight, pinstriped shirt with two breast pockets and a zipper that begins at mid-chest. Across Mike's belly, where his shirt has met so many sheep, lanolin has stained and worn the pattern away and has molded Mike's suede shearing slippers, oily black, to his feet. His thick, smooth, muscled hands remind me of baseball mitts.

Mike swings a pen door open and, seconds later, pulls a sheep—backside down, belly up—onto the floor. She sits upright, facing us,

Sheep penned beside the shearing floor at the Hopland Research and Extension Center.

and Mike shifts her weight slightly, onto one hip. The sheep's legs splay open, which will enable Mike to begin by shearing wool off her belly. He tucks her right foreleg between his legs and hooks it behind his right one. Safely held, she watches us, calm, blasé, unperturbed. Mike, too, is calm, and the entire set-up feels like a dream sequence, slow motion, no big deal. Mike pulls the cord, the handpiece shakes to life, and he makes one stroke from the top of the sheep's chest to the bottom of her belly.

Gary says, "Watch Mike's hands." While shearing, Mike's hands always move. His left hand smooths the sheep's skin taut to prevent nicks, while the handpiece in his right floats over the sheep. We begin to call Mike "the sheep whisperer." He so totally controls the sheep that she appears to fall asleep during shearing: her eyelids close for thirty seconds at a time. He shears so calmly, evenly, and methodically, so early in the morning, that I think I might fall asleep watching it. Mike shears two sheep in less than ten minutes—done slowly for our benefit—and does not appear to have exerted himself. Mike is in his sixties.

Neither the US Census nor the Bureau of Labor Statistics includes a line item for "sheep shearer," so numbers are hard to come by, but—as I'd learned from author Clara Parkes and at the Fibershed Wool Symposium—sheep shearers are considered a dying breed. Gary sums it up with a joke: "First thing you do to get ready for shearing every year is call your shearer, see if he's still alive. They're all old." Our instructors estimate that, at best, the world has five thousand shearers. It seems plausible, considering that eighteen of us are attending a shearing school offered for just five days, once per year, and the fact that even minimal attendance is not guaranteed from one year to the next. Some students are repeats who cannot count as "new."

Gary claps his hands, rubs his palms together, and yells, "All right! Let's get to it!" Mike's two-sheep demo will serve as the full extent of introductory material. I didn't think we students would shear on the first day. My agricultural fairy tale included a two-day, introductory classroom session on sheep breeds and their anatomy, and careful review of precise diagrams showing a sheep's major arteries and organs. It is not to be.

My pastoral enchantment evaporates, giving way to dread that threatens to become panic. Suddenly, my rural adventure has gravity: this is serious business. The weight of responsibility to these living, bleating beings grows as I realize my naïveté. I have adored the popular idea of sheep, those cute yarn growers to pet at county fairs and share as Facebook photos, but in fact I know nothing about sheep, not sheep themselves, their bodies, their instincts, stripped of the romantic, rustic yearnings we put on them. And I won't have a chance to learn it before I have to shear one. I feel nauseated and unsteady, as if I'm in the first few minutes of the flu. I bend at the waist and lay my forearms and head on a short pen wall. I try to think, and I resist the urge to run out of the barn and bail.

This discomfort hints at why I ought to stick around. I am deeply dissatisfied with the extent to which modern American culture seems more comfortable "knowing that" (or not even, when the act of Googling stands in for knowing) rather than "knowing how." In haste and short-sightedness, we exported not just manufacturing jobs but craft skills and traditions of making, traded shop class and home economics for credit-powered consumption, planned obsolescence, and disposability, the table saws and sewing machines from high school classrooms sold for a song. Poet Edwin Muir wrote "men are made of what is made," and, in the United States, we make less than ever. When people see me knit in public, their first reaction is almost always, "wow, I could never do that!" followed by "my mom did that" or "my grandma did that." Our default expectation is that making is exceptional rather than normal, even though we know it wasn't always this way. But had I, too, become accustomed to this culture, more comfortable with buying yarn than doing something difficult?

In college, a section about Martin Heidegger and the hammer, which a philosophy professor at my urban Jesuit university astutely included in an ethics class, appealed to me. Heidegger bridged the gap between my blue-collar roots and my family-mandated, white-collar aspirations by stating that we achieve our closest relationship with a tool or skill not by looking at or studying it, but by manipulating it. Only in physical use do we achieve what Heidegger called readiness-to-hand. Nothing is without context, without its particular situation in the world: Any practical, hands-on skill is inextricably tied to experience. Skills can only be lived.

Gary is the most talkative instructor, so I plant myself beside his shearing station. The other instructors embody the shepherd stereotype: meditative, solitary men who rarely speak and intervene only when necessary. That is not what I need right now. I want a red-faced drill sergeant barking out orders loudly and often, screaming at me if I screw up, and Gary is the nearest thing to it. His stream of imperatives reassures me: Gary is in charge. He will stop me from doing something wrong.

Gary resembles an old-time German brewer with the build of a warrior. Jolly and outspoken, he has wide, rosy cheekbones, is nearly bald, and—though somewhat portly—seems made of dense matter, solid, immovable. You'd never want someone with Gary's muscle and strength running at you head-on, and I believe I may have seen a statue that approximates him in either Wales or Scotland, a shield in one hand and a sword in the other.

The barn noise is more reminiscent of a Detroit machine shop than a farm: four shearing motors, four buzzing handpieces, and fifty penned sheep drone on simultaneously and loudly. Rain drums the metal roof. Students shout over the din, periodically yelling "Pull!" to ask each other to yank the cords that turn the shearing motors on and off. I wonder how barns ever got a reputation as quiet places.

I try to soak up proper shearing technique and motions. Sheep on its back, three strokes down the belly. Mind the teats and cover them with the hand that isn't holding the shears, and don't cut your hand while you're at it. Go out the right leg, then back up the same leg. Sink your fist into the sheep's hip socket to straighten out its leg and reduce the likelihood of cutting a tendon on your return trip. Be very careful around the tail. Look for the pink part and start above it. And for God's sake, don't cut the vulva.

Late morning, the shears and even Gary go quiet. The rain has slackened, no one shouts, and stillness grows. It must be time to break for lunch. My eyes sweep over the shearing floor and stop at the brightest color in the room: thin drops of poppy-red blood trail along, then bloom into a wide, viscous puddle with Mike, the sheep whisperer, sitting in the middle of it. He tenderly cradles a ewe in his arms and in the crook of his bent, spread legs. They might be attending a birthing class.

Blood slicks Mike and the ewe so thickly that it's difficult to tell who's bleeding, but it's her. Each huge gulp of her breath powers a pump of her heart that pushes more blood to the floor. An artery. It's a very unusual, especially miserable accident. The student who cut the sheep crouches helplessly beside her, neither hiding from us nor looking away from his awful mistake. I feel sorry for him, and frightened. He's more experienced than most of us. He took a shearing certificate home last year and shears professionally. If that guy can make this mistake, aren't the rest of us even more likely to do the same? Moments ago, my worst case scenario was nicking a sheep. Now I am certain I will kill one.

The sheep lies still, breathing heavily. Why doesn't she panic? Why is she so calm, when I feel so lightheaded I have to lean against the pen wall to stand?

A curved needle glints in Mike's bloodied hands, which he uses to stitch the sheep's artery and then, on top of that, her skin, gently and deliberately. He could not be more careful if he were tending his own child. And then, quietly, Mike begins to tell us how to do the same thing. I force myself to stay on my feet and focus: Mike is right. We must know how to do this. It is irresponsible not to know. Large, curved needles are easier for you to grip and easier on the sheep's skin. Carry unwaxed dental floss in your kit for thread, and make sure it's the unwaxed kind. It will disintegrate nicely, naturally. Sew with the baseball stitch used in taxidermy: push the needle down in one edge of skin, then—going under the thread—bring it out the other edge. Don't tug too hard to pull the edges closed. Sheepskin is delicate.

Mike ties off the dental floss, bites right into the bloody stuff to cut it with his teeth, turns the sheep onto her hip, and lightly pats her rump. She stands, staggers as she gets her bearings, and hops out to the side yard to join her flock. We collectively exhale and resume breathing. A few men turn, wipe their eyes with their cuffs, and walk a few paces away to hide their emotional relief.

Gary pipes up again. "You know, sheep die. They do!" My lips pinch together, and I shoot him a look. I do not want to hear it right now, but Gary looks me in the eye, points his index finger at me, and continues: "Let me tell you about the sheep I've had die on me. Had a sheep die right between my knees of a heart attack while I was shearing it. One time, I had a lamb start to have a heart attack and I gave it CPR and it lived. . . . These things happen and you don't get to know how it's gonna turn out." Gary adds that food and water make heart attacks more likely for sheep. "Imagine if I fed you Thanksgiving dinner and then asked you to stay bent over for an hour. You wouldn't feel too good, would you? When the sheep have all this food and water inside, it can push up against their organs when you're shearing them. They got four stomachs in there! You've got to ask people not to feed or water their sheep for ten to twelve hours before shearing."

Students return to the drops. I let every other student shear before me, delaying the inevitable. Eventually, shortly before lunch, Gary looks at me, waves me over, and hollers, "All right!" I yell my confession, outing myself as the agricultural fraud I am: "I've never handled a sheep before!" Gary rolls his eyes, puts his hands on his hips, and shakes his head before asking, "And you wanted to do this again why?"

It all seems ridiculous here, now. Because I'd heard about a shortage of sheep shearers. Because I want local clothing, yarn, and fabric and am tired of "knowing that" instead of "knowing how." Incredibly petty stuff compared to my present problem: how to get a sheep that weighs as much as I do out of a pen.

Gary hollers, "Well?! Go in and get that sheep!" He opens the pen door and waves at me to follow him in. All morning, I've gazed at pen walls and, inside, the sheep's relative heights, yet their true, far taller sizes did not register until I stood beside them. In that close pen, I am gobsmacked by the reality of relative scale: their heads nearly reach my waist, and I am five feet eleven. "Pony sized," I say to Gary with a nervous laugh.

The sheep run around and slam into my legs, hooves pounding the tops of my feet, covered in soft, felted wool slippers that offer no protection. No video could possibly convey how large, hot, fast, and determined a single sheep can be. "Show you how to catch one," Gary says. He slips the palm of his left hand firmly beneath the sheep's jaw, cupping it. "If this does not work," he says, "though it usually does, stick your thumb into the corner of the sheep's mouth, clear through until your thumb exits the other corner. They got a smooth spot between their incisors and molars without teeth in it. Do it on this one so you feel it."

I stare at him. Stick my thumb into a sheep's mouth? "Get on with it!" Gary says. Gingerly, I tap my left thumb around the edge of the sheep's mouth and, just as he said, I feel a gap between her teeth and push my thumb through, like a bit on a horse bridle. He's right: it's smooth, feels like the space my wisdom teeth left.

"All right," Gary says, his palm and four remaining fingers still holding the bottom of the sheep's jaw. "Now you put your hand where mine is, get a feel for it. Gently. Doesn't require much force. Your hand can almost rest on the sheep's jaw. They don't want to walk forward into the pressure of your hand, so they stop. They will back away from it, though, so put your right hand on her tail." The sheep's jaw is level with my hip, so I have to extend my arm only a little to cup my hand around it. Touching wool on a living, breathing being feels more like submerging my hand in warm oil than touching yarn. Miraculously, the sheep does not move. I smile at Gary. "Okay, good. Give her back," he says, taking over.

Gary cups the sheep's jaw again, and turns her head toward her right shoulder, the sheep's nose pointing toward her back. "This causes the sheep to lower its butt and begin to lay down, in order to become more comfortable," Gary says. "As she begins to sit down, you want to use that being off balance to your advantage." Gary pushes his right knee into the sheep's left hip and, at the same time, gently pulls the sheep's right haunch toward him: a synchronized push and pull in opposing directions. The sheep's turned head, the pressure of Gary's knee, and the sheep's right leg being lifted off the floor causes her to lose balance and, at that precise moment, Gary swiftly flips the sheep over onto her back. "Your turn!" he says, as the sheep stands up. Right.

Somehow, flocked tightly together in an enclosed pen, the sheep have room enough to run fast and easily escape me. They get an assist from the lanolin, literally slipping through my fingers. Around and around the pen perimeter they go. Some attempt to climb or jump right over me, and their 120-pound bodies easily push me over. In the melee, one ewe "hides" by sticking her head beneath another sheep's belly; one attempts to scale the pen wall by climbing another sheep, resting her forelegs on its back; and still another makes like a trained protester and goes dead weight, flattened to the pen floor, head buried between two other sheep. I cannot properly grab a sheep's jaw and don't want to pull at their wool, which can hurt and bruise them. Arms crossed, Gary blocks the pen door to keep the sheep from escaping onto the floor and slamming into shearers.

Eventually, I realize my best bet is to sidle alongside a sheep and use my full body—especially my two knees—to catch and brace the sheep against the pen wall, and then cup my hand around her jaw. In this manner, short of breath and sweating profusely, I finally catch one. At last. I huff, pause, glance up at the barn lights, and cannot believe how hard this is. Covered in lanolin and dirt, my hands and arms shine.

My heart rate slows, and I assess my caught sheep. Rigid, she stares into the distance, as if I am not present, waiting for me to let up so she can escape. Somehow, I am supposed to move all 120 and some pounds of her from standing, pinned against a wall, to laying on her back, me with two forelegs in my hands. "We don't have all day," Gary reminds me. "Go on and turn her head." I do, a little, but fear turning her head too much. She doesn't sit down at all, won't budge. Gary helps me turn her head, and she moves to lie down, but I don't have the strength to finish flipping her over. I sweep the full length of my right leg beneath her body, hoping to guide her over and aid my arms. For this, I sincerely apologize to her aloud, repeatedly. "Stop apologizing!" Gary says, for the first of many times.

Allegedly, sheep go limp and become docile when flipped over. Folks hypothesize that the sheep, a prey animal in an unnatural position, suspects it is dying and lies still to play dead. One guess is as good as another, but if it exists, this mythic docility does not present itself. Students in general don't seem privy to mellow, obliging sheep. The ewe kicks with her legs, trying to get free of my hands.

Gary steps aside. While I push the pen door open with my butt, Gary will prevent other sheep from following mine out to the shearing floor. "Sheep love an open gate," he says. I am supposed to drag the sheep about six feet, to the nearest shearing station, but she does not move when my feet do. I step backward. Nothing. Every subsequent step creates more space between us, because I am moving and she is not. She slumps into the gulf between us. Thank heaven the pen doors block sight of these antics from the other students, who have walked in one minute and exited with a sheep the next.

My brain clicks into gear and some cerebral nether region says "momentum." I take tiny, rapid, shuffling steps, jogging backward, and the ewe's butt begins to slide across the floor. I'd really thought the lanolin would help more. We make it to the correct spot beside the shearing motor, where Carrie, a classmate, is ready to pull the machine on. I huff and puff and sweat, trying to push the sheep's right foreleg between my legs to rest behind my right thigh. "Stick your butt back," Gary yells. "It creates some space to drop that leg through. Then come forward again to keep that leg in place." Right again. The tiniest movement makes all the difference.

I take a moment to breathe and feel proper shearing position in practice, a revelation. The sheep's butt sits between my slippered toes, my quads and hamstrings scream around my bowed knees. That morning, it looked as if shearers' arms did most of the work but, in reality, legs hold and control the sheep. This leaves the shearer's hands free, the left hand to pull the sheep's skin taut, and the right hand to guide the handpiece.

Just when I think I've got it right, the sheep begins to slide down, butt first. This win encourages her: she flails about, attempting to rejoin the rest of her flock, whom she can see just outside the shearing area. My every instinct is to back away and let go, but Gary tells me to press gently down into the sheep, to lean even farther forward. "Gotta pinch your legs in," Gary says. "Don't have her held enough. You should be able to shift your legs and knees back and forth like you're dancing, and not have her go anywhere." He demonstrates, his hands in the air, shaking his knees left and right.

I pull her back up and get resituated. My legs, back, and arms form three sides of a rectangle, my fist gently nestled in the hip joint to get the sheep's leg out straight. For a rough approximation, fill a plastic sack with nine gallons of water and nine gallons of sand. Try to keep it upright and still using only your knees, bent ninety degrees at the waist, your spine straight. Stay that way.

Gary tells Carrie to pull the shears on and calls out the moves I should be doing. "You know you'll start with the belly wool, then go out the first leg, and toss the wool because it's the dirtiest," Gary says. I shear down the belly, carefully, picking at it, moving wool out of the way so I can see better. I finish that, and prepare to go out the sheep's right leg, which I can barely reach. "I'm going to fall into her!" I say. "Then you gotta bring her more toward you," Gary replies. "Let her brisket roll into your right knee, reduce the distance between you and that leg." It works. "Roll that handpiece around the curves of the leg so you don't hamstring her," Gary adds.

I return up the same leg toward the crutch (crotch) area, removing sticky manure tags that look like mud-dipped pinecones, trying not to drive the teeth of the shearing comb into the plywood floor. I shear the other leg and hip haunch all the way over to the spine. "All right," Gary says. "Now, while you got her head controlled there, by your knees, shear the top knot, two strokes." Gary means the wool on top of the sheep's head, between her ears. Called "wigging," it allegedly gives the ewe a clue to seek shelter and contributes to the success of her lambs: the missing flap of wool on her head creates awareness of "Oh, it's raining. We should seek shelter."

Next, I shear around the ears, holding each ear with my left hand. "Bend the ear over each eye," Gary says, and shows me. "You protect the eye socket, and can see real well around the ear and not cut that." Time for the neck. "Step forward with your right foot, put it right between the sheep's legs and your knee in that brisket." I can't make the shears move, frozen in fear that I will part the wool to find I've cut the length of the sheep's neck, repeat the morning's ghastly event. Blood pounds in my

ears. "I can't do it!" I say, but Gary hollers, "Oh yes you can! Keep going!"
He does, however, pull the shears off for a moment, and shows me how
to turn and hold the sheep's head, making the neck skin as taut as possible, and where to begin to get a clean start at the top of the brisket.
"You sheared the top of that brisket when you did the belly," he reminds
me. "So now you got a clean start there, wool's gone, can see what you're
doing and get that comb down against the skin. And don't press down
on her windpipe!" Gary tilts his chin far back, then runs his hand over
his own windpipe. "Try that," he says. "Don't feel good. So don't do it
to her with the handpiece." I make the first stroke up her neck, part the
wool, and let it fall forward over her shoulder. An inch of wool remains,
but no cut, saints be praised.

Gary guides me through it marvelously, laying on the filthy shearing
floor to nudge my feet into proper position. As in yoga or dance, a shift
of an inch makes all the difference in form, technique, ease. Most of the
other instructors and students have left the barn for lunch outside, but
Gary sticks with me. It takes an eternity. On and on, indefinitely. Half of
my back is ice cold, frozen. Sweat pours off the bottom of my chin and
nose like streams from a watering can.

I shear the shoulder and foreleg and lay the sheep down on her side,
ready for the "long blows," clear across the full length of her spine, back
to front. Gary shoves my feet beneath her body, and the point of the
slippers becomes clear. "Raise your toes up," Gary says. I do. "You can
feel her with your feet, move her around, tilt her toward you to make it
easier to reach over her back." Fascinating.

The long blows mean I'm more than halfway through, and I think
the shearer who invented this technique, Godfrey Bowen, put it there
to give the shearer and sheep a break. The shearer gets to stand up for a
few seconds of back relief, and the sheep lies stretched out on her side,
a normal and comfortable position. I enjoy the long blows, sustained
strokes from the sheep's spine from tail to neck, smooth. I smile at Gary,
squatting beside me, hands on his knees. "It's the fun part," he acknowledges. With my left hand, I lift the sheep's head around my left calf to
lengthen her neck and avoid nicks.

I am in the home stretch but have to lift and roll the sheep forward
to sitting on my feet in a slouched, bowed position, her head and neck

Raw Targhee fleece and one foxtail, sheared by the author at the Hopland
Research and Extension Center.

tucked between my knees. This bowed shape also makes her skin as
taut as possible. I shear from her shoulder down to her tail, in horizontal strokes. With every stroke, Gary, who has resumed lying on the
floor, calls out, "Tiny step back, tiny step back," pulling my heels. I scoot
backward—an inch at a time—to roll the sheep forward, head dropping
behind the back of my knees as I shear down her body. And then, the
last stroke, the outside of her last leg. I pull the shears off, release her,
and gently pat her rump as a signal that she's free to stand and go. She
pops up between my legs, facing the door, and runs away, giving a sassy
little hop and a kick of both rear legs that plainly means, "Screw you!"

I do not nick the sheep, not even once.

Gary wipes the sweat off his face with a towel, claps my shoulder, and
says, "Good job. That's your first sheep." I quiver on the plywood, knees
knocking, so utterly spent and with my back in such agony that I stay
bent over. I cannot believe I can raise myself to standing or lift a single

foot to take a step. I turn toward the pen wall and use it to pull myself upright. My hamstrings feel disconnected from my glutes, my limbs in distinct sections. I'll be surprised if I can lift my thermos of water. I start to laugh, a deranged, half-crying laugh, out of relief that I am done and the sheep is not dead, and at the full force of knowing, so immediately, that nothing I have ever done has been hard. Not double shifts waiting tables, nor emptying grease traps; not cleaning wealthy people's houses, or three jobs and five classes to get myself through college, or solo back-packing trips in remote regions of the West, alone in a tent in Utah during a thirty-degree night, vomiting, with a teeth-chattering fever. Nothing in my life was ever hard.

John Sanchez told the truth at the wool symposium: "There's easier ways to make a lot more money. 'Backbreaking' is too light a word for it." For all this, I would normally be paid just $3 to $7 per head. I will never feel guilty about buying a $50 skein of yarn. Yarn should cost three times that, for what it takes to get the wool off.

THREE

Kindred

I scrub my hands and forearms at the long steel sink in the barn and join the rest of the students at lunch outside, sitting on the roots of a big oak tree. It feels like the first day of school, most of us shy and quiet as we get to know one another. Like me, a woman named Carrie opens a full-sized box of Cheez-Its. Faced with our twin selection, we say—in unison—that we don't normally buy processed food, but only indulged because we're shearing, which makes both of us laugh.

Each of us is curious about why other people are here. Who else is crazy enough to spend an entire week learning a dirty, old-fashioned skill in a struggling industry? Who else wants to share a world with other dying, esoteric practices, like book binding and thatched roof construction? Even our instructors can't explain why they've continued to shear, offering only vague remarks like "It gets under your skin" or "Shearing gets in your blood. We call it wooly worms."

As we get to talking, I gather that students have one of three primary motivations for learning to shear: (1) they have sheep to care for, whether their own or someone else's; (2) they need or want the extra money that shearing work can provide; or (3) they are, like me, fiber-loving women who spin and/or knit, adore wool as key to our craft, have no prior agricultural experience, and yet hope we might prove helpful to the local wool economy.

Marie, Darryl, Annie, Daniel, Alexis, and Alice have sheep to care for but do not fit any of my existing notions of what an agricultural worker is. Marie looks as if she's just returned from a casual stroll down an Alpine glacier. The picture of healthy living in plenty of fresh air, she has shoulder-length, wavy, dark brown hair, fair skin, bright pink cheeks, and broad, strong shoulders. She is a nonresident apprentice on a locally famous, exceedingly private (and thus somewhat mysterious) back-to-the-land commune. Rumor has it the near-mythic intentional community was founded by an heiress to the Dole fruit fortune, who used her inheritance to purchase twelve hundred acres on the Pacific Coast in the late 1960s. The founders moved on years ago, and today, the community includes an ecologically managed sheep and wool operation that sells yarn, wool pillows and comforters, and handcrafted lambskin vests. After shearing school, Marie plans to spend time working in shearing sheds in New Zealand.

Darryl, a gentle giant with short dark hair, dark eyes, and a sunburned neck and forearms, is a man of few words, listening more than he speaks. He is an agriculture vocational teacher at Mission Viejo High School in Southern California, which offers agriculture classes.

Annie—tanned, gregarious, perennially smiling—wears a green, hooded cotton sweatshirt and running shoes, her long blond hair in a ponytail. She recently graduated from Cal Poly in San Luis Obispo, where she studied animal science. She works as assistant livestock manager at Swanton Pacific Ranch, thirty-two hundred acres owned and operated by Cal Poly in Watsonville, California, near the beach town of Santa Cruz.

Daniel, in his early thirties or so, has blue eyes, reddish hair, and freckles. Genuinely friendly, he sports already permanent smile lines, and a tie-dyed shirt beneath his overalls lends a Nor Cal hippie air. Daniel leases an apple orchard in Covelo and has nineteen sheep. He says he stops them from eating apples right out of the trees by tying one foreleg to a rear leg, which lets the sheep roam and graze but not perch on their rear legs. (People claim sheep cannot stand on two rear legs, and Daniel believed them until he looked out from his porch and saw one doing just that, eating apples from branches.) I get the impression that Daniel—well read, traveled, observant, thoughtful—has seen a lot of the world without judging any of it.

Alexis and her husband could be poster children for young greenhorns trying to break into humane agriculture. They lease land in the Capay Valley, not far from Sacramento, where they opened their Skyelark Ranch in the spring of 2011. They raise, butcher, and sell pastured chickens and lambs, and they run a flock of rare-breed California

Red sheep that grow unusual, cream-colored yarn with a copper cast and a subtle, almost metallic sheen. "We had trouble finding a shearer so here I am," Alexis says. She already shears well, halfway through the first day, so serious, intent, and no-nonsense about the task at hand that it's intimidating. Alexis, petite but not delicate, with bobbed reddish hair, is clearly no stranger to handling sheep. I have no doubt her agriculture operation will be successful, given the woman behind it.

Alice hails from Boonville, California, an eccentric, idyllic spot in the hills between Hopland and the Pacific Coast with its own dialect, Boontling. Exceptionally pretty, maybe in her early thirties, Alice has long brown hair, vintage glasses, and a small dog that behaves well in the shearing barn. She's previously sheared her small flock of sheep with hand shears, large scissors I find almost more frightening than the electric ones. The blades on hand shears are so long, it seems as if it would be easy to puncture the sheep's skin. Impressed when Alice tells me she has sheep, I naively ask, "You have land in Boonville?" Land in Mendocino County doesn't come cheap. Alice laughs loudly, in genuine surprise. "Hell, no!"

Alice is the first of several people I meet who own sheep but not a speck of land. I cannot wrap my urban head around the logistics of this, so Alice spells it out for me. Alice lives in a movable trailer. It's easy to find land on which to graze her animals, but that land is not necessarily land that a person is allowed to live on, even with an obviously impermanent structure like her trailer. Wealthy, urban, remote landowners, who might visit their property only a couple of times a year (if ever), happily engage someone like Alice to manage their land with grazing, which provides fire control, lawn mowing, and fertilizing manure. The same absentee landlords do not want an unsightly shepherd's trailer or tent anywhere on the property, either not knowing or not caring that a grazing flock requires the protection and tending of a shepherd, who in turn requires shelter.

Indeed, three women in class are effectively homeless. Like Alice's flock, their sheep have more secure housing than they do. Two women obtain shelter and some money by staying with various friends or house and farm sitting, for which there is a real need in rural areas. Farmers rarely get a vacation because it's hard to find a reliable person capable of livestock handling and care, if they can afford the same. When the shepherdesses cannot couch surf or farm sitting is not available, they sleep in the covered beds of their pickup trucks or in tents at campsites. Shepherds in the truest sense of the word, nomadic, each woman moves with her sheep.

In the 1800s, male Basque herders walked the length of California with their dogs and slept on the open range for months at a time. Today, women herders live out of trucks and trailers. Though each operated in different eras and contexts, I wonder whether the herders themselves are all that different from each other. I admire their fortitude. There is no one like a homeless shepherd to make you examine your courage and your commitment to living as you please.

Mark, Jordan, Randy, and Henry plan to earn extra money from shearing, and Randy and Henry are already quite good at it, having attended shearing school before. They're wildly funny, entertaining storytellers. Mark is a big Native American guy with a long, black pony-tail and glasses. He lives in Sebastopol, California, and has sheep and so many professions that I consider him a Renaissance man. As some-one accused of being a dabbler with too many interests myself, Mark's views on vocation appeal to me. According to him, "If there's something you're good at, you should just do it, and it doesn't matter how many things there are." Mark lives his words. He grooms and trims horses. He used to shoe horses, too, but stopped because he makes more money trimming the hooves of sheep, goats, and horses. For trimming horses' hooves, he makes $50–$60 per animal. Mark is also a social worker on a local reservation, a therapist who works with violent men one-on-one, a certified yoga instructor, and a father to four children, ages five months and twelve, fifteen, and thirty-one years. "The thirty-one-year-old's not mine," he adds, "but a nephew that I raised." In a few days, Mark will add "sheep shearer" to that list.

Jordan reminds me of some family and neighbors back in Michigan. He's skinny and sports a long mohawk and hunting gear: camouflage pants, army green jacket, and a fluorescent orange stocking hat that screams "Don't shoot, I'm not a deer." At first glance, an unkind person might call him "white trash," but they'd be woefully wrong.

Raised in South Carolina in a large, fundamentalist Christian family that later moved to California, Jordan stayed when they moved on again, earning a GED and working and living on-site at a Sonoma County winery. Jordan lives by his hands: he makes wine from leftover grapes and obtains almost all of his own food from a huge garden and hunting. For additional income, he shears sheep and hunts rats. Jordan takes his pack of rat terrier dogs to farms and, in short order, rids entire properties of rats, without using poisons that permeate the food chain and kill owls, mountain lions, other wildlife, and pets. Jordan's ratting services are so effective, often eliminating rats for years at a time, that he puts himself a little more out of business with every job. He has an incisive, unusual wit, is observant and appreciative of craft, and is so thoroughly self-reliant that he seems meant for a different time of trapping, open spaces, fewer constraints, and greater freedoms.

An honest-to-God cowboy from Oakdale, California, Randy used to rodeo in the 1970s, leaving most of his fingers canted at the first knuckle. His hands, head, and neck—permanently tanned and more sun spotted than I thought possible—appear almost square, and I believe that touching him would feel like tapping stone. Randy became interested in sheep shearing because his then-girlfriend trained sheep dogs and "her demo sheep needed shearing."

Randy is also a talented metalsmith who makes belt buckles and barrettes. Although it's probably not the first word that would cross your mind if you passed him on the street, he is an absolute gentleman. All morning, Randy noticed the weaker, less-experienced shearers expending all of our strength getting the sheep out of the pens and onto the shearing floor. At lunch, he offers to catch and flip them for us in the afternoon, so we can spend more time "learning the actual shearing, getting the moves down." Embarrassed, I acknowledge Randy's offer might be helpful, disappointed at the fact that it's true. Picking up on this, Randy politely stares into the distance, not at me, as he says, "It's tough. It is. It's tough for me and you must weigh half what I do. I have a lot of respect for you."

Randy has stories for miles, each one so unbelievable that we forget our exhaustion. On one trip, he says, he'd "just gotten off the plane and ended up killing a boar." We all stop chewing and chatting, not sure we heard him right. Randy continues. "I'm walking off the plane and my shoes aren't even tied on right, because I sort of untied them for being on the plane, you know. And this guy I'm staying with in New Zealand says he senses that there is a boar nearby. There was a slope, like, and I guess some dogs went after it, and they chased the boar down. So this boar comes running down the hill, and this guy I'm with is yelling, like, "Randy, here!" So he throws me a knife, and this boar goes right between my legs, and I kill this boar, which is a very small boar I guess, and I could barely keep my feet in my shoes!"

Randy laughs so hard he can barely finish the story.

"So we get to the guy's house, and the guy's got an eleven-year-old daughter. She says, 'Oh, you killed a boar?' I say, 'Yeah, yeah I guess I did.' She says, 'There's the first boar that I ever killed!' And she points to the wall and it's twice as big as the one I just killed, which apparently is not even big enough for us to eat, like, they fed it to the dogs!"

Randy smacks his thigh and laughs while the rest of us stare in disbelief. He continues, telling us that when he arrived in New Zealand as a beginning shearer, he asked someone to help him finding shearing work, and a guy said "'Oh yeah, yeah. You're a shearer, I can get you some work. How many do you do in a day?' I said, 'Oh, about thirty.' The guy says, 'Oh, you mean like three hundred?' I said, 'No, thirty,' and the guy's laughing, like, 'Oh, I don't know if I'm going to be able to find you work, only doing thirty head a day!'"

More laughing.

Henry, not yet twenty-one, is blue-eyed, blond, and heart-stoppingly handsome, with one overall strap forever falling down. The Extension Center could probably sell a calendar with nothing but photos of Henry and fund the shearing school—perhaps the entire facility—for at least a year. Henry attended shearing school last year, handles the sheep gently and well, and is always willing to jump in and help another student in a tricky spot. His parents own a feed store and raise hogs. Henry also competes in roller derby.

There's also an "old timer," so-called by Gary, who is a friend of Mike McWilliam, our instructor. Old Timer and Mike drove down to Hopland from their homes in coastal Oregon. Old Timer has a wide, friendly face with high cheekbones, a Santa-sized belly, a long gray beard and long gray hair, and a T-shirt with a wolf on it beneath suspenders. It is a better-than-average wolf shirt, so I ask him about it. "Oh, I just love wolves," he tells me. "I have one at home." I raise my eyebrows. "It seems to run in the family. My grandma had a wolf too." Leaning on his hand-carved wooden walking stick beside the sheep pen, looking out at the hills, he continues.

"She went out to bring the cows in one night. This was in, like, the early 1900s or so. She gets her shotgun, walks out there like usual, and sitting out on the edge of the herd is this wolf. Cows are unharmed. And the wolf slowly walks toward her! Well, she's too afraid to move. She doesn't want to kill it, wonders if she could even draw her gun in time. And do you know, it comes all the way over and sits down beside her, 'bout six, seven feet away. She stands there for a long time, doesn't know what to do. But she can't stay out there all night. She still has her gun, so she walks back in with the cows, and the wolf comes along, but it don't do a thing. It lays on the front porch!"

"No!"

"Yes, ma'am. So she walks down to the end of the driveway to get the mail and stays there, so she can tell her husband when he pulls up, 'There's a wolf on the porch, don't shoot it.' Well, the wolf stayed on for years and years. All the people knew about it, and you know, when a wolf's got a territory, you're safe from other wolves and coyotes, too. Everybody knew the person who shot it would get shot himself, so nobody did. And one day, it just walked away, probably to die."

"And . . . that was your grandmother."

"Yes, ma'am."

"Then . . . how did you get your wolf?"

"I come upon a litter in the woods. Found mom shot dead a little ways away. Just horrible. Three of the litter was still alive. Took them all home but only one made it. He stands taller'n me when he puts his front paws on my shoulder, I'll tell you. When someone new comes over, he can be real intimidating. But if you come in with me, it's all right, and then if you sit on the sofa, he'll sometimes lay on the sofa with you, with his paw on your leg, just lookin' at you. But he would'n hurt ya. Just feels like he will, for a while."

If I leave shearing school with nothing more than stories, that is enough. If Old Timer is yanking my chain, I do not mind.

As Jordan puts it, I am one of four "fiber ladies" in class, in addition to Carrie, Nancy, and Heather, who had, like me, thought, "Sheep shearing! Now that might be something I could do for money." I feel somewhat less crazy for their company. Carrie, my fellow Cheez-It eater, is quiet, gentle, and sweet, a slip of a woman in her early fifties who is much stronger and younger than she looks. She has worked in the East Bay Municipal Utility District (specifically, the water department) for seventeen years. Carrie will retire in a few years, after which she'd like to spend her time shearing. She's taken shepherding and wool-handling classes, spins yarn, and describes herself as a military brat.

Nancy lives in Oakland and heard about shearing school through Fibershed and A Verb for Keeping Warm, a yarn and fabric shop in Oakland. An accountant by trade, Nancy recently quit a miserable job, used up her savings in order to take some much-needed time off of work, and is looking for something else she'd like to do. She's friendly, tall, skinny, nimble, and strong, like someone you'd see on a yoga poster: no observable fat, serious biceps, and naturally curly brown hair piled atop her head, pineapple style.

Heather, a licensed acupuncturist and massage therapist from New Mexico, shuttered her practice, took off, and—for the moment— lives on the road and out of her vehicle. She travels throughout the American West and learns to do new things, with no itinerary or agenda save for classes in certain places at certain times. Since she is not licensed to practice acupuncture or massage in any state except New Mexico, Heather supports herself by offering these services for whatever amount people would like to donate—or for no money at all. She sets up her folding massage table behind her SUV at lunch, not far from the barn, and offers acupuncture and massage to her classmates. Given how my back feels after just one sheep, I suspect Heather will be busy. Though I didn't expect to see a massage table here, I'm relieved there is one.

We may, admittedly, be idealistic—and perhaps deranged—for wanting to shear sheep in this day and age. But the shearer shortage points to a much more dire problem. The American sheep industry is dwindling: in the United States, sheep numbers have plummeted since World War II and wool production has declined 64 percent since 1987.[1] As Robert Irwin of Kaos Sheep Outfit, a contract grazing operation in Northern California, describes,

> Wool and lamb are not our main revenue anymore, I've gotta be honest

with you. If I relied on [selling] wool and lamb meat to feed my family, I would be a lot thinner than I already am and I'm pretty thin, so I don't have a lot to lose. Wool has been worth almost nothing to the sheep producer for a long time. When my uncle was first starting out in the 1960s, his wool check was as large as or equal to his lamb check. I ran thirty-nine hundred feeder lambs last year, managed a thousand ewes, and had three hundred of my own ewes, and my wool profit margin was $4,500 and I sheared the sheep myself. Wool is losing. It makes up 17 percent of the processing system in the United States and it's declining steadily, not at a small number but at a large number, every year.

Robert speaks of what we try not to think about: the point of no return, the point at which something becomes so small that it makes no sense for anyone to participate anymore. With sheep numbers down, for example, no one has a compelling reason to become a shearer. In turn, the presence of fewer shearers makes it harder for people to keep sheep: anyone who wants a flock will have trouble finding a shearer and may have to learn to shear themselves, provided they can physically do so. Even in Australia, sheep numbers "have diminished to a point where we can't maintain the number of shearers," farmer Stan Hulme told BBC News Online in 2004.[2] Robert elaborates:

> That is what we call the death call, because if the sheep numbers drop below a certain point the infrastructure around it falls as well. We don't need to worry about vaccines. The FDA won't approve them, because there won't be the [sheep] numbers for the people to come up with sheep panels, to the guy that makes sheep crooks, to the guy that makes feeders, to the guy that bales the hay. There won't be enough animals in the United States to do any of that. The whole thing.... A harvest facility in Dixon, California, needs three thousand lambs a week just to stay alive. It pulls from seven states and it's barely afloat. That company is barely going. When that falls, we have no large unit to sell our lamb through.

That old, familiar, Detroit recession feeling: fear. And, especially for people born in the 1970s and later, the sense that we're too late to the party, that something precious is already mostly gone, whether it's the wool industry, decent wages, affordable housing, or a stable climate. Though undoubtedly upsetting, the more I learned, the more questions

I had. I knew what the problems were, but how had they happened? How did we get here? Outcomes are not reasons.

I began with the obvious, big reason all around us, and on us: synthetic fibers. Walk into any department or big box store, check as many clothing labels as you'd like, and the extent to which synthetic and semi-synthetic fabric dominates our modern wardrobes becomes clear. Most closets contain far more imported polyester, acrylic, Lycra, and nylon than pure cotton and wool. Synthetic fibers are manufactured, though most technically begin as natural materials. Rayon, for example, comes from wood pulp, while polyester comes from petroleum and ethylene glycol (derived from the hydrocarbon ethylene, a colorless, flammable gas). This synthetic state of affairs became normal only during and after World War II.

World War II influenced the US sheep and wool market in several big ways: it created a spike in wool production, a long-lasting demand for synthetics, a rural-to-urban population shift, and the foundations of international trade policies that—decades later—would contribute to the decline of the US wool and textile manufacturing industries. Historically, war (any American war) is a boon to the US wool market, creating high and sudden (albeit temporary) demand for wool. The 1941 Berry Amendment went further. It requires the Department of Defense to procure certain items produced within the United States, to maintain the safety of servicemen and women, and to ensure they are not harmed by dangerous or faulty goods produced in other nations. This includes American-grown wool, a mandatory component in military uniforms and items like blankets.

The characteristics of wool fiber itself mean at least as much to troops in remote, rough conditions as they did to early humans. Wool is not flammable and does not melt like synthetics do, making burn wounds far worse for soldiers. Warm when wet, wool provides more comfort to troops crawling through trenches or wading through swamps. It dries quickly, a boon when items must air dry, and does not stink like synthetics do. The latter may sound trite, unless you're a soldier who has gone days or weeks without a shower or water to spare for laundry. In order to provide all of that US-grown wool for war goods, US farmers raised a record high number of sheep in 1942.

World War II and its restrictions also created consumer demand for synthetic fibers, though they had been invented decades earlier, in the 1880s. World War II put the United States and its allies at war with trade partners that usually provided other raw materials, namely rubber and silk from Japanese-occupied Asia. The fact that the United States couldn't obtain rubber and silk, and that wool went to military use, meant rationing. Citizens had to "make do and mend," reworking and sewing old clothes into new garments, unravelling old sweaters to reknit into other items, a new stitch pattern selected to hide worn spots in yarn. In the 1930s, as fascism strengthened its hold over Europe, Dupont created nylon as a replacement for silk. Polyester was introduced in 1941.[3]

Like the human US rural population, sheep and lamb numbers declined in 1945 with the end of World War II. A report titled "Sheep and Wool Situation in California, 1950" observed that, between 1942 and 1950, California's sheep numbers dropped from 2,977,000 to 1,602,000—a decline of almost 50 percent in less than a decade.[4] A nationwide, record-high sheep inventory of 56 million head in 1942 reached 6.2 million head as of January 1, 2007, at the time the lowest level in recorded history.[5] The dearth of domestically and locally made yarn during my 2007 shopping made more sense in light of this fact.

After World War II, the United States began to minimize tariffs and other trade restrictions, and to promote the General Agreement on Tariffs and Trade. Established in 1947, this agreement promoted global postwar trade, world peace and stability, and the wealth of US corporations. Decades later, the revised agreement of 1986–1994 allowed full US access for textiles and clothing from developing countries, and the flood of cheap imports began in earnest.[6] This is one reason why clothes manufactured during the 1980s had more "Made in USA" labels than they do today.

Around the same time, in 1992, the elimination of the Wool Incentive Program, which imposed a tariff on imported raw or processed wool, created a precipitous drop in US sheep production. These taxes went into a pool that annually generated $90 million to $100 million for wool producers, a subsidy payment from the US government to US wool producers that provided a critical safety net. To calculate the share of the pool to pay to US wool producers, the government took the total number of imported pounds of wool, divided that out less what the government kept, and sent the remainder to wool producers.

Lest this seem like government interference in a free market, it's worth noting that US wool producers had to compete with overseas producers whose governments already subsidized their wool production, whereas the US government did not. The Wool Incentive Program, then—as Mike Corn of Roswell Wool put it—"made wool a fair trade, free but fair." Aided by subsidies from their governments, overseas wool producers and textile manufacturers exported their wool goods, and the US government taxed imported wool on the way in, subsidizing US wool production. Fair wool trade ended with the end of the Wool Incentive Program: US wool producers didn't stand a chance.

Mike Corn, a manager at Roswell Wool, works as a commission wool broker in Roswell, New Mexico. Roswell Wool gathers wool from the ranches of wool producers, sells it at auction on their behalf, and earns a commission for doing so. But Mike Corn isn't just a wool broker: he's got skin in the game as a sheep rancher and wool producer. The Corn family has run sheep in Roswell since the 1870s, and today, more than 50 percent of the sheep in the Roswell area belong to the Corn family. This gives Mike a broader and longer perspective on things. He describes the "tailspin," the slippery slope that began in the American West in 1992 with the elimination of the Wool Incentive Program:

> There's generations of lamb and wool buyers and they used to make dad-gum good livings, but not so much anymore. If you look back to USDA figures, from 1992 to 2000 it fell out of bed. And sheep ranchers moved on, straight to cattle. Less labor. Cattle, as long as they've got water, they're fine. Turn your sheep man into a cattle man in a click of a finger, but try to turn a cattle man into a sheep man? Can't do it. Every day you gotta ride fences, check on predation—demoralizing. Good word to use, demoralizing. You got fifty sections, coyote predation over here, you're concentrating on it, find the killing, find where the coyote is living, catch him. Think you can take a day off and go over to the other side, and you find they're eating you up over there. Average ranch out here is twenty-five thousand acres and that's small, that's not a place you can make a living on. That'll run about three hundred animal units, so that's fifteen hundred sheep or

three hundred cows or a combination thereof. That's not enough animal units to support a family. It doesn't pay the bills plus make your mortgage payment. Just doesn't jive.

Unfortunately, the elimination of the Wool Incentive Program was not the end of it. The Multi-Fiber Arrangement was replaced with the World Trade Organization Agreement on Textiles and Clothing in 1995,[7] scaffolding for the sharp decline of textile manufacturing in the United States. In 1995, just three years after the elimination of the Wool Incentive Program, the 1947 General Agreement on Tariffs and Trade became the World Trade Organization, and certain wool and textile products from four categories—"tops and yarns, fabrics, made-up textile products, and clothing"—were "integrated."[8]

Since the mid-1990s, US imports of textile products have grown rapidly, while textile milling has shifted to China, India, and other countries with lower labor costs and no requirement for mills and dye houses to clean up their toxic waste.[9] In 2011, the worldwide textile industry produced 85.9 million metric tons of textiles. Man-made fibers accounted for 61 percent of total textile production. Most growth in man-made textile manufacturing has taken place in China, responsible for 63 percent of total production in 2011.[10] The US ranked as the third-largest man-made fiber producer, behind China and India, though it's important to note that "producer" does not mean "manufacturer." Many of the world's largest apparel retail and marketing firms boast US headquarters, but have limited or no domestic manufacturing capabilities. In 2011, US textile factories employed just 151,000 people, and in 2010, the US was responsible for just 1 percent of the total $350 billion of global apparel exports.[11]

These discouraging statistics, however, didn't fully reflect my personal experience. Whenever possible, I had diligently purchased used or US-made everything since 2001. By 2009–2012, it seemed easier to find US-sourced and manufactured apparel made of natural fibers. Significant improvements in online searches and shopping during the intervening decade certainly helped, but wool product availability and selection genuinely seemed better. New companies like Ramblers Way, Duckworth Wool, and others touted 100 percent US-sourced and made lines of goods. Did I imagine it?

I asked Mike Corn and he concurred, seeing some positive signs for the US wool industry. "Yep, sock companies and the knit fabric industry in the US is gung-ho right how. Hasn't been this way for a long time. I think it's gonna continue because of rising costs in China, as those countries develop." Labor costs overseas are rising, so apparel makers may not save as much money as they thought, to say nothing of quality control challenges across great geographic distances.

Mike also links higher availability of US-grown-and-sewn garments to a US superwash facility at Chargeurs Wool USA in South Carolina. "Superwash" refers to a shrink-resistant polymer treatment that alters the fiber in wool products, allowing them to be machine washed and dried without shrinking and felting. Before the superwash process was reintroduced in the US in 2011, American wool had to be shipped 7,227 miles to China to be chemically treated, then 5,070 miles to England to be spun into yarn, and 4,094 miles to South Carolina, before it could be industrially knit into socks that could be machine washed and dried.[12] Mike points out that these miles mean long product turn-around times:

> There is cost, speed, and efficiency, and those things are costs all the same. If China buys some wool from me on an order to make material, they gotta buy it over here, wait 30 days from confirmed sale to get it loaded and headed on a ship, then 30 days across the ocean. That's 60 days. Off the boat and over to a warehouse where it sits for 30 days. That's 90 days. Then scour, process, combed top[13] to material, another 60 days. Now you're at 150 days. Take it to the cutter, make a garment. That's 180 days. They're pushing a year before they can get the material back to the United States. Textile industry's coming back just because of logistics. Apparel companies will pay more because they can get it in their hands faster.

I wondered if these gung-ho numbers in the wool sock and knit fabric industry might explain the ever-so-slight increase in the numbers of US sheep and lamb. According to the February 6, 2015, ASI newsletter, "The sheep and lamb inventory in the United States on January 1, 2015, increased by 1 percent from the same time in 2014, reported the National Agricultural Statistics Service in its annual Sheep and Goat inventory report." The last National Agricultural Statistics Service report to show any increase in sheep numbers was published in 2006.

Slow fashion and conscientious consumption trends may also play a role. They are convenient terms for a growing sense that, as Wendell Berry noted, "One man's producer is another's consumer, and even the richest and most mobile will soon find it hard to escape the noxious effluents and fumes of their various public services." Attributes that make synthetic fabrics attractive also make them damaging to the environment. Unlike natural fibers, synthetic fabrics do not degrade. This creates a major problem for our oceans and waterways, and for us: tiny plastic particles wash away from our laundry only to appear in the fish we eat,[14] and in 90 to 94 percent of drinking water samples as well.

Mike describes a threshold similar to that of which Robert Irwin spoke. In Mike's opinion, the death call for the US wool industry would be the closure of the last big mill in the United States. "If we lose Burlington, we're shot." Burlington, with locations in South Carolina, North Carolina, and Vermont, is the largest domestic mill. It is still one of the largest processors in the world, responsible for a large amount of military products and—along with Pendleton Woolen Mill—one of the largest domestic buyers from Roswell Wool.

One purchase does a textile-supply-chain's worth of good. When you buy a 100 percent grown-to-sewn US garment from Ramblers Way, for example, your purchase supports the mill where the fabric was woven, a mill that pays taxes and is subject to US environmental regulations and labor laws. It supports jobs at both the mill and Ramblers Way office, those at Roswell Wool in New Mexico, the truckers and wool warehouse workers, the wool growers across the United States, the shearers who removed the wool, the sewers (or sewists, the term many are adopting), and the people who delivered a finished product to you, whether at a local retail establishment or through the mail. You've supported the wool grower's stewardship and care of their land and animals, as well as the economic and environmental quality of life for other members of the wool grower's community who need to breathe that air and drink that water. If we lose all of this, we may never get it back. Would we deserve to?

FOUR

Imposter

A downpour begins as we finish lunch. Gary hollers, "You never shear wet! Never." A heavenly reprieve. Rainwater combines with sheep lanolin, which I thought might make for oilier, easier shearing, but it makes the floor dangerously slippery. Wet-shorn wool rots, molds, and—because wool is warm when wet—creates a fire hazard. Wet wool can heat to the point of smoldering, and it usually contains hay, grain, or animal bedding (wood shavings and sawdust) that easily catches fire. Wet wool can stain or change color significantly, and these colors cannot be washed out. "Worst of all," John says, "handling wet sheep creates wool boils, nasty, painful boils on the shearer's arms and legs." Moisture causes chafing, and prolonged wetness leads to a loss of layers of skin, which results in skin sores. The water-and-oil combination in the wool causes human skin to draw bacteria—and anything else that was on the sheep—into its pores.

Since we cannot shear this afternoon, we learn about the business end of things: how much shearers charge, how to establish a shearing business, and what equipment to buy. Most shearers have a setup fee, known as a farm or ranch call. They charge between $35 and $80 to show up, sometimes more depending on driving distance and time, gas costs, setup and breakdown, and wear and tear on equipment. In addition, shearers charge between $3 and $10 per animal to shear, depending on the size of the flock (the smaller the flock, the higher the per-head charge) and whether the sheep is a ewe, ram, or lamb. Rams are larger, heavier, full of testosterone, and more dangerous and difficult to handle.

Shearers may also increase per-head charges if a sheep has horns, is in poor condition, or has not been shorn in a long time. Fleeces are heavy: depending on a sheep's breed and size, one year's fleece may weigh five to twenty pounds. Two or three additional years' worth of wool growth, then, can add ten to thirty pounds or more. This increased fleece weight pulls the sheep's thin skin, making it looser and thus easier to cut the sheep accidentally. The longer the time between shearing, the slower the shearer must go.

John and Gary tell us about sheep they've sheared that had not been shorn for three to five years, their fleeces laden with treasures like metal staples and bottle caps. Besides the damage these can do to sheep, they also pose a danger to shearers and their equipment. Fast-moving shears turn metal objects into shrapnel, destroying a shearer's forearm and hand, and breaking or bending the comb on the handpiece. Combs don't come cheap at $15 to $50 each.

If a shearer can handle a lot of sheep, John says, like 70 to 150 sheep per day, and charge $5-$7 per head, they can make $500 to $1,050 plus ranch call on a single job. The faster the shearer, the higher their hourly pay. In most regions, sheep shearing is seasonal work, but the American West's size and climate variability makes it possible to shear almost year-round, provided a shearer is willing and able to travel a bit farther afield. A shearer could conceivably shear in California's hot Central Valley from January through June, working farther north and toward the coast as these cooler areas become warmer later in summer, and "crutching" some flocks in late fall, before they lamb in late winter.

I cannot conceive of shearing a hundred sheep in a single day. I cannot conceive of shearing ten. The difference between one and five sheep, and between five and one hundred sheep, feels equally cavernous, impossible.

Shearing equipment of the sort we use at school, with a motor, drop, handpiece, combs, and cutters, starts at about $1,500. Gary says a shearer can recover this investment in a couple of jobs, in just a week or two. I groan, silently. Ha. I would need years to shear enough sheep to earn $1,500, at least one very long, slow year.

Tuesday, the second day of shearing school, begins with a so-called apple fritter from a gas station, the only business open before 6 a.m. at the northernmost tip of the Napa Valley. It is just me and the Mexican vineyard laborers, the people who keep the wine industry—and most of US agriculture—going. I arrive early and chat with other students outside the barn in the sweet-smelling morning. Puffs of coffee steam, and the sheep's breaths and ours, mingle in the cold air.

Our instructors bring good tidings: we will start by "shearing" yesterday's sheep again, but with our bare hands. We will make the same patterns and strokes as if the shears were on, but they won't be. Since we sheared the wool off yesterday, we will be able to see and feel everything, and to pay more attention to the sheep, proper positioning, our stances, and how to shift our weight more effectively, all without the added worry of the shears.

I am so relieved I feel giddy. My ignorance of sheep anatomy has kept me in a constant state of anxiety because I know I don't even know how much I don't know. Periodically, for example, one of the instructors casually says something like, "Oh, ewes have a big vein running over there, so shear in this direction. That way if you cut them, you don't cut the vein." Oh! They've got a big vein there? You might have mentioned that sooner.

"Shearing" with my bare hands, I can feel the sheep's anatomy. Dim lightbulbs flicker on as I begin to connect body and brain. Yesterday, for example, when I was in the middle of a stroke, Gary had said, "OK, stop! Stop!" Today, when making the same strokes with my bare hands, I understand why he stopped me: I can feel that I've reached the sheep's shoulder bone. I have sensory information to guide what I should do with the shears later. I would gladly shear bare-handed all day, safe inside my new comfort zone, but alas, it cannot last.

I've set a modest Tuesday goal: to get at least one sheep out of the pen and onto the shearing floor by myself. I almost free my second sheep unassisted. I know the trick to getting the sheep down and out of the pen lies in the timing and coordination of turning the sheep's head, which makes the sheep move to sit down, and using my knee to make the sheep lose balance and turn over, but I don't quite get the job done.

Late morning, I drag my deadweight, second sheep of the day out to the shearing floor. My arms shake, gone to jelly, and I can barely hold the shears steady. The sheep between my legs behaves, at least. Once I get her into the correct shearing position she, miraculously, just sits there. She almost seems to say, "All right, greenhorn. I will sit still and take one for the team so you can learn to do this already." She feels relaxed. Does this mean I've achieved the correct position, that I don't even know is correct, to get her to behave this way? If so, I don't know what it is I've done right, so how will I be able to repeat it?

I want to reward the ewe's patience by shearing her as quickly as possible, but speed is antithetical to safety. As time stretches on, I feel I will never finish. I have no concept of how long I've been shearing. Twenty minutes? Forty? And I am not even halfway done. Sweat and tears of frustration sting my eyes, and then, even worse, I nick the sheep's neck. I scream for Carrie to pull the shears off, and stroke the sheep's head and apologize, a constant stream of "I'm sorry, girl. I am so, so sorry."

I force myself to look at the cut, really look at it. It is smaller than my thumbnail and only a little bit of blood is visible, but this does not change the fact that I have nicked my first sheep. I quake from exertion and guilt and look at Gary with tears in my eyes, but he only yells, "Don't look at me! She's fine! Keep going!" I cry and shake and shear, repeating my apology to the sheep until Gary hollers that crying won't help the sheep and she has no idea what the hell I'm saying. He is right. The sheep does not connect my crying with a nick she does not seem to have felt, and crying does not improve my shearing. I can barely see.

I stand up straight, the sheep held by my legs. Attentive Carrie has already turned my shears off. Yes. I will rest my back a minute, calm down, and think straight. My back is so busted I can barely raise my chest. I wipe a forearm over my eyes without noticing or caring that it's full of lanolin. The patient sheep stares up at me, and I feel her every breath beneath my left palm, lightly resting on her left shoulder. Gary is right. She isn't even bleeding anymore. I must be a real trial, the high-maintenance, semi-hysterical city dweller in a barn full of able-bodied, level-headed agriculture people.

Gary tries to reassure me by describing how sheepskin is different. It appears to have two distinct layers, which I can see. A cut through the first layer doesn't create much blood, and I can see another solid layer of skin beneath it. Both layers look like thin membranes. Gary says that, thanks to lanolin, cuts heal completely within a few days, with fresh air and sunlight preventing infection. My cut probably was not painful because, as compared to human skin, sheepskin has a lower density of nerve endings. Sheep really do not notice small cuts, so they do not react, which does not give the shearer a signal that anything happened. Which is probably why this cooperative, mellow sheep is still sitting here.

Carrie turns the shears on and I finish the sheep's neck with one more stroke, before moving on to her left foreleg and shoulder. I take my time, and too much. By the time I finish the long blows, my sheep is, understandably, trying to get away. I feel horrible about it and almost start apologizing again, but think of Gary.

I marvel at the adrenaline that comes with trying to control an animal and remember to do so many other things at once: maintain the correct position, keep the sheep's skin taut so as not to nick it, keep the shears going, keep the comb pointed down and the back of the handpiece up, make sure all the teeth on the comb are down on the skin, don't push the shears, bend at the waist, push your knees in, keep your feet beneath the sheep, don't set the sheep on its tail, keep the sheep comfortable, don't make second cuts (a second pass to remove wool left behind on your first pass, which shortens the staple length of the fiber and wastes wool). It is a full-body, full-brain experience. I cannot see how I will ever get this. Carrie puts a hand on my shoulder after I finish, and it's all I can do to not break down. Avoiding eye contact with other students, ignoring high fives, I practically run to the sink in the back of the barn to hide my frustration and embarrassment.

That day, Tuesday, I shear only two sheep, one in the morning and one in the afternoon, fewer than almost everyone else in class. Carrie tries to console me by noting that Henry and Jordan partially sheared some of her sheep, so she cannot count them as full ones, but I am mortified. Wednesday must be my turning point. No excuses. I can no longer blame my lack of familiarity with the barn and the sheep.

Some people in class, like Alice and Alexis, ultimately shear in order to take care of their sheep. I envy this motivation. I may feel less timid if I had sheep at home, familiar sheep handled often, responsibility for a flock. I decide that tomorrow, Wednesday, I will envision my sheep of the future, all day. Come the prospective sheep arrival, I will wish I'd sheared more than a handful, certainly as many as possible, before trying it on anyone else's sheep, particularly someone expected to pay me. I make a deal with myself: I cannot ever have sheep unless I learn to shear, and shear well, by the end of this week.

On Wednesday, all we do is shear, all day, without pause, three to four students at a time, one student per station. Students who are not actively shearing pull the shears on and off, pick up fleeces, and sweep the floor before the next sheep comes out, to keep things moving faster. No more easing into class, no more long breaks for detailed explanations from instructors: by now, they expect us to know the motions well enough to keep going, to practice and make bodily memory. John announces that, today, our instructors will begin to evaluate us for certification.

The work is relentless. I am dead on my feet by 10 a.m., but the sheep keep coming. Just when each pen contains two sheep, rather than five or six, and we see we're making progress, the barn door heaves open and Jim, the shepherd, appears with several dozen sheep, opens the livestock gate, fills the aisle behind the pens, and packs each pen again. Good God, how many sheep are there? The pens never empty. No matter what time of day, no matter how many hours have passed, there is always another sheep waiting, ears poking out.

I look for the sheep we've sheared, desperate for some visual clue to show the scale of our collective accomplishment but, as we finish, each sheep exits the barn and Jim soon moves the group out to graze open pasture. We see only what we have not done, and that is all that matters. The work will not be done anytime soon, not at the end of today, and not at the end of tomorrow, and we had better keep going if we want a hope of finishing by Friday.

I am not where I want to be, skill-wise. I don't seem to shear any better than I did on Monday. I still have to pause periodically, think through my transition steps. My body does not instantaneously know what position or stance follows the one I'm in. I make too many strokes with the handpiece where others use fewer. I do learn a fitting new phrase from another student that sums it up nicely: "Turned out you was shittin' in knee-high cotton." You thought you had yourself covered, but everyone can see you.

As Carrie and I pull the cord for another shearer and cheer him on, Carrie gets a call that something has come up with her elderly father in hospice. She has to leave that day, late in the afternoon, and I do not want to think about shearing without her. Carrie has given us so much support, compliments, encouragement, reassurance. She has been a one-woman relief crew who offers to take over shearing a sheep midway through to give people a break, or finishes shearing if someone is all out of everything. I walk out of the barn with her and stand in the parking lot while Carrie digs around for a business card, wiping tears from her eyes but trying to keep it together. I feel oafish and ridiculous in my felted, soiled slippers, bulky work pants, and soaked, stained shirt. My legs feel swollen, my hips bigger than usual for having been on my feet all day. Choking up, Carrie tells me, "You're doing a good job. You have to finish class for me, you have to, because I can't and I really want to." We hug and, as her car pulls away, I stand on broken, pokey acorns, reeking of sour sweat and manure, and cry. I cry for her dad, for her daughterly devotion, for my patient, nicked afternoon sheep, for my inability and hubris.

And I have to go in and get another sheep from the pen full of sheep faces. Bottomless, endless pens, so many sheep. Each ewe seems fatter than the previous, though I know they're all about the same size. Immediately after Carrie's departure, I pull a boxer of a sheep with mastitis. She wallops me as soon as I flip her. I try to wrangle her into proper position but, as I lean her back and attempt to place her right foreleg behind my right thigh, she bucks so intensely that my left foot lifts off the ground. I nearly fall on top of her. She's a real acrobat, rebounding off the floor, powered by hip thrusts. Since I am bent in half, my head dangles over her teats and burr-laden rear legs like a speed-boxing bag, and she absolutely pummels me, kicking me in the arms, sternum, chin, eye, and mouth to her heart's content.

After several minutes of this, even Gary nods, crosses his arms, and says, "You got a fighter, there." Raised, red welts and open cuts cover my arms, I taste blood, I think one of my teeth may be loose, and I have not yet started shearing. Unfortunately, neither of us get a shearing reprieve for her having mastitis.

For the first time all week—and which I did not think possible given my love of yarn—I begin to lose my temper. I have tried everything I can think of to make the sheep as comfortable as possible. I make sure she's not sitting on her tail, see if she prefers to have her head up or leaned over to the side, see if she likes sitting up or would rather recline. No matter. She beats the hell out of me. She has mastitis. I can only add to her trouble. I pause and announce, "Might be easier to put this one on my dinner plate than finish shearing her." Gary laughs and says, brightly, "Supposed to shear 'em before you butcher 'em!"

At a certain point, it becomes a simple matter of endurance, of getting through one second, then the next. I lose sight of trying to shear well, of improving my technique. Any focus on footwork and form seems a luxury, so distant and idealistic compared to the next stroke, and the next, and the next.

When I finish, my forearms swollen to pink and red and purple ovals, a wet paper towel held against my cut lip and chin to stanch the bleeding, I allow myself a meager hope for some slack. It is nearly 4 p.m., class ends at 5:00, and each pen has two or three sheep in it. The student who just pulled shears for me has also noticed the pen levels. "Sure is getting late," he says. "They probably won't bring any more in." His speaking these words, aloud, gives me hope. "Yeah," I say. "Those are probably it for the day." I imagine one of the instructors saying, like a manager on a Friday, "You guys got through a lot today. It's 4:30 p.m. Go get a beer. The sheep will still be here in the morning." I replay this line in my mind as if doing so can make it come out of John or Gary's mouth.

The other student looks as pissed off as I feel when, minutes later, the barn door slides open and dozens more sheep run in. No, no. No reprieve. I want to scream, cry, and stomp out of the barn. Fuck this. We will shear until 5 p.m. no matter what we feel like.

Beside me, Randy rocks back and forth, heels to toes, looking at the ground. He lets out a low, whistling breath. "Dig deep," he says, almost inaudibly. "Dig deep, girl. We gotta." It's at the point of having no reserves, of everything gone, that we must force ourselves to get back on the shearing floor to help someone else handle a sheep, or hold a sheep so someone else can take a break or readjust themselves into proper shearing position. We shout the words of encouragement we now know so well, an unconscious litany on autopilot, incantations that make me think I will drop dead if I stop repeating them: "No, it hasn't been as much time as you think! You're faster than that. Think of how far you've come since Monday. You're almost done! That sheep looks better than your last one. I don't see a lot of wool on that sheep."

After we finish, I want to ask some other students out for a beer, burger, or both, but am too shy. I soon realize I should have, because I can't control the steering wheel very well. Though my hands and arms shake uncontrollably, I make it to Cloverdale, suck down the root beer float in two minutes flat, cry more than I have in years, and stop at a drugstore to buy a pack of Salonpas, topical pain relief patches redolent of camphor and menthol. I plaster ten patches across my lower and mid back, dosages be damned, turn the heated seats on to stop my back from seizing up, and re-embark on the hour's drive to my father-in-law Tim's house, where I am staying for the week.

When I reach Tim's house, I walk from the car directly into a skin-itchingly hot shower. While soaping up my left calf, I notice two perfectly hoof-shaped bruises, so sharply outlined they could be tattoos. I can even see where the sheep's hooves are overgrown and need trimming. I laugh. The hoof prints strike me as hilarious and endearing, like a sheep's cleverly designed maker's mark on a piece of pottery. I take a photo of them. Scrubbed and soap scented, wrapped in pajamas and a sweatshirt, I find that Tim has made minestrone soup for dinner, which he serves with buttered sourdough bread and red wine. We eat it outside, in front of his backyard fireplace, already roaring. I inhale two bowls, a salad, and half a loaf of bread.

Dinner is marvelous, a wonder. The previously mundane stuff of daily life seems brand new, resplendent, as if I'm seeing and smelling all of it for the first time. I ache with gratitude: Clean, hot water. The texture of a washcloth. Soup. Salt. Butter. Wine. A chair, any chair, anything that is not the ground, to sit on. The spoon, the fire feel like major marks of civilization. Is this a mania or a nervous breakdown? Is this what it means to break a person in order to build them up, what Randy meant when he likened shearing school to boot camp? I've so lost my moorings, I no longer recognize myself.

I stare at the vibrant fire, hot in my face as the Milky Way appears, its white stripe denser, brighter as the sky darkens. I admit it: the absence of hard, physical labor in my life makes it easier to take things for granted. Can collective lethargy explain our culture of always wanting more, of not knowing the worth of things we already have? Daily, physically demanding work clarifies and simplifies. The basics become the things that matter most, but then, they always are: only our perception of their value changes.

I relish being well and truly done at the end of the day. For the first time in a decade, home means done, a haven. Sleepy with fire, wine, blankets, and bread, I consider how easy it would be to sleep in, to not attend shearing school tomorrow, but the thought feels half-hearted. I want to finish, but why? Out of pride? Obligation to Carrie, because she asked? I don't know. My original motivations disappeared three days ago, when they met reality. Ultimately, I did not go through three days of agony only to quit now, with fewer days ahead of me than behind. I understand why there aren't more sheep shearers, though. That much is clear.

Thursday morning, I pass out Salonpas patches to any classmate who wants them. Within thirty minutes, Jordan becomes their number one fan. Today, we have half as many classmates, and fewer people in the barn means more sheep for the rest of us to shear. Some folks who cannot continue say they will show up for the rest of the week anyway, to lend moral support. We are deeply moved by this gesture, that they do not head back to more comfortable places and relax. Using her drop spindle, Heather "spins in the grease," making raw wool straight into yarn, and knits it into a beer cosy for Mike.

Come lunch, I am genuinely glad I came back. I can't say I'm any good at shearing, but I'm not as bad as I was on Monday. Strangely, my back recovers more quickly with each passing day. I realize our bodies are supposed to do more physical work than they usually do, but the speed of the adaptation comes as a surprise. And, with one day left to go, I am hell-bent on finishing. My mood is bright, buoyed by the fact that I get to see my husband, Ian, at the end of the day. It's easier to get through the sheep with something big to look forward to. That morning, I packed baby wipes, a clean set of clothes, and a garbage bag for my soiled clothes and slippers, and I plan to use them.

I shear three sheep, decently, and don't nick any. I am disappointed it's only three, though, and say so to Jenny, the kind former shepherd at the Extension Center who, with her charming, red-headed toddler, drops in to observe our shearing. "I'd at least like to break into the double digits, have a ten-sheep day," I tell her. Jenny laughs and asks, "Why?! Who wants to shear ten sheep in a day?" She continues, laughing, "I sheared ten sheep in a day, once, and I barely stood up for the next three!"

I depart thirty minutes earlier than usual, drive south, and—hoping to banish any remaining manure smell—roll the convertible top down while I wait for Ian at a ferry landing on San Francisco Bay. I stare at the water as if I can conjure his boat from the fog and waves. Nothing can touch my happiness. We feast on fish and chips and blueberry wheat beer in icy pint glasses at a brewery across the street, and he drives us back to Tim's house as the sun approaches the top of Mount Tamalpais on its way down into the Pacific. I can't stop looking at my sweet, dear guy, his profile a silhouette, pink and orange sundown streaming past behind his head. All is right with the world.

On Friday, the tall metal tower of a baling machine thumps away noisily, pressing collected fleeces into white nylon bags. While it's off, we pile our sheared wool into the baler. When the bale bag is full, the baler roars on, exerting tremendous force and pressure to form the wool into neat, elongated, 450-pound cubes.

I feel relieved, yet depressed. Class ends just when I'm getting the hang of things, just as my body is adapting to more laborious days. I cannot fathom making it through another week of this, but that's exactly what I want. If I followed this week with one more week of school, I think I'd be all right at shearing. Madness. How can I even consider this? Like John said: wooly worms.

After shearing all morning, it is time for a "graduation" ceremony on the shearing floor. Throughout the week, our instructors have watched how we've come along, not only in terms of the number of sheep each of us can shear but how skillfully we handle the sheep, how accurately we achieve the proper shearing positions and transitions, and how well we shear. Students will receive beginning, intermediate, and advanced shearing certificates, though I do not expect to be among them.

It may be common elsewhere in our culture, but shearing school is not a place where everyone gets a trophy for participation. Every outcome was earned and depends on our ability. I do not feel I've gained a skill so much as endured exposure to a new one, which does not make up for the fact that, in my estimation, I've done a thoroughly inadequate job. Getting something you don't deserve casts you in stark relief to people who do. However much a piece of paper might claim some arbitrary similarity between two people, one is better at something than the other, and everybody knows it. John calls students' names, and they walk onto the shearing floor, shake hands with John, Gary, and Mike, face forward, and hold their certificates in front of their chests for a photo. I am so proud of them, I clap, hoot, and holler with abandon. And then, John calls my name. I don't budge, but stare at the instructors, disbelieving. Gary yells at me. "Get up here!" I hug him, he who stayed with me and saw me through it all.

I have never been more proud of anything than the beginner-level sheep shearing certificate I hold in my hands. I may be the first person in my family to graduate from college, and I may have spent seven years earning MS and PhD degrees part time while working full time to pay for them in cash. But those pieces of paper cannot hold a candle to my shearing certificate. This is due, perhaps, to the difference between—in the words of author Matthew Crawford—well-founded pride versus gratuitous self-esteem, the difference between a crew and a team, and the fact that, in being one of a community of shearers, the social character of work isn't separate from it, but intrinsic to it:

> A carpenter faces the accusation of his level, an electrician must answer the question of whether the lights are in fact on, a speed shop engine builder sees his results in a quarter-mile time slip. Such standards have a universal validity that is apparent to all, yet the discriminations made by practitioners of an art respond also to aesthetic subtleties that may not be visible to the bystander. Only a fellow journeyman is entitled to say "nicely done."[1]

We each jot our contact information on a group list and pass it around on a clipboard. I commit to making Jordan some shearing slippers and he gives me two bottles of homemade wine as a down payment. Later that evening, my family and I will find out he's a talented winemaker.

John announces that it's time for a group photo outside, in back of the barn. We find four full bales to sit or stand on. Each bale contains the fleeces of forty-five to fifty-five sheep. I had no sense of the scale of our accomplishment until I climbed a bale and and sat on it, legs dangling above the ground. Even as novices, we've managed to shear over two hundred sheep for about two thousand pounds of wool—measurable, quantitative evidence that we've done something. The existence, size, and contents of the bales cannot be disputed.

After our photo, we head over to a small on-site kitchen for a potluck lunch. People leave early for their long drives home, to Oregon, Nevada, almost to Mexico. Later, I tell my husband that I can't be a shearer, that I have a certificate that says I know how to shear but I don't. I can't responsibly claim that I can shear and charge someone money for it. It would be dishonest. Ian echoes Gary's words, says I need to think of shearing like dancing, that it takes ten thousand hours to get good at something, but I tell him I'm not meant for it. "Maybe if I were a young, able-bodied man like Henry, who's grown up with livestock," I say.

A few days later, Jordan emails our class with an invitation to a shearing day at the commune on the coast where Marie works. I would love to see my classmates again, and I recognize the rare opportunity to indulge my curiosity about the enigmatic hippies. I also feel like a fraud. I don't want to admit, least of all to my more skilled classmates, that I won't be shearing again. It would be more honest to distance myself, to avoid the appearance of any claim to being like they are. I stay home, depressed, thinking of the fun everyone else is having, missing the kindred spirits who got me through so much.

In the weeks that follow, I look at each face in our group photo, all of us perched and arrayed across the wool bales that contain the fruits of our week of labor. I wonder where the homeless herders sleep these days, whether Carrie's father is still alive. I recall that I bought a barrette from Randy and he still hasn't cashed the check I gave him. (Later, I hear a similar story from another shearer: Randy wouldn't cash his payment for a belt buckle.) But it's not just my classmates I think about. Where did our bales go? What became of our fleeces?

FIVE

Bale and Sale

The word "clip" is to wool what "harvest" is to food: both a quantity—as measured in weight—and an event, the days or weeks of labor required to complete it. The clip is the wool sheared from a particular flock or band of sheep (one band is one thousand sheep), as measured in pounds of raw fleece, in the grease. It also describes how much wool a region or state produces in total. Today, approximately 70 percent of the California wool clip is exported annually. (It ranges from 50 to 80 percent, and this has been true since the early 2000s.)

But how, exactly, does all of this export happen? After wool is sheared and baled, each bale needs a buyer and to physically move from farm to factory. This process involves shearers, wool handlers (the people who run freshly shorn fleeces from the shearing floor to the skirting table, and then skirt each fleece, removing manure, paint, and vegetable matter), and wool classers (trained and certified folks who evaluate wool attributes in order to assign quality grades to individual fleeces and full clips); community wool drop sites, traveling wool baling machines, coordination of trucks that ship wool clips from multiple ranches, and wool coring and sampling machinery; warehouses in Roswell, New Mexico, and Bakersfield, California; a wool-testing lab in Denver, Colorado; auctions, wool buyers, container ships, and the Port of Long Beach. A startling amount of these logistics depend on one man from New Zealand.

In the wee hours of a midsummer weekday morning, a text message from an unfamiliar area code and number pops up. "Hi, have made it to California. I will be sorting and baling wool for much of July. You are welcome to catch up! Ian." There was only one Ian it could be: the wool-wise Kiwi who spends part of each year in California and other western states as a field representative for Roswell Wool, the commission wool broker. Immigration issues had temporarily delayed Ian's usual seasonal arrival from New Zealand, but he was usually hard to track down and catch up with, anyway. Ian himself often didn't know where he'd be the following day, or if he'd be there at all, until the night before. It wasn't until 7 p.m. one Thursday night, for example, that I knew Ian would be a few hours north the next morning.

Roswell Wool is a commission wool broker. Through auctions, they sell wool to buyers all over the world on behalf of wool producers. In 2000, Roswell expanded its operations from New Mexico to California. The wool export market is why a California presence makes sense for Roswell: the larger the export market, the greater the need for Roswell to obtain and sell sufficiently large quantities of wool to attract big, overseas manufacturing buyers.

Mike Corn, manager at Roswell Wool, describes a "big old warehouse" in Roswell but says, "There's not much wool in it anymore. It's all in Bakersfield." Roswell bought Cal-Wool, a cooperative warehouse, around 2000 because there wasn't enough wool production in New Mexico alone to sustain Roswell's business. It also doesn't make sense for Roswell to truck California wool to New Mexico for an auction, only to truck it back to California to leave the Port of Long Beach, bound for Asia. Mike says that, initially, California wool producers felt pessimistic about Roswell buying Cal-Wool but, after Roswell sold more wool in its first year than Cal-Wool did in its last, they were willing to give Roswell a try. Cal Cotton (Calcot for short), a cotton cooperative with members in California, Arizona, New Mexico, and West Texas, leases warehouse space to Roswell in Bakersfield. As Mike puts it, "They market cotton so I thought, at least they got an idea of what to do."

Roswell does a lot more than store wool in warehouses and run auctions, though. Roswell is involved in every aspect of wool quality, with the exception of breeding, lambing, and shepherding. They—and specifically Ian MacKenzie—are responsible for many steps in the wool supply chain, including preparation for and organization of shearing days, supply delivery, baling, organizing freight trucking, sampling and testing wool for quality attributes, and more. For half the year, Ian lives on the road, towing a baling machine behind a heavy-duty white pickup truck on a custom-made "baler trailer." These preparations are made primarily for big ranching outfits with a thousand or more head of sheep. If a ranch lies in Ian's general direction, he'll drop off supplies, meet with shearing crews, make sure they have the packs and other supplies they need, and bale and coordinate shipping for the wool if needed.

On shearing days, Ian ensures the sheep are penned and sheared in an order that increases wool quality and the likelihood of a higher sale price at auction. White sheep are sheared first, then white sheep with black faces, then black sheep, then hair sheep. Each batch of wool is kept separate from the others and the shearing floor swept clean between each sheep, because black wool and hair are considered contaminants by the commercial wool industry.

Industrial manufacturers want to buy wool that will scour and dye both well and consistently, and black wool and hair don't. While black wool can be dyed, the final color doesn't look the same as it does on white wool. When a company like Smartwool makes wool shirts in a certain shade of turquoise, for example, they want that shirt to be the exact same color no matter what store it's sold in, consistent throughout. Black and colored wool is, by contrast, appreciated by some hand spinners and fiber artists for its variety and its natural ability to make attractive color blends in hand-spun yarn.

Hair sheep have hair, not wool, and hair does not absorb dye. If you've ever dyed your hair, you know that chemicals are required to open the hair shaft to accept and hold dye, and that dye doesn't last. Ron Cole, a wool consultant and educator, illustrates the point: "A man drives bales of wool up to the gate of a mill. The man at the gate asks, 'Were there any hair sheep in the barn?' The driver answers 'No.' 'Were there any hair sheep on the ranch next door?' The driver says 'Yes.' 'Turn around,' the man at the gate replies." That's how much of a contaminant the commercial wool industry considers hair.

If Roswell fails to maintain high wool quality, Roswell or the wool producer may have to pay claims. Let's say that someone bought several bales of wool and one bale contained a black fleece. That buyer can file a claim against Roswell, which Mike Corn says he's had to pay. It's not common but it does happen, and when it does, it's usually because of black wool or hair contamination.

As a shearing day proceeds, wool handlers and classers sort and skirt wool, classifying piles by grade, according to wool quality guidelines. Just as at shearing school, bellies (wool from the belly of the sheep) are sheared first, immediately removed from the shearing floor, and placed in their own pile. Top knots (the tuft of wool atop the sheep's head) and cheeks are also tossed aside by the shearer, as these can be coarser and contain some hair or kemp, a weak, brittle fiber that, like hair, does not take dye.

Full fleeces are rolled up, thrown, and skirted on the skirting table by trained wool handlers. Vegetable matter like hay and feed is shaken out, and paint and manure tags removed by hand. Pieces of removed wool, called "pieces," land in another pile and receive the label "PCS" on their own bale bag. If a wool classer is present, full fleeces are skirted, handled, categorized, and piled according to grade. The term "grade" encompasses attributes like length, strength, crimp, and fineness, and accounts for weaknesses or breaks in the wool. The "A Line," also called the "main line," is the standard wool quality within the flock being shared, the bulk of the clip. All of the other wool piles are of higher or lower quality (finer or coarser, shorter or longer) relative to the A Line.

After shearing is complete and all fleeces sorted and graded, the wool is baled by grade, like with like. A higher grade brings a higher price for the seller, which explains why the skilled people who skirt fleeces and grade wool are so important: their work affects the grower's wool reputation long after the bales are gone. By taking all of these steps early on in the process, Ian lays the groundwork for wool quality and the best possible sale price for a sheep rancher's wool. The quality and price realized—the money in the rancher's pocket—will be higher because Ian and Roswell did what they do.

I finally catch up with Ian at the Mendocino County Farm Supply store, where we will bale wool for two days. While large ranches with hundreds or thousands of sheep produce enough wool to warrant use of a baling machine onsite, and produce enough bales for a large truck to do a pickup, the same would be overkill (and financially out of reach) for people who produce smaller quantities of wool. But small and mid-sized producers need a way to sell their wool. Some of them put their wool in large, cylindrical jute bags, label them, and drop them off at the Farm Supply.

I hear the rattling din of the baling machine as I park my car. Regretfully, I did not think to bring ear plugs. It's early summer, not even 8 a.m. and already pushing one hundred degrees. A colossal wildfire rages several miles to the east and a pyrocumulus cloud—a fire cloud that looks like a mushroom cloud—rises over the uplifted volcanic rock peak of Mount Saint Helena against an improbably clear blue sky. Rail tracks border the Farm Supply on one side and a tiny municipal airport occupies the other. Cal Fire planes land and take off every few minutes, their buzz barely audible over the noise of the baling machine.

On the other side of the tracks, in long dry grass and trees behind a single-story business, an itinerant camper awakens. He rolls up his blankets, packs his bag, and walks north along the tracks, blurry from heat reflecting off creosote. Stacked against a cyclone fence like gigantic white blocks, bales of wool bear "HREC" labels, and it hits me: they're the bales from shearing school, dropped here to hitch a ride on the larger truck that will come.

I find Ian tossing wool into the baler and remember that grease-weight wool is surprisingly heavy. I expect to do more heaving than tossing. A ratty, threadbare hand towel hangs from a portable shade structure so Ian can mop his brow. I add my own identical towel and am relieved Ian brought shade. He is red-faced, sweating profusely beneath a white cowboy hat, and wearing jeans, steel-toed boots, and a button-down checkered shirt. We're similarly dressed and laugh to find we both "got it at Goodwill." Just behind Ian and the baling machine, two stacks of jute bags, full of wool, are piled more than a story high against an exterior wall and beneath an awning. I could climb the bags to the rafters. We have a lot to do.

When wool producers dropped off these bags, they filled out forms with their contact information and the quantity and type of wool: "12 Months Lamb, Blackface (BF), Whiteface (WF)," for example. Ian and I need to sort all of the wool dropped off by multiple growers into like piles, according to label and wool attributes, weigh them, and evaluate the contents of each bag to confirm they match the label. Then, we must weigh how much wool each producer contributes to the bale, to ensure the producer is paid fairly for his or her share of the bale when the bale is finally sold at auction. Finally, we will combine the small bags of wool into larger, standard-sized bales.

Ian and I climb the high, malleable stacks of jute bags, some packed more tightly than others, each bag longer than a person is tall. I fear my steps on the soft bags will send others rolling down on me, or that my foot will slip between bags and I'll fall. Together we drag the bags, heavy and cumbersome, down to the ground and stack them in groups closer to the baler.

As we pull bags down, Ian reads the wool grower's name from the bag label while I find the corresponding drop-off slip on a clipboard. I tell Ian how many bags of what type of wool that grower dropped off to see if we've found all of the bags. We'll start baling by volume, with growers who dropped off enough wool to make their own full bales. After these bales are made, we'll move on to smaller batches from multiple growers that need to be combined in order to create a single bale of a specific type of wool. We pass information from bale bag and drop-off slip to bale label, which Ian affixes to the top end of the bale.

Ian is an expert wool classer. He's called "old butterfingers" since his finger tips are, somehow—at the ends of hands and forearms that look sunburned and purple patched beyond repair—as sensitive as a laboratory micrometer. A micron is one millionth of a meter, and a measure of wool's fineness: the lower the micron count, the finer the wool. The higher the micron count, the coarser the wool. Ian can feel the micron count of wool within half a micron's accuracy.

The wool we're pushing into the baler is not great stuff. It's short, just one to two inches long. Some of it is tender, easily snapping apart at weak points. Much of it is dirty, full of blown soil and vegetable matter—manure tags, straw, and, the worst contaminant of all, polypropylene, which comes from all of the plastic on today's farms, namely ropes.

Ian reads wool staples—full-length pieces of wool—like tea leaves. By looking and tugging at a staple, he can suss out its geographic origin, its region in California ("This is Los Baños" or "Rio Vista, this") and sometimes the specific ranch ("Think this is Jenny's wool"). He knows the climate, whether or not the wool came from a range sheep, the breed, and if the wool comes from a crossbreed of two or more breeds of sheep. I wonder: Has anyone had their hands on more American wool?

Ian will look at a piece of wool, squint, see a line in it, and say, "This was about four months ago." He will then ask a wool grower, "What happened about four months ago?" The grower thinks for a moment and answers, "We moved them off pasture to hay." Ian may be a man of few words, but it is a wonder to watch and listen to him work. His hands know so much.

Ian estimates that the wool we're baling will fetch about $1.20–$1.80 per pound. It will almost certainly go to buyers in India or China, be scoured, and be used in products where consumers won't see it, like wool mattress stuffing. Ian says, "At least there is a buyer." He has a point, but $1.20–$1.80 per pound is not a lot of money. It covers the cost of the shearing but not much else, certainly not the food and water that the sheep need to grow the wool, to say nothing of the rancher's or shepherd's time. It's another chicken-and-egg scenario I keep seeing. Wool growers do not have an incentive to produce high-quality wool when prices are low, and they realize lower prices because their wool quality is low.

Ian prepares the baling machine for the next bale. Roswell Wool supplies Ian with new, proper equipment, including bale bags with labels and metal hooks to securely close each bale. Ian drops the bale bag into the center of the baling machine. He locks the bale bag into place on all four sides by closing four metal bars down on the flaps of the bag, and we're ready to go.

We weigh a jute bag containing 170 pounds of wool and drag it over to the baling machine. Before we cut into a bag, we record the description of the contents, which the wool grower has written on the bag with a Sharpie. On a yellow legal pad, Ian writes the destined bale number in the left column, the grower's last name, the grower ID number, the type of wool, and a Roswell classification number that describes the quality and class of wool as Ian observes it. Inside the bag, fleeces are layered in cylindrical disks, which I throw and press down into the open bale bag. When the wool has filled the baler, we turn on the baling machine, press a lever down, and the metal top of the baler (a flat, metal square) comes down and compresses the wool. I don't want my hand anywhere near that top coming down. The baler will take an arm off.

Ian and I cannot really talk while we work. The baling machine is too loud.

When the wool cannot be compressed any further, Ian turns the machine off, closes the flaps of the bale bag, and uses bale hooks to lock the end flaps together. He grabs a fat black marker and refers to the yellow notepad to label the end of the bale with the wool grower ID, wool classing number, type description, and the label "Youngmark"—which turns out to be the last name of Jeff Youngmark, whose ranch in Dunnigan, California, serves as a wool drop-off and pickup site for multiple wool growers. Ian explains that all of this wool, from so many different growers, is being labeled as one lot so that there will be sufficient quantity of wool, of similar type, to create an auction lot of large enough size for a big buyer.

We release the bale from the machine and I grab a corner of it with a metal hay hook, piercing the bale bag to drag it into position. Using the hook, I tip the bale up enough on its side to get it started, and then run, "rolling" the rectangle that is almost as high as my waist, pushing and running along the pavement until the bale reaches its resting point near the other bales. Momentum makes up for my insufficient strength. I should sell this as agricultural parkour to city folks. Rolling a 450-pound bale, quickly, across blacktop on a hundred-degree day is work.

And so on, for two days, until the jute bags are gone. On the evening of the second day, Ian presses wool and other things into the baling machine for transport and hand cranks the baler up onto a custom trailer. As I attempt to lift an old tire onto the truck, Ian tells me to stop, to save my back for shearing. He wants to reach the Youngmark site in Dunnigan before nightfall. He pulls away, and I notice the license plate on Ian's truck says "Roswell."

In the next few days, a freight truck will arrive, the bales will be loaded, and when the truck arrives at the Roswell warehouse in Bakersfield, California, the bales will be sorted, from tags to super fine. Mike Corn says, "You pull the puzzle apart once you unload the truck. Short, coarse, fine, medium, who knows how many groupings there will be. It's very important that we have producers label packs properly, labels on the fastened end, and labels sewn to the pack. Name, the brand to draw on, the type of wool in that bale, and bale number." Now I understand why Ian was so careful about accurate labeling.

At the warehouse, each bale is weighed and two types of test samples taken: a core sample and a grab sample. For the core sample, twelve small cores—half-inch diameter tubes—reach out like mechanical eels, insert themselves at various points in the bale, and extract samples in the shape of miniature donuts. All bales must be cored to 80 percent of depth, to international standard. The grab sample is pulled from the bale with a grappling hook, and looks much like the arcade game in which you try to steer a hook to grab and lift toys. The core sample is sent to Denver, Colorado, where it is evaluated for yield and fiber diameter (micron count) at the Yocom-McColl lab. The grab sample is sent to Roswell, which Roswell uses for physical viewing at its auctions, to enable buyers to make a visual appraisal.

Five to six wool sales are held at specific times of year, which coincide with peak shearing seasons of spring and fall in the West: late March, April, and May, and then late September and early November. Wool seldom sits for more than thirty days before it is sold, and all wool at a Roswell sale is offered to the entire wool trade, not just to any one buyer. All Roswell sales take place in sealed bid format, not an outcry auction system. In a sealed bid auction, all bidders submit sealed bids to the auctioneer simultaneously. This means that no bidder knows how much the other auction participants have bid, nor does Roswell announce the price that was offered. The Roswell auctioneer might say something like "Burlington high on Lot 1" but give no price.

Sealed bid auctions take time. Buyers submit bids on premises that day, and it's slow going. It is difficult for the auctioneer to get through more than thirty lots per hour, so anyone interested in Lot 150 on page five has a fair wait time, since the auction begins with Lot 1.

Despite its secrecy on price, the sealed bid system is completely transparent to those directly involved. Producers who attend the sale see buyers face-to-face. The wool producer knows what the buyer paid, which is the bid that was offered less itemized deductions and freight costs. In the warehouse system, producers have high awareness of how their wool was marketed and sold. Mike Corn doesn't "sell a lick of wool without first talking to the wool producer, which is tough because very few people send people to the sale." As Mike says, "It's the customer's wool," so he always asks first, even if they tell him, "If you think it's fair, sell it."

Mike and Ian call each and every producer before a sale is finalized. With two hundred or so people to call and fifteen to thirty minutes per call to confirm all of the sales and prices, it is a time-consuming effort and more of a courtesy than a necessity. But, as a wool producer himself, it's what Mike does. "I run this business to make money for my wool, but if I run it to make money for my wool then it should carry over and make money for my customers. Decisions I make on how my wools are marketed, and who they are marketed to, should benefit all of my producers' customers."

At the end of the day, some wools get more than they deserve and some don't. All wool, however, is sold on reputation more than the information in the Roswell auction catalog. The first thing a wool buyer (and especially a US wool buyer) wants to know is, "Whose wool is it and where did it come from?" Wool buyers purchase wool based on its past performance, and the black book with a list of wool producers from whom wool should never be purchased is real. Certain producers have a reputation for using too much paint to mark their sheep, for example, or for poly contamination, or—on the other hand—for having the longest and strongest wool in the country.

California's perceived wool quality has risen, in part, because Roswell now operates in the state and thanks to the way Roswell runs its sales. "When we first come in and bought Cal-Wool, they had been selling all wools private treaty, forever. And their perception with the outside wool buying community was that 'California's got a pile of shit wool.'" A private treaty wool sale takes place completely outside of the competitive auction system. In a private treaty sale, a wool buyer purchases wool directly from wool growers, then resells that wool under their own brand, whether through the auction system or directly, through private sales, to mills, overseas manufacturers, or other entities. The problem is that a bunch of wool from wool growers is put together, and the lowest quality wool sets the standard for the lot. Higher quality wool doesn't make up for lower quality wool, which lowers the price the buyer pays for all of it.

When Roswell first expanded into California, Mike Corn found that California's poor reputation for wool wasn't entirely accurate.

"California" was always said in a negative way, but I said, "That's not what I'm seeing here." I get out there, and even those Bakersfield wools were 20 micron, 4 inches long, little tender. The further north [in] California you got, the stronger it got. By the time you got up to Firebaugh, best you got in the country. Los Baños and Firebaugh on up toward Rio Vista, it's good wool. When we took over, producers' wools were sold on their own merit, and they started getting their product out there with their name on it, and some of the California wools started to do better. Once they started getting wools sold on their own merit and not pooled they started seeing a difference. It was great news for California wool.

After the sale, Roswell pays the producer less a sale commission, coring and testing charges, and any costs of supplies like bale bags. But Roswell doesn't charge a wool grower anything unless the wool is sold. Roswell finances freight, shearing, and baling supplies for a period of time, sometimes thirty days, sometimes six months. The wool buyers—those winning bidders from the auction—pay after they are invoiced and have a full thirty days to pay. This means that Roswell pays wool producers before it has been paid by wool buyers. Mike Corn doesn't necessarily like it, but it's the way it's always been done. The cost of doing business is having money out thirty days.

Mike says, "When we first started in 1993, all the wools were still in burlap bags and sold and stayed in the country, the United States. Now it's all in nylon packs and 60 to 80 percent is exported." Most California wool is exported because, with few to no labor and environmental regulations, it costs less to mill and process into fabric overseas than in the United States. At the time of this writing, China is the largest wool producer and the largest textile processor in the world, but is having growing pains. Labor costs in China are rising, and some wool that was processed in China is now being processed in India. "Wherever it's cheaper is where it's gonna go," says Mike. And so, most California-grown wool goes on to the Port of Long Beach, one of the busiest container ports in the United States (second only to the Port of Los Angeles).

In addition to auctions, some wool growers also have the opportunity to contract sell (presell) directly to a buyer, like Pendleton. Wool producer Lani Estill and her family run a few thousand head of sheep in California's high desert country, on the Bare Ranch in the Surprise Valley, near the Nevada border. The Bare Ranch has what's known as "a reputation clip," wool of very high quality, which is why a high-caliber buyer like Pendleton might be interested. In order to obtain the best price for her reputation clip, Lani sends their previous year's wool testing results to Utah Wool Marketing, Pendleton, and Roswell.

A representative from each of these prospective buyers (including Ian McKenzie) examines the Estill clip to see if it looks like last year's. Each representative then tries to get Lani a good price. Lani says the ranch does better "putting it out there and making them compete a little bit," and that they have sold directly to Pendleton (which has mill operations in Pendleton, Oregon, and Washougal, Washington, with company headquarters in downtown Portland) for the last two years. She feels better when her wool stays on the West Coast: "Yes, I care. I want our wool to be here, West Coast preferred but the United States, definitely."

When a direct buyer like Pendleton buys a wool clip that Roswell might otherwise get, it makes Roswell's business that much harder. The volume of wool produced in the United States is getting smaller and smaller, but Roswell needs to source and sell a certain amount of wool to stay in business. Nobody likes losing turf, especially the few people left in the already diminished US wool marketing and warehouse business.

From Mike Corn's perspective, the US wool industry has been hit hard. There are so many challenges that, to Mike, it still feels like a net loss. But, from the perspective of Lani and others, some domestic wools are profitable again. As the Livestock Conservancy, an organization devoted to the conservation of rare livestock breeds, points out,

> For the first time in quite a good number of years, it's actually now profitable to raise wool, and especially if you have a heritage breed....If you take, for instance, Lincoln Longwool sheep, beautiful lustrous wool but very resilient, strong fibers, so they were used to create carpets and socks. And so if somebody's looking to create a carpet that's going to stand the test of time, Lincoln Longwool's going to be the way to go. Or you could have Santa Cruz sheep fiber, which has been likened to natural Lycra, and so it's very stretchy, and a wonderful fiber if you're looking for something that's going to have the properties similar to the Lycra....It can be a challenge for the beginner spinner, but for a spinner that knows what they're doing it's a fabulous product. So there is good news in some areas where heritage breeds are actually beating out the commercial ones.[1]

I wanted to know more about wool like this, high quality, special wool, sometimes from heritage breeds, that was profitable. What happened to the 30 percent or so of the California clip that was not exported, that came from producers who didn't want their wool to be sold overseas? How did smaller producers, without multiple bales worth of wool, make money from their clips? Did they make money?

Ian McKenzie closes a new bale of wool in Ukiah, California.

SIX

Husbandry

"The vet is coming about 9:30 to euthanize the goat. Just a heads-up in case you want to come a little later (if you even get this)."

I do not get it. I am already on my way to Vacaville, California, to meet Robin Lynde and her flock of sixty-five or so Jacob sheep. Vacaville sits on the western edge of California's Central Valley, separated from the Napa Valley by Lake Berryessa. For about half the year the Central Valley is searing hot, drought-dry, and dusty. Even when I drink as much water as I can manage, wear a sun hat, and stay in the shade, my lips darken and crack. Though it is early in the morning and the summer, it's going to be a scorcher. Heat mirages ripple off the pavement and cows stick to the shady side of the hills. A week ago, the temperature reached 108°F.

Since shearing school ended, I've been too petrified to shear for anyone. I want to be more comfortable with—and skilled at handling—sheep. I am, however, ready and willing to clean pens, stack hay bales, and do whatever else in order to learn more about sheep firsthand. I figured free labor (albeit unqualified) might be useful to someone. In this case, it is less than free for me: I've paid Robin to let me work on her land, with her sheep, and to learn.

Robin offers something called Farm Club, a deceptively simple name for an innovative fiber program. Farm Club is structured much like community supported agriculture (CSA) programs are for food, in which CSA members pay a farmer at the beginning of the growing season for a share of the anticipated produce harvest, and receive shares of fruits and vegetables once harvest begins. The CSA members provide the farmer with up-front, steady income no matter the outcome, and some CSAs accept contributions of labor in lieu of some or all cash subscription costs.

Similarly, members of Robin's Farm Club pay an annual membership fee early in the year and, at the end of the first wool-growing season, receive either a raw fleece from one of Robin's sheep, roving (wool fiber ready for hand spinning, fluffy and similar in appearance to pillow or toy stuffing), or yarn, as well as the opportunity to work on scheduled days. I thought it was a brilliant idea and a win-win all around. Robin got additional income and many hands to make light work, while Farm Club members got quality time with sheep (lambs included) and the local yarn, fleece, and roving we wanted. I hoped participation in Farm Club would train me to properly handle and tend to sheep.

Just past new stucco sprawl, a megachurch, and a Genentech office, I exit Highway 505 and turn onto a two-lane county road bordered by an irrigation canal and rectangular brown fields. I'm intimidated and a bit nervous, a dilettante who has paid to play in Robin's world. Robin is a true fiber professional, a successful and well-known wool grower, shepherd, craftsperson, and entrepreneur who has created and manages multiple lines of business. In addition to producing high-quality yarn, roving, fleeces, and sheepskins, Robin is a master weaver who creates blankets, shawls, and more, some of them with yarn she spins herself. She teaches classes on spinning and weaving in a complete yarn shop and studio that sits between her house and barn, where she also sells looms, spinning wheels, books, and other equipment and supplies. Robin travels to fiber festivals to show her sheep (and, not infrequently, win ribbons), and she sells some of her lambs each year. She sells sheep to people who are starting or adding to flocks of their own and sends about eighty lambs to butcher each year and sells the meat. All of this work provides income and keeps the Jacob breed, a rare and ancient one, alive.

A clearly displayed sign, illustrated with the silhouette of a four-horned sheep, marks Robin's neat and pretty property, as do pomegranate and lemon trees and a substantial garden of greens. I park on gravel near a wooden gate, the entrance to the back of her house and the front of her shop, shaded by maple and locust. Robin's farm business, Meridian Jacobs, is so named for her land along Meridian Road and the Jacob breed of her sheep, which graze six flat, irrigated acres of her total ten. I walk toward the gate but stop when I see two protective sheep dogs headed my way from the back of the property. Rusty is an aging brown and white border collie, a trained sheepherding dog, and Maggie is a new arrival, a butterscotch-colored rescue mutt, cautiously curious and skittish.

Robin follows them, thin, wiry, and all muscle, with sharp features, big brown eyes, and silver hair cut short beneath a baseball cap. As soon as I see her, I know something is wrong. Though she walks deliberately and calls to the dogs, she's also wiping tears away with the cuffs of her bleached shirt sleeves. Robin explains that the vet is coming to put down the goat. "You sure picked a day to come," she says, wryly.

"This is not what I signed up for," I think. My first experiences with livestock have been that of near or actual animal death: the cut sheep at shearing school, and now a goat at the end of her life. Any farmer will tell you that farms are full of dirt, manure, blood, and death, but I seriously underestimated the frequency with which they appear.

The goat and I are namesakes: she, too, is Stephanie. As a kid, Stephanie was the 4-H dairy goat project of one of Robin's sons, Chris. Stephanie is the family pet and not, as I'd hoped, one of many thousand head of livestock, which I wanted to believe might somehow make her death easier. Chris and Robin's husband, Dan, are inside the house, preferring not to see Stephanie's last moments.

Robin and I reach the barn, near a hedge of blackberry bramble, past a hot metal roof where sheep skulls dry. Robin points out that Stephanie shares her pen with Little Chicken. Little Chicken is exactly that, almost half the size of a normal chicken. She lays very few eggs and, when she does, sits on them forever. When I see Stephanie and Little Chicken together, Little Chicken beside her rotten eggs on the ledge above Stephanie's pen, I am suddenly sad for Little Chicken. I wonder if she'll move on from the goat pen after Stephanie dies or if she will age in place, alone.

Stephanie glimmers. She is the color of wheat and pale barley and seems ephemeral in the dust motes and filtered light of the barn. Robin gestures to her and says, "It's time. It is. I mean, she can't lay down anymore. She's stuck standing." It's true. Stephanie's bones and joints no longer work. Every few minutes she shifts the weight in her hips from side to side, paws the straw beneath with a front hoof, and attempts to lie down only to find her body unable to deliver her to some rest. Stephanie's eyes look desperate, bewildered, and depleted. She leans her head against a hay bale and looks at us, but doesn't eat. It is heartbreaking. All I can think to say is, "Better too soon than too late."

Nancy, the vet, tanned and freckled, arrives in jeans, a baseball cap, and a faded tie-dyed tee. I want to ask exactly what to expect, but refrain. Nancy and Robin already seem to know. Robin, tears on her cheeks, decides Stephanie's last moments should take place in a corner formed by hay bales in the center of the barn, near a gate that swings out to pasture. I tell myself to toughen up and be useful. Don't cry. Don't make it about you. Be useful to Robin.

Robin leads Stephanie over and sits down on a hay bale where she can feed and cradle Stephanie, who is still stuck standing. I squat on the barn floor beside Stephanie and pet and scratch her side and belly, while—on her opposite side—Nancy readies a syringe. Stephanie, enjoying the attention, munches grass from Robin's hand. Nancy injects Stephanie behind her left shoulder and, in a split second, Stephanie's legs buckle. Finally, she can lie down.

I should be so lucky. We treat dying animals more humanely than we do dying people.

Robin and I lift the very heavy Stephanie into a wheelbarrow and roll her out to pasture, to a hole that Robin started digging earlier that morning. The sun is white in my eyes so I keep them down, aimed at less reflective soil and away from Stephanie's face and body. Robin and I attempt to place Stephanie in the hole but it's not quite long enough for her. We lift her back into the wheelbarrow and I dig while Robin goes to ask Dan to help finish up.[1]

Stephanie's body is in the wheelbarrow beside me and, eventually, I take a good, long look at her. Though I've sat with dying people as they passed, I've never seen a dead animal that wasn't a fish, roadkill, or hunted. Stephanie's eyes are half open and her long tongue lolls out the side of her mouth. Her teeth look loose and show her age, ground down with a lot of space between them. Human death, segregated in the hospital, the nursing home, the morgue, is so rarely in plain view. Not on a farm. Digging the hole in dirt as I am, it's impossible to ignore that death and rotting are necessary for the life of the soil, critical food for other living beings. I am comforted by how up-front and undisguised

Stephanie's death, and specifically her body, are, and by the knowledge of a minuscule soil world that will receive her. There is less dignity in a suddenly vanished life, whose departure no one saw fit to witness, so perhaps it's fortunate that I could witness Stephanie's. It is an honor to have a bit of time to see her as she is, for what she was, for what she will continue to be to the land on which she lived.

A teary-eyed Dan relieves me, and Robin and I walk back toward the barn where the sheep have gathered. First we will vaccinate ewes and then halter-break lambs. Unless they are pets who know humans bring food, sheep want nothing more than to get away from people, so they walk away from us and toward the barn. The flock headed into the barn for vaccination is composed entirely of ewes, female sheep at least one year of age and older. Wethers (castrated rams), rams (male sheep at least one year of age and older), and ram lambs (under one year old) are penned separately to mitigate the danger they pose to other sheep and to control when breeding, and thus lambing, occurs. If not kept apart from the rest of the flock, the rams could impregnate ewes (including their mothers and sisters) at too young an age, or too soon after they've given birth.

Robin's Jacob sheep look quite unlike the Targhee sheep at shearing school, which are what probably comes to mind when you hear the word "sheep." Created in the 1920s at the USDA Sheep Station in DuBois, Idaho, Targhee are white fleeced and large framed. They were cross-bred from Rambouillet, Corriedale, and Lincoln sheep to create a hardy sheep well suited to the rough conditions of the western range and that produced high-quality meat and wool. Jacob sheep, by contrast, have ancient origins. They are named for the spotted sheep mentioned in the Bible (Genesis 30), when Jacob keeps all of the spotted sheep from his father-in-law, Laban's, flock around three thousand years ago. In spite of their name, however, no genetic evidence links these sheep to the biblical flock.[2]

Jacob sheep are very rare and considered a threatened breed by the Livestock Conservancy, which has a five-stage scale that describes the status of particular breeds of livestock: critical, threatened, watch, recovering, and study. Threatened status means that fewer than one thousand registrations of the breed take place in the United States each year, and

Jacob sheep head out to pasture at Meridian Jacobs farm in Vacaville, California.

that the known global population is fewer than five thousand animals. Such is the case with the Jacob sheep.

Jacob sheep, categorized a primitive breed, have survived with very little human intervention. They are spotted, with brownish-gray and white, or black and white, fleeces. They are frequently mistaken for goats by the general public because of their prominent and often large horns, of which they might have between two to six (but usually two to four). Both Jacob rams and ewes have horns, the rams' larger. Of sheep that have four horns, two might stand straight up on top, like parallel six-to-twelve-inch unicorn horns, while two more horns curve out to the side and down, sweeping back behind the ears or curving beneath the jaw.

Many Jacobs have spotted legs and distinctive facial markings, the most striking of which are symmetrical: a wide, white stripe down the center of the forehead and black nose, for example, with cheeks and eyes surrounded by black on each side. Most Jacob fleeces are spotted black and white, and a rare few have an almost purplish-gray cast, like dusty pale lavender. I attribute this unusual color to the dim light in the barn until Robin tells me the sheep is a "lilac," a color pattern in which the markings on the sheep's face are gray-brown instead of black, and the dark wool is also a gray-purplish brown instead of black.

The Jacob sheep's spots and tall, curving horns made them attractive to the British landed class, who kept Jacob sheep on their land for appearance's sake. This attraction may have helped preserve the breed. Today there are two major types of Jacob sheep. Those in Great Britain have, over time, undergone breeding shifts to make them more productive meat animals, so they are now significantly larger, while those in North America are still smaller and closer in appearance and other characteristics to the old-style sheep.[3]

A few Bluefaced Leicesters ("BFLs" in fiber parlance) are mixed in with Robin's Jacob sheep, and they are obviously different. Bluefaced Leicester sheep are one solid color, don't have horns, and have longer ears that stick straight up from a high point on their heads. Their faces aren't very wooly, and their bodies are both taller and rounder than the Jacob. The BFL body shape is different, too: the neck is longer than that of the Jacob and the face broader. The BFL's longer nose is reminiscent of that of a bull terrier dog, whereas the Jacob's noses are shorter and their faces more diminutive, almost cute.

Robin got a BFL ram several years ago and now has three of his offspring in her ewe flock. Robin discovered crossbreeding accidentally, when one of her Jacob ewes accidentally bred with a Merino ram in a truck during transit. The result got Robin thinking about crossbreeding, and she decided BFL would be a good Jacob cross. Robin's BFL-Jacob lambs were bigger and, since Robin sells about half her sheep for meat, the larger size was a boon in that regard. As far as long-wool sheep breeds (bred for their ability to grow long, lustrous, loosely crimped wool) go, BFL is on the finer end of the spectrum with a nice hand that makes it pleasant to work with.

Robin and I will treat the ewes with Covexin, a one-time vaccine injection for clostridial diseases (the bacterium that causes tetanus and botulism), and administer the flock's third day of sulfadimethoxine and Safe-Guard treatments, oral drenches recommended by Nancy based on fecal samples from some of Robin's sheep. Sulfadimethoxine is an oral antibiotic used to treat infections in sheep, coccidia in this case. Coccidia are protozoan parasites that live in the cells of the sheep's intestines. They are passed in the feces and picked up by other sheep through contaminated feed and water.[4] Safe-Guard is a dewormer used to treat the barber pole worm, a parasitic nematode (roundworm) that causes anemia, bottle jaw, and death in infected sheep and goats.

My job is to measure and fill all three syringes (the Covexin injection and two oral drenches) based on each sheep's weight, which is logged on a weight sheet affixed to my clipboard. Robin catches a sheep and reads me its ear tag number. I find the sheep's ear tag number and corresponding weight on one of the sheets on my clipboard, then fill the syringes with the appropriate dosage. I hand each syringe, one at a time, to Robin while she holds the sheep, injects Covexin behind the right foreleg, and places each oral drench gun in the sheep's mouth for it to swallow. After Robin finishes I use a grease pen to draw a line on the sheep's forehead so we can glance at the flock and see who isn't fully treated and needs to be caught.

And so we proceed from one sheep to the next. Each sheep is caught just long enough for Robin to inject its armpit area, shoot oral drenches into its mouth, mark its head, and send it on its way. We work together seamlessly, focused and without much chitchat, and it's quite pleasant. The sheep are too loud to make much conversation possible, anyway.

Robin does all of the animal handling. I am wary of the Jacobs' prominent horns, which could hit me in the chin or the face if they jump. Robin calmly walks among her flock, the sheep moving away from her but unable to go very far. She catches sheep by grabbing one of the sheep's horns, then slips her other hand beneath the sheep's jaw to control it before straddling the sheep over its shoulder area. Robin's Jacob sheep are—unlike the Targhee at shearing school—short enough to straddle. This puts a sheep's neck and shoulders between our thighs and its head and horns in front. The sheep's horns effectively capture it: The sheep won't run forward into the pressure of our hands on its jaw, and the horns conveniently catch on the front of our thighs, preventing the sheep from escaping through the back, though this method does create spectacular inner thigh bruises.

I ask Robin how she does all of this herself, between measuring out syringes, catching sheep, administering and recording medications, and marking sheep. Does she somehow manage to control the sheep with her legs and do the rest herself? "It takes a lot longer," she says.

How did the term "unskilled" ever come to be paired with "agricultural labor?" This may be only my sixth day in a barn, but I am already painfully aware that the skill required to work well with sheep will take years to get right, and many more to master. It requires dozens of fine-tuned, well-timed movements in combination with those of the animals. So far, agricultural labor is distinctly not work that just anyone can walk in and do efficiently or well, and the term "unskilled" is an insult.

After the sheep are treated, Robin and I clean the sheep pens with a pitchfork and a shovel to scrape the urine-soaked, ammonia-scented, matted hay and manure—which is quickly becoming soil—into piles. We pitch it all into wheelbarrows we've brought into the barn and placed alongside the pens, and they fill quickly. I roll the heavy wheelbarrows out to the big manure pile. The sheep and Amaryllis, the donkey, join me there. They know that green alfalfa feed, buried in the pens, has been turned and is now available for the taking. There they stand, munching atop the manure pile, the blue sky and brown hills like a portrait studio backdrop. What would the English landed gentry make of this scene? Regal Jacob, indeed.

The morning flies by and becomes afternoon. It is very hot, and the barn feels stuffy and close. I don't mind any of the work. Cleaning pens may seem unappealing and mundane, but I like knowing it contributes to the health and cleanliness of animals. The smell of manure doesn't bother me, and I'm struck by how different a clean, healthy farm smells compared to the largest cattle feed lot on the West Coast: Harris Ranch in Coalinga, which Californians commonly refer to as "Cowschwitz" when passing on I-5. The two are not even comparable.

Since the main chores are done, Robin offers to show me her yarn shop. I leave my mucky shoes on the porch and am careful not to let my soiled clothes touch anything in her well-ordered, civilized space. When she and Dan purchased the property in 1999, it did not have a yarn shop or people coming out for lessons, but Robin's hobbies grew into a flock and fiber business. As she describes, "I've always sold some wool and I've always done some weaving, and selling stuff at the Artery (a gallery in Davis, California), stuff related to the fiber business but not the farm. This business as it is has been about ten years. It sort of became...I had a store, and then I could teach classes out of here."

Robin's flock produces medium to medium-fine fleeces (29–30 microns on average). They're easy to clean with one wash and one rinse, whereas many raw fleeces require at least two to three washes and a rinse. Robin's medium-fine wool has a wide range; it's a good fit for many kinds of fiber projects. It's not fine enough for underwear, for instance, but is suitable for gloves, hats, blankets, and sweaters. Even Jacob britch wool (from the sheep's hindquarters) can be used for outerwear or rugs.

The Jacob's colored spots also make its fleeces interesting to work with. Hand spinners can buy a fleece and sort the colors, or they can spin the multicolored fleece randomly to obtain variegated colors, or colors that blend to gray. Robin says that "dyeing Jacob wool is cool because the white and gray take color differently. With the exception of britch wool, Jacob black wool is not coarser than the other colors. The different colors behave in roughly the same way, so it can all be used in the same project without difficulty." Robin's fleeces are also easy for beginner spinners to handle: the Jacob wool's middle-of-the-road qualities make it easy to learn to spin with.

Recalling my San Francisco yarn shop and quest for local yarn, I ask Robin, "Can you afford to sell wholesale?"

"No," she answers. "Some shops seem...negative that I won't sell to them, but I can't sell my yarn to a yarn shop for $15 per skein. I need to sell for $30 per skein. If a yarn shop wants to buy my yarn for $30 per skein and sell it for a higher price, fine, but I can't sell it for less." After a pause, she adds,

> I want people to think about where the fiber came from and what went into the whole production of it. It is grown here, and I have my hands

on through most of the processes. I grew the sheep, I grew the wool, I'm trying to do stuff that makes me a living. Where are you spending your money? Are you spending it in China or are you spending it here? Start to recognize that it's here, locally. There are true costs where, if you buy from China, we're not paying those costs. That's why it is priced as it is. No, you can't get this at Walmart. It's wool, not acrylic or a blend. Not to get snooty, like in wine country, but you know where it came from. It's an honest, agricultural, California product. It's got character. It's unique. Jacob sheep in the whole world of wool are unique, and the Jacob sheep I have are unique. It is different.

Robin's words remind me of a passage I read years earlier in a Wendell Berry essay, in his book *The Unsettling of America*. In it, Berry contrasts exploiters and nurturers:

> The standard of the exploiter is efficiency; the standard of the nurturer is care. The exploiter's goal is money, profit; the nurturer's goal is health—his land's health, his own, his family's, his community's, his country's.... The exploiter wishes to earn as much as possible by as little work as possible; the nurturer expects, certainly, to have a decent living from his work, but his characteristic wish is to work as well as possible.

I had appreciated Berry's words in an abstract way and, now, here was Robin, who embodied them. Robin put so much care into each animal and her land, and into her yarn and wool products. It was striking to observe, in our work that day, what is ecologically normal—sheep grazing on grass, pasture management attentive to the plants that grow and what sheep like to eat—instead of what's culturally normal, which is to treat our air, water, and soil as trash bins rather than valuable resources, and to force our livestock into confinement. Robin's efforts point out how little care I see in daily life in general, whether it's the poor quality of a manufactured product or the way we treat our too many cheap possessions. Robin cannot imagine having to leave her land every morning to go to a traditional job and work for someone else, and the greater world—her family, her community, my region and state—is better off for it.

I'm surprised when Robin points to some yarn she had milled and spun in my home state of Michigan. She reiterates the need for a local mill, which would save her a great deal of money and time. To reduce weight and save on cross-country freight costs, Robin skirts and scours her fleeces before shipping them from California to Michigan. She recently purchased 241 pounds of raw fleeces she wanted to process into yarn and roving. Skirting each fleece removed a total of 57 pounds of vegetable matter, manure, and low-quality wool, and washing removed another 50 pounds, leaving 127 (rather than 241) pounds of wool to ship. Skirting alone saved Robin $260: mill scouring for 176 pounds of skirted wool would have cost her $915.20, rather than the $655.20 she will instead pay the mill to scour 127 pounds of wool.

Robin still has to pay the mill to scour the wool on premises (required) at the rate of $5.20 per pound. "Freight will be less but I don't know how much," she says. "I may be breaking even on my time, however." And that's just scouring, before the additional wool processing required to transform raw wool into a finished product like yarn (carding, combing, spinning, dyeing), as well as shipping costs to get finished products back from the mill.

I leave with four undyed skeins of Robin's Jacob yarn as part of my Farm Club membership, alternately lilac gray and silvery brown as the sun and shadow shift through the window of my moving car. The next time I visit my family in Michigan, I think, a road trip to a wool mill is in order.

SEVEN

Mill

I may be a native Michigander, but it wasn't until I became one of Michigan's many economic refugees in California that I heard about the Zeilinger Wool Company in Frankenmuth, Michigan. Robin Lynde had described how she and other California wool producers shipped their fiber thousands of miles to Michigan for processing at Zeilinger Wool because there were so few wool mills left in the United States. I was simultaneously horrified at how little wool processing infrastructure California had and pleasantly surprised to find that Michigan still manufactured something that other people wanted, despite the relentless export of manufacturing jobs overseas from the late 1970s to the present.

Wool mills had been established in the western United States in the 1850s, the result of American westward migration. Mormon settlers built the first Utah Territory wool mill at West Jordan in 1853, while the first mill in Oregon, the Willamette, opened in 1857 at Salem. California's first wool mill—the Pioneer Woolen Mill at Black Point (also referred to as the Black Point Mill)—opened in 1858.[1]

When the Civil War broke out in 1861, the demand for wool for military uniforms skyrocketed. This made some western wool producers wealthy and some mills profitable for the first time. The first wool mill in Oregon, for example, "obtained no profit from it until after the civil war began."[2] The completion of the Central Pacific Railway in 1869 linked California to the rest of the country by rail. Western producers shipped bales of raw wool to East Coast mills, but the feasibility and profitability of this arrangement was tenuous at best, affected by federal tariffs[3] and freight rates set by the railroads. Initial freight rates from the West to the East were less expensive, but only temporarily.[4]

Some of my California predecessors asked the same questions about the California wool industry that I have: How can it possibly make sense to grow wool here, process it elsewhere, and bring it back? More than a century ago, people were frustrated that just a fraction of the wool grown in California was processed within the state, despite the increase in California wool production. Although "the wool clip had increased threefold, from 9,500 to 30,500 tons" between 1870 and 1876, "about one fifth of the wool produced on our coast is consumed in our coast mills....The greater portion of the remaining four fifths is sent away not only unworked, but even unwashed, to be cleansed, spun, woven, dyed, cut, sewn, and returned to us, quadrupled in price, as clothing."

An 1897 editorial in the *San Francisco Chronicle*[5] described wool mills as an economic opportunity for the city, citing advantages like location (proximate to shipping ports and rail lines, an established hub of the West Coast), cost efficiencies, mild weather and consequent reduced energy needs, a local abundance of high-quality wool, and job creation. The *Chronicle* points out that processing wool on the West Coast would occupy twelve mills, each averaging two hundred pounds of wool per day, and employ five hundred people "at an average of not less than $2 per day....It would indirectly employ tailors, carpenters, machinists, blacksmiths and other craftsmen." The editorial goes on to compare two mills, one in San Francisco and the other in Lowell, Massachusetts, penny to penny, and finds a savings of six and two-thirds cents per pound in the San Francisco mill's favor.

California got its wool mills, as did other parts of the West. In 1882, California historiographer John Hittell—employed by both the *San Francisco Chronicle* newspaper and A.L. Bancroft & Co. during his career—published a bean-counter-style inventory of western industries. Hittell does not always come across as a trustworthy source, given his shameless California romanticism and boosterism,[6] and his blatantly pro-capitalist and anti-labor sentiments. Still, his nearly thousand-page tome, *The Commerce and Industries of the Pacific Coast of North America*, is one of the few historical sources of data available on wool mills—and every other type of industry—in the West in the late nineteenth century.

In 1882, Hittell wrote that the Pioneer and Mission Woolen Factory in San Francisco[7] was "the largest establishment of the kind on the Pacific Coast" and that the West had a total of twenty-eight wool mills, thirteen of those in California, with a total sixteen hundred employees. However, Hittell lists the location of only nine California mills—two in San Francisco, and one each in San Jose, Stockton, Santa Rosa, Marysville, Merced, Los Angeles, and San Bernardino. Oregon's five mills were in Oregon City, Dayton, Ashland, Brownsville, and Dallas. In Utah, Hittell names nine (although he refers to ten): Salt Lake City, Beaver City, Brigham City, Ogden, Big Kanyon Creek, Springville, Manti, Provo City, and St. George. And western wool mills were busy: by the 1880s, some had deep order backlogs. In December 1881, for instance, one mill would need until September 1882 to fulfill its East Coast orders for wool blankets for the cold winter there.[8]

Hittell makes clear the extent to which western wool mills relied on low-wage Chinese labor, though he does not find this problematic. To Hittell's way of thinking, low wages enable greater mill profitability. He notes that demographics from Utah's wool mills skewed the story on the overall ethnic makeup of wool mill employees, and gives the western wool mill "number of hands employed at 2,150, of whom 700 to 800 are Chinamen, and the remainder white operatives. The proportion of Chinese to white labor would be much greater, but for the fact that, in the woolen mills of Utah Territory, white labor is employed exclusively." Indeed, the San Jose Woolen Mill employed so many Chinese people that it effectively named a neighborhood, one of San Jose's six Chinatowns, fittingly called Woolen Mills Chinatown.[9]

The majority of California wool mills closed between the 1890s and 1950s, for various reasons, many not well or reliably documented in the historical record. According to available sources, however, many wool mills closed because California was new and undeveloped territory, with all of the associated challenges and costs that accompany starting infrastructure from scratch in rough country, from building roads to finding and using clean water to finding sources of energy to a lack of hard currency in circulation. Other reasons included inexperienced management and/or mismanagement, low profitability, mergers and acquisitions, changes in federal tariffs on wool that hurt domestic producers, rail freight costs (in general, as well as some that penalized wool growers in particular), mill fires, and changes in consumer preferences.

The Zeilinger Wool Company, by contrast, has operated since 1910, surviving many of the above factors as well as two world wars, the Great

Depression, and the recession, housing market collapse, and financial crises of the early 2000s. How had they done it?

I am curious enough to plan a visit to Zeilinger Wool on one of my trips back to Michigan. Every autumn, I feel the call of the cold Lake Michigan shore like a salmon seeking its natal estuary. By September, I am desperate to see colored leaves, smell fresh snow, and enjoy the few open businesses free of summer tourists, who visit small, Bavarian-styled Frankenmuth, Michigan, for three things: Tony's restaurant and its excessively large portions of food (like a sandwich served with twenty strips—nearly one full pound—of bacon), a three-day polka festival, and Bronner's CHRISTmas Wonderland (exact spelling), the largest Christmas store in the world, filled with ornaments, nutcracker dolls, Advent calendars, and an astronomical collection of Hummel figurines.

In late October, one of my oldest and dearest friends, Becky, and I borrow my grandmother's Buick and head up north to my childhood stomping grounds of Traverse City. We will spend a few hours in Frankenmuth with Kathy Zeilinger, owner and operator.

It is an eye-wateringly cold, windy day in late autumn when Becky and I stop at an unheated antique mall on our way to the mill. We are making good use of the Buick's heated seats and sipping hot vegetable soup out of a thermos. Blue sky peeks through low, gray clouds while yellow leaves and light snow swirl along street curbs and in tornado-shaped clouds above the fallow Midwestern plain. We find Zeilinger Wool in a residential area, occupying three large buildings just a few miles down the road from Frankenmuth's tourist attractions.

A set of slightly fogged double-glass doors marks a mill store open to the public, its cozy contents made all the more attractive by the weather outside. Calico-patterned wool comforters hang from the ceiling and are draped over a wooden bench. Wool pillows of various sizes have been stuffed into sharp navy-and-white-striped cotton fabric, and the shelves are full of cones of finely spun sock yarn; wool socks in navy, cream, and brown; knit scarves and sweaters; roving dyed in every color of the rainbow; and sheep's milk soap. Kathy Zeilinger herself works the counter. She is petite, with a big smile, high cheekbones, bobbed soft brown hair, and a trace of the "Oh yah?" accent common to the Dakotas and Minnesota, but also found in Michigan, where our vowels sound more nasal, like in Chicago. Do not mistake her friendliness and feminine warmth for a lack of competence: Kathy is an expert in wool. She is also stereotypically midwestern: sharp, completely on top of every detail, hardworking, organized, and reliable.

Kathy has reason to be proud: Zeilinger Wool can celebrate more than one hundred years and four generations. Kathy is the third generation to own the mill, following her late father, Arnold Abraham, and her grandfather, William Abraham. Kathy's husband, Gary, and their son, Jon, also work at the mill, and Jon will one day shepherd the business.

William Abraham founded the wool mill in 1910 and soon made socks, yarn, and comforter stuffing (batting[10]) for World War I. He ran the mill through 1950 when Kathy's father, Arnold Abraham, took over until 1976. At that time, Kathy was too young to run the mill, and her brothers and sisters had pursued other lines of work, so Arnold sold the mill to someone outside of the family. Kathy then worked for the new owner at what had been her father's mill.

After ten years, the new owner "went more commercial," making garments and other items not related to wool, and opened the Frankenmuth Woolen Mill. It was then, in 1986, that Kathy and her husband started their own mill, the Zeilinger Wool Company. Though it may not have been family owned for more than one hundred years, then, "it's been family on premises the whole time," Kathy notes. She thinks continuity is part of what has helped the business last as long as it has. Comforters, mattress pads, and bed pillows periodically need to be laundered and reconstructed: the fibers never die. Customers "always come back, so I have people that Grandpa sold to come back four, five times, and they're always thankful we're here."

The Zeilinger Wool Company has occupied the location we are visiting since 1986, during which time the Zeilingers have added two buildings to the original. The store, carding, and laundering operations occupy the first floor of the building we stand in, and upstairs is the area where comforters, pillows, and socks are made.

Zeilinger Wool provides a full selection of fiber-processing services, not only for wool but for alpaca, llama, mohair, buffalo, and even dog hair. When the company started accepting alpaca fiber several years ago, business increased 25 percent. "Everyone started getting alpacas and didn't know what to do with their fiber," Kathy explains. Alpaca fiber is processed in the same manner as wool, and the color divisions are the same as those for non-white wool. Zeilinger Wool accepts all kinds of wool, including colored wool fleeces, whereas some mills will only accept white wool, which was what Kathy's father preferred. "He didn't like to do dark fleece, it was always white wool, white wool. We had a hard time convincing him to process wool that was not white."

Zeilinger Wool accepts wool for processing at any point in its life-cycle, as they have since 1976. If a customer has scoured their wool at home, for example, and ships it, the company will process the wool from that point on. Other customers might scour and dye their wool, and then send it for carding. Some customers even send their own dyes, in custom colors, and the company uses them to dye either the customer's own wool, or wool provided by Zeilinger Wool. In addition, the company manufactures and sells all of the products I see in the store: a huge variety of bedding, socks, yarn and more.

Kathy directly credits hand spinners with much of the mill's success. "It's just phenomenal. There are so many spinning guilds, and young people are getting into fiber more. There are a lot of knitters. It's not just an old person's craft." The popularity of spinning in the late 1970s and one phenomenal spinner, sheep producer, and customer, Gloria Bellair, led Gary Zeilinger to begin making roving and dyed wool. "I just don't know why roving continues to be overwhelmingly our biggest ... it's unreal," she laughs, her palms upturned. "And I know that there's rooms and rooms at people's houses filled with roving, because ... people want to do something with their wool, especially if they really love their animals for the wool, they want something done with it."

On the day Becky and I meet Kathy, she and her husband have recently returned from two fiber festivals: the New York Sheep and Wool Festival in Rhinebeck, New York, one of the largest fiber festivals in the United States, and the Southeastern Animal Fiber Fair (SAFF) in Asheville, North Carolina. The Zeilingers attend eight to ten fiber festivals per year, both as vendors (they'd nearly nearly sold out of their wool roving in Rhinebeck and Asheville) and as a pickup and drop-off service. Along with delivering finished orders at the festivals, they had returned to Michigan with three thousand pounds of wool from Rhinebeck and fifteen hundred pounds of wool from SAFF to process for customers.

Kathy says that picking up wool to process is "a bread and butter type thing, because we go to where the mass amount of people are, that are only interested in roving, batting, yarn and all that, so that's a good thing." Given how much Robin Lynde had to pay to ship her wool to Michigan, it strikes me as both savvy and kind of Zeilinger Wool to pick up wool at festivals, leaving the wool grower to pay for only the processing services and return shipping of finished products that weigh much less than grease-weight wool. Kathy says an added benefit is that it gets her and her family out of the mill and into the world for a bit, too: "I'll get to see something, and see the shows. They're fantastic."

Most of the wool that Zeilinger Wool receives for processing arrives by mail from across the United States. The company receives a lot of orders from the states of New York, Michigan, nearby Indiana and Ohio, and big wool-producing states like Wyoming, Montana, and Colorado. "It comes from every state in the union and Canada. And you're going to say 'How much?' and I'm going to say 'I have no idea.'" Kathy throws up her hands and laughs. "I would say a good five thousand pounds a month, at least, times twelve, so that's sixty thousand pounds a year, but this is probably a low estimate." For a sense of scale, one small sheep's fleece might weigh one to three pounds, an average fleece eight pounds, and a large one ten to fifteen pounds or more.[11] Depending on fleece weight, then, Zeilinger Wool processes tens of thousands of fleeces each year. Most raw wool is processed into roving[12] and batting, products that hand spinners use.

Kathy says the type of wool they receive for processing indicates "the fad of the spinner. They all went into Shetlands, they all had Shetland sheep. Before that it was Border Leicester, right now it's going toward Cormo, before all that was Romney; so it all depends on what the spinner wants, or the sheep person buys their sheep and sometimes we recommend what the wool producer can and should do with their wool."

No matter the delivery method, upon arrival at Zeilinger Wool, the wool is weighed, which is its grease weight unless it has already been scoured. Next, the wool is tagged according to who the customer is, what they want done, and the color of the wool. (Wool color helps "decide which building it's going into," so colored fibers don't contaminate white fibers and affect dye that might be applied later.) Zeilinger Wool's tagging system consists of a simple manila card on which everything is documented from beginning to end, so that the customer knows they got their own fiber back. They once tried to computerize it, but, Kathy says, "Nothing worked as well as the manila card. My grandpa started it, and my dad, and my sons wanted to change it millions of times, and it doesn't work."

The wash room is the first stop for wool, where fiber is washed in 180°F water. Most wool needs to be washed a couple of times, to remove the lanolin. Kathy says, "We really try to educate people that 'what comes in, goes out.' So if you have a lot of chaff, we're going to work on it to try to get it all out, but sometimes it's impossible." Scoured wool is placed on drying racks until it is completely dry, and then is brought downstairs for picking, carding, and end-product manufacture, into either roving or batting. Some wool moves on to the yarn mill to be made into yarn, then socks. Customers can have their wool processed and machine knit into socks just like those I'd seen for sale in the Zeilinger Wool storefront.

And those socks are popular—so popular that the company can't keep up with the demand to process wool into socks. Socks have "so many repeat customers. Because once they sell 'em, it's a product that they have on their farm or at farm markets, and also they sell them to shops. Everybody can use a pair of socks." And she's right. Everyone wears socks and will try them out as a "starter" wool garment because they're not too expensive. However, finding skilled labor is a challenge. Zeilinger Wool has eight or nine sock-knitting machines but cannot run all of them because they have just one sock knitter, a woman who

goes crazy all week trying to make socks, and we're two years behind on socks, that's how many people want socks made out of their fiber. We have contacted the South, where all the laid off sock knitters are, and nobody'll move north. It's just unreal. And we don't have that many sock knitters because nobody made socks up here. When my dad and grandpa had sock-knitting machines, they were hand cranks, it's nothing that you would use now.

Zeilinger Wool has about twenty employees, family included. They run one shift but wish they could run two. "It's too expensive. Labor is our biggest expense, because this is all so labor intense." The company also has to invest in training, because it's unlikely someone could obtain wool mill experience elsewhere these days. "The wool processing industry has shrunk significantly in the United States in the last twenty years," Kathy says. When mills closed in the United States and moved overseas, skilled wool processors had no reason or need to pass on their knowledge. Decades of accumulated, nuanced, tacit knowledge—from the delicate humidity and static electricity controls required to process wool well to the best way to tweak a setting on a particular piece of equipment—were lost.

A shrinking domestic market may actually have contributed to Zeilinger Wool's success. The company does not have a lot of domestic competition: starting a new mill requires tens or hundreds of thousands of dollars in equipment, and knowledge about how to effectively use the heavy machinery is scarce. Knowing how to run and maintain mill equipment inside and out, and having deep experience in wool processing, are skills that live on in Kathy, Gary, and their family. When I ask if Zeilinger Wool ever thought about using overseas labor or facilities, Kathy quickly shakes her head and says, "We never even considered it. Our main aim is to have a high-quality product, so we take care of our machinery, we know our product, and it takes years of experience." Zeilinger Wool's skill, quality, and experience has paid off.

After seeing the company's midsize operation, which is not industrial scale, I notice that there are a lot of businesses that call themselves "mills" that don't do what Zeilinger Wool does—wool processing at scale, with a complete line of processing services. In practice, the simple word "mill" seems to have a wide variety of meanings. Sometimes it describes a small home operation with a few top-loading washing machines for scouring, a table-top drum carder, and a few soup pots for dye. Some mills spin wool into yarn, some do not. Some farmers and fiber artists use the term "mini-mill" to distinguish smaller operations from those of Zeilinger Wool's size and larger. Mini-mill is not a derogatory term—these cottage-industry-style operations are critical to keeping fiber-processing skills and know-how alive—but is a convenient, shorthand way to communicate the fact that smaller-scale processing and possibly more limited services are on offer. Folks who start small wool mills often have no choice but to teach themselves and learn by doing, by trial and error over time.

Robin Lynde learned this firsthand. She started out processing her raw fleeces with a small, local mill a reasonable distance away from her farm. At first, the mill did a good job with Robin's fiber, processing it into roving. As time went on, though, Robin noticed there were times when her fiber got processed quickly, while her friends' fiber waited for years. Then, Robin experienced some quality issues.

> I was really careful about labeling my bags. I knew it was unorganized in there. I have all my separate bags. I had one with lilac Jacob wool, and I don't have that much lilac. It's rare, really special. Well, they processed that side-by-side with britch wool, and that screwed up everything, because they put best and worst together. And the mill just said "too bad," but did not get that that was a big problem for me and that they messed up. And the yarn would have a lot of knots in it. They did not do well with finer fibers or wind it onto cones, which I want for weaving. So I tried other mills, in Oregon and California. One did a pretty nice job with it.

Experimenting with mills and their output may be necessary and worthwhile, but it creates additional work for people like Robin. And inconsistencies across product lines are a problem. If a skein of yarn from one mill is two hundred yards long and weighs three ounces per yard, for example, while two hundred yards from another mill weighs four ounces per yard, that's not the same quantity of yarn even though the yardage is the same. Not only are the two yarns not identical (and thus should not be combined in a project requiring a high degree of consistency throughout, like knitting a sweater), but the customer buying the latter yarn is getting, and should pay for, more wool. Someone like Robin then has to price different products from different mills accordingly.

Zeilinger Wool has an excellent reputation and business is booming, to the extent that they are often too busy processing customer orders to produce their own wool products to sell. It takes the company a while to get its own products back in stock. Their volume has increased so much that, as of October 2014, the company was taking three to four months to complete a customer's order, though they will do rush orders. Kathy says, "We don't like the three to four month wait because we always want the customer to have it but . . ." What can she do? They're busy—so busy that, in early 2016, Zeilinger Wool stopped taking new orders altogether for a short while.

Zeilinger Wool is a critical piece of infrastructure in the American fiber-product supply chain. Perhaps more importantly, it also enables a certain type of livelihood to exist and continue, and—by extension—the cultures and communities of the people who practice that livelihood across the United States. Zeilinger Wool, and mills like it, enable small fiber producers to do something with their raw fiber and to realize income from their investment of time, feed, animal care, and land stewardship. It's not a stretch to say that Zeilinger Wool even helps the survival of rare sheep breeds unappreciated by a commercial industry that craves homogeneity and standardization. Our domestic manufacturing infrastructure (or lack thereof) impacts farm income, breed diversity, the choices people have about how to earn a living, and the variety of wool and fiber choices available to craftspeople and hobbyists, whether in the form of yarn or clothing.

Many small flock owners are also hand spinners, weavers, or knitters. They are wool people first, usually people who live and work in the same place with their sheep, on land for which they also care. They are not detached investors, far removed from the products and consequences of their investment decisions, with little or no direct involvement. They raise sheep primarily or exclusively for their fiber, and their products reflect a firsthand knowledge and appreciation of unusual colors or other fiber characteristics, made for equally discerning customers. If artisans find a particular breed and preparation of wool interesting and enjoyable to work with, and are pleased with the results, the demand for that wool—and for the continued existence of sheep that produces it—grows as well.

If, on the other hand, a dearth of wool processing mills makes it too difficult for small-scale wool producers and fiber businesses to realize income for their work—which they require in order to keep doing what they're doing, in the way that they're doing it—then these producers are increasingly and inevitably pushed toward selling raw wool on the commercial market, overseas and, consequently, to breeding and raising a flock that meets that market's needs, rather than those of the hand-spinning, weaving, knitting, and independent fashion design markets, who want interesting materials to work with and need a place to be able to buy and responsibly source them.

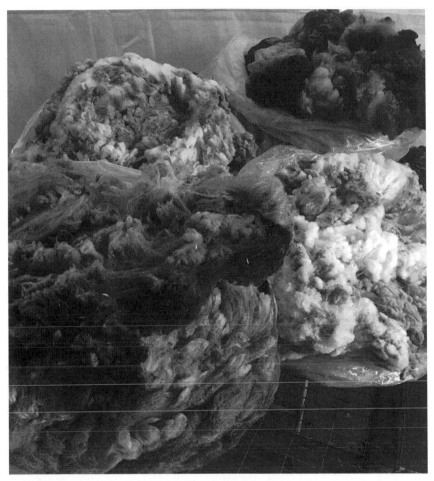

Raw fleeces at the Fibershed Wool Symposium.

Today, Joann Fabric and Craft Stores, Michael's, and Walmart do not sell roving for hand spinning. Most of the yarn they sell is made of synthetic, acrylic fibers and manufactured overseas. A 100 percent wool yarn is rare and, if it's on the shelf, usually isn't available in great variety or quantity. What is profitable for these stores, and affordable for their customers while still enriching the shop and the manufacturer, is not always the same thing as what is best for the project someone wants to make, or what is most appropriate for the artisan's region, culture, climate, season, or gift recipient.

I remain amazed, for instance, that highly flammable acrylic yarn is explicitly marketed as a good choice for baby sweaters and blankets. What's best for the big box store is not necessarily best for the baby. The aisles are evidence of diminished, rather than expanded, consumer choice—bigger increasingly tends toward "only," not "more." Zeilinger Wool processes unusual fibers into a wide variety of products conceived by passionate business owners, and works with them to design and customize them for customers.

The degree to which Zeilinger Wool is a processing linchpin—for some small and midsize wool producers, one of few high-quality mills for people all over the United States—makes me feel uneasy about what would happen if something happened to it, or to the trends of hand spinning and knitting that have driven so much of the company's business. The Zeilingers themselves will grow older and may not want to work as hard, or may be unable to do so. It's not as if it would be easy for anyone else to pick up and take over running the mill, unless they'd worked on site for years, learning the ropes. It's not as if anyone can just purchase the equipment and an industrial-size building in which to operate it. It is so much harder and expensive to rebuild infrastructure from scratch, rather than keep even a portion of it.

I attempt to stave off my concern with—what else?—shopping. As Kathy rings me up for a wool comforter, two wool pillows, and two cones of sock yarn to ship to California (the wool socks are staying with me), I am impressed with the high quality of what I'm getting and am glad to be giving Kathy my money. Every purchase should feel so good: a fair price, top-notch stuff, and no apparent exploitation under way, run by lovely, hardworking people who have nothing to hide and welcome you in to see their operations with open arms. But I am unsettled by the extent to which one piece depends on and benefits from another, and how precarious each piece seems in its rarity.

EIGHT

Apprentice

A few months after visiting the Zeilinger Wool Company, it is March and peak lambing season at Robin's, a busy time that calls for Farm Club workdays. Lambing ewes have been moved to securely fenced pastures adjacent to the barn, where newly born lambs will be protected from coyotes, birds of prey, and life-threatening cold temperatures and rain.

Seen from the rear, the ewes for whom delivery is imminent look like horses with sharply protruding saddle bags on each side: twin lambs, large mounds on each side of the ewe's spine, so near the surface of the sheep's thin skin that I half expect to see noses and outlines of hooves. The ewes in early labor are agitated, bleating loudly, pawing and stomping at the ground while turning around in circles, not lying down, unable to get comfortable.

My instinct is the same as it is with a human friend in labor: give her space, let her do whatever she needs to get through this, and don't interfere any more than necessary. Robin says she does the same. "It sounds superstitious, but things seem to go more smoothly when I'm not here. They seem to have more problems when I'm in the barn, almost like they know I can help them if they need it. They don't actually, of course; I just find more things to interfere with." Though the spinning, pacing ewes have not yet delivered, their rush of maternal hormones has begun. They call to and nudge lambs who are not theirs, much to the consternation of the other new mothers who butt the early-laboring ewes away from their babies.

It's a busy morning. Ewes are dropping lambs more regularly, quickly, and easily than I expected. Much of what I've read about lambing was based on breeds and lambing practices in northwest England, which included more human involvement—like pulling lambs out—but that wasn't the case here. Some ewes, for example, approach Robin's barn, pause, deliver a lamb, lick it off and nudge it, walk a few more steps, and deliver another. The lambs are on their feet almost immediately, and we have to work quickly to pick them up, hold them in front of their mother's face so she can smell and get the urge to follow them, and shepherd everyone into their post-labor-and-delivery quarters: a private, warm, and safe pen with clean straw where everyone can get on with the critical business of latching on and nursing. The slimy, six-to-eight-pound lambs are so much tinier than I expected, all long skinny legs and tail.

We are barn orderlies, following Robin's direction to keep everyone moving and to free up pens for the newest mothers and their lambs. We move ewes and older lambs to larger pens with room enough for a few families, but we do it carefully. Some new mothers get ornery quickly and—with their Jacob horns—head-butt curious lambs who aren't their own with such force that they stun or, more rarely, kill them. Robin monitors ewes for this behavior and, if she sees it, does not move them into group pens.

We deep clean the recently vacated pens, which are soiled with afterbirth, blood, and the usual manure and urine. We scrape it all out, lift it into a wheelbarrow, spread a chalky layer of hydrated lime over the exposed concrete, add wood shavings and absorbent straw, and bring in the newest ewe moms who have just delivered lambs, or are about to. As soon as a lamb is born and the mother has licked the afterbirth away from its face, we pick it up and weigh it. Robin records each lamb's date and time of birth, sex, and weight beside its mother's name on a whiteboard.

We stay vigilant and listen for weak lamb voices, so we can find any who may be stuck or accidentally separated from their mothers. Their voices are high pitched and desperate, but easily drowned out by the deeper bleats of dozens of older sheep and our conversation and work noise. One of the dogs, Maggie, seems obsessed with something in a barn wall. We assume it's a rat or a bird's nest, but Robin finds a lamb stuck inside the wall pocket, where the sliding barn door normally goes. Later that morning, I find a lamb with its head pinned beneath the bottom of a wood wall that divides two pens. I could barely see the lamb because it was bedded so far down in the deep straw and lying flat to accommodate its neck. Listening often provides the only clue that a lamb might be around.

I'd looked forward to holding the impossibly cute newborns, but my enjoyment evaporates when I see the stress it creates for the mother. When a person stands and holds a lamb, the lamb is three to four feet above the ground. Since sheep can't fly, a ewe doesn't instinctively look up in the air to find the lamb she now perceives as missing. Instead, able to hear her lamb but unable to see or smell it, she goes crazy, round and round in circles trying to find her missing baby, and calls to it desperately and ceaselessly. I cannot stand to witness this. If grown folks must hold lambs, they ought to at least sit down on a hay bale and hold the lamb at its mother's face level.

There is one lamb for whom I make an exception. When I arrived, a little lamb in a red sweater lay in the corner of a pen beneath a heat lamp, all by his lonesome, motherless. Early that morning, Robin found what looked like a dead lamb and two live ones, who were up and nursing. The lamb lay flat on the ground, cold and still and splayed, membranes over his face. Robin said she "pulled the membranes off the nose and surprise! That lamb wasn't quite dead yet."

She grabbed the lamb, carried him to the house, set a soup pot in her kitchen sink, filled it with warm water, and placed the tiny lamb in the soup pot, his limp head and neck resting on the countertop. She rubbed him as he came to. Once he was clean and looked like he might live, Robin laid him on a heating pad on her kitchen floor and covered him with blankets. Rusty the sheepdog kept watch, while curious cats hovered nearby. Robin successfully revived the lamb, and he lived. I nickname him Mr. Lonelyhearts, because he is all alone, motherless in a red sweater. I hold him as much as I like. He gets a lot of love from humans, if not ewes.

After several hours, the pace slows a bit; new families are getting established in clean pens, and it's time for Robin and her Farm Club members to eat lunch. I've been working with Joy, a gentle, soft-spoken, and warm woman from Davis, California. She is petite, bespectacled, and has a whimsical, elven aspect. As we clean up, Joy tells me she has two sheep that "really need to be sheared. It's been a year, and it's hard to get someone to come out for two sheep. I only have two. They're little guys, like pets. They'll be really easy."

The author holds approximately six-week-old Bruce the Jacob lamb at Meridian Jacobs, Robin Lynde's farm. Photo by Gynna Clemes (who is now Bruce's mom).

Robin Lynde revives Bruce the Jacob lamb in warm water at Meridian Jacobs. Photo by Robin Lynde.

I freeze, standing behind a livestock gate. Joy means me. More frightening than shearing (and possibly hurting) someone else's sheep is the
unknown, the idea of visiting someone else's property with customer,
land, and sheep size and condition unforeseen. At shearing school, our
instructors had tried to mitigate this by preparing us for our first jobs.
They listed questions to ask our shearing clients in advance: How many
sheep do you have, and of what breed? How many are rams, ewes, lambs,
and wethers? When were they last sheared? Do you have a sheet of
plywood I can shear on, or should I bring one? Where is your nearest
power supply? We were supposed to tell customers to bring sheep into
a barn or pen the night before—so they would have a chance to calm
down after being herded—and to refrain from feeding and watering
them overnight, so they wouldn't feel full, suffocated, and stressed in
the morning.

During one of our shearing school lunch breaks, however, Jordan had
told me, "It's never like that, like they say. I never even have a barn. I'm
always shearing in the wild, on the ground, in the middle of a field, dragging sheep across the dirt. Sometimes they're not caught, not penned,
even though I tell people I don't chase sheep. I'm happy if the ground
is level." I'd looked shocked, but Jordan's expression told me he wasn't
kidding. "Really! Half the time I'm on a hillside!" Gesturing with half of
a sandwich, he'd continued:

> You can get your shearing kit together, you can have all of your supplies
> and your training. Even so, you've got no idea what situation you're actu-
> ally facing until you're on someone's ranch and have a chance to see and
> touch their animals. Even the owners can be wrong about things. They
> don't always know exactly how many sheep they have, so you can't rely
> on that. When you ask how much the sheep weigh, they'll tell you, then
> you'll get out there and find they don't have a scale and they don't go
> around lifting their sheep.

Jordan had shrugged and continued eating.

These days, it's rare to walk into any situation without an inkling
of what lies ahead. We have Google Maps with its street and satel-
lite views, Yelp reviews, and TripAdvisor treatises with such detail that
we know what almost any place, anywhere in the world, might be like

before we get there. In the absence of such tools, my mind fabricated unfounded visions of events that looked more like police visits than shearing jobs and included meth labs, warehouses of cartel marijuana, armed squatters, and being raped in a barn in the middle of nowhere.

None of this, of course, was likely to happen at Joy's. She wasn't a stranger at all. Several other Farm Club members knew her even better than I did, and had for many years. Even better, here was Joy herself, standing just the other side of a livestock gate. I could ask her anything, and she probably wouldn't bat an eye if I wanted to drive out to Davis to check out her sheep and property in advance. But can I manage to do the reasonable, sane thing and ask her questions while we are chatting and working together in Robin's barn, face-to-face? Of course not. I am too busy freaking out and stammering.

I haven't sheared a single sheep since shearing school. I haven't bought any shearing equipment. I am a shearing impostor. Hoping to convince Joy of this, I tell her, "You know, I'm really slow and haven't sheared in a long time." It doesn't work. "That's okay," she says. "Take all the time you need." I stare some more. Joy is exactly the kind of person for whom I started shearing, the reason I went to school in the first place. I'm in a position to help her. Who else is going to do it? I either did this for a reason, or I didn't, and if I say no to Joy, I didn't. I can't say no.

I tell Joy we'll schedule her shearing for the day after shearing school ends, in mid-May. That way, I can attend school again and get one full week of practice before shearing Joy's two Shetlands, Periwinkle and Zinnia, whom Joy says weigh only about eighty pounds each, small as sheep go. I will also need something to shear with, but I don't want to spend $1,500 or more for the type of rig and handpiece at shearing school, so I buy a portable, handheld Oster Shearmaster (an oversized version of the Oster clippers I use to cut my husband's hair) for a little over $200, two combs, and one cutter, just enough equipment for Joy's two sheep. Maybe I can even practice with my equipment at shearing school.

May rolls around and, as Joy's shearing day approaches, I work myself into a state of abject panic and gutlessness. The first two days of my second year at shearing school are, again, difficult, and I feel I should be doing better even if I haven't sheared in a year. It begins to seem worse that I know Joy personally. If I hurt Joy's sheep, everyone will

Jacob ewe and two lambs at Meridian Jacobs in Vacaville, California.

know—Robin, everyone in Farm Club, and everyone they know. Maybe I won't even be allowed to participate in Farm Club, banned from helping Robin with her sheep. My fear and doubt mount to the point that I convince Sergio, an alpaca and llama shearer who is also attending shearing school, to come with me. I offer to pay him, in addition to what Joy will pay us, to do what should be my job. I email Joy with a message that is mostly true:

> If it's all right with you, I'd like Sergio (a fellow shearing classmate who is local to you) to shear with me. I am confident of my ability to shear your sheep, but Sergio has done an absolutely fantastic job and has seven years of experience shearing alpaca and llamas. It would be nice to have some

support as a newer shearer, as I want to ensure the best possible outcome for your Shetlands.

If Joy is disappointed or concerned she doesn't show it; she is very supportive of this idea. But, more embarrassingly, I have an ulterior motive. Since Sergio lives near Joy, he might shear for Joy in the future, absolving me of all future shearing accidents, responsibility, risk, learning curve, and imagined sheep deaths (which, by this point in my imagination, resemble Gettysburg).

As soon as I'd hit the send button, I was disgusted with myself rather than relieved. As each day of my second year of shearing school goes on, I realize I do have some clue as to what I'm doing. My fear is gradually unseated by total exhaustion, body memory, and automaticity. This time around, my body knows what it is supposed to do, where it should be, and when. My feet at least know where to land, even if they don't always make it, even if my transitions from one position to the next are less than graceful, and I have to stop shearing while making them. And that counts for a lot. I even level up my shearing certification to Beginner Level II.

But it's too late. I've involved two other people, Sergio and Joy, in my anxiety trip and created a messy cascade of events. By Thursday, I want the job to be mine and no longer want Sergio to come, but I don't want to jerk both of them around with more changes to the job plan. Why can't I think like a man? None of the male shearers I know would behave this way. No matter what their ability, they advertise on Craigslist, show up to shearing jobs as promised, shear to the best of their ability and with confidence, take the money, and do not worry any further about how imperfect anything might be. They get the wool off and that's what matters: you either get the job done or you don't.

On Saturday, I awake at 4:30 a.m. and meet Sergio in Joy's driveway in Davis, California, at 7 a.m. Joy and her husband live in a deceptively suburban-looking area, with a front yard and driveway that obscures twenty acres of land, a barn, and gardens. Their property is breathtaking, beautifully kept. A small section of their acreage contains a covered sheep pen, more of a large shed really, which is enclosed on four sides by a tall chain-link fence with a door for people to go in and out. Joy's sheep have excellent protection from predators.

Joy has set up a small, homemade skirting table where the vegetable matter from the fleeces can fall through. It resembles a work bench, but with chicken wire where shelves would normally be. Joy's husband has already laid a clean piece of plywood down in the fenced area and run an extension cord, plugged in at the barn, all the way out to the sheep pen. There is no shearing setup to do. Just when I think Joy's arrangements can't possibly get more deluxe, Joy offers to walk the sheep out—on halters—to the shearing plywood, where they can be flipped in place. Joy's place is a shearer's dream job. It's as if she designed it to ease new shearers into the idea and get us hooked. I am a bit sad that it's my first ranch call, because I doubt it will ever get better than this.

Sergio does all of the shearing and I'm profoundly disappointed about it. In less than twenty minutes, it's over. Periwinkle and Zinnia are several pounds lighter, much thinner, and their fleeces are lovely, silvers, oatmeals, and dark grays glimmering in the sun. Joy and her husband, Jon, ask us to stay a while and have breakfast, and I do. They've warmed croissants, cut strawberries, and brewed fresh coffee for us. They are downright lovely people. After less than an hour all told, it's time to turn around and drive home.

I feel utterly ridiculous. I am over myself and my fear. I was handed the perfect shearing job for the perfect customer, and I gave it away. This morning, after five days of shearing school, I felt completely at ease and ready to shear, and I didn't. Now I'm impatient, eager to make up for my mistake by getting back out in the world and behaving like a professional. Immediately after leaving Joy's, I drive a few miles to Higby's Country Feed store and finish stocking up my shearing kit. I sincerely wish I were driving to another shearing job, but some additional combs, Kool Lube spray for hot metal, wound spray, blood clotting powder, motor oil, gauze, and disinfectant wash will just have to do.

The following weekend, I accompany Jordan on one of his shearing jobs. A text message from him arrives at 6 a.m.: "Bring sunscreen or a hat. We are not in any barn." Other messages Jordan sent bore portents like "There are not good corrals so we will have a rodeo." When I'd asked how many sheep we'd be shearing, Jordan only replied, "I am not sure of the numbers but need to call and confirm anyways. They have Jacobs and also a few Cashmere goats. Shearing mocs won't be much good.

Boots or hiking shoes preferable. You are welcome to bring your own gear and we will likely need three to four hours. I usually hoof trim as well."

I ask how many sheep again. Jordan's message reads, "I don't know. She is an invalid."

Invalid. As I brush my teeth, I remember a story Jordan told me nearly a year ago during my first visit to shearing school. "Is this with the meth head son?" I type.

"Yup."

I'll get that social worker ranch call after all. At least I won't be alone. "This will be interesting," I type. "Aw hell. Well...we'll do our duty."

He replies, "At least they have been sheared the last two years by me. The first time I sheared they had three years' wool."

Jordan and I have arranged to meet at 7:30 a.m. on Saturday at Hardcore Espresso in Sebastopol, a couple of miles from our shearing destination. When I arrive, I send Jordan a text message: "Early to coffee. Every grower in the county must get coffee here."

In the local vernacular, "grower" is not a synonym for farmer. It means only one thing, which is "pot grower." I didn't expect to find some of Humboldt County's notorious Emerald Triangle as far south as Sebastopol. There are a lot more high-end, brand-new vehicles than is typical for agricultural areas: one Land Rover, for instance, and several massive pickup trucks that I'm not sure how people manage to climb into. Inside, jarring, electronic circus music plays too loudly for the time of day, so I take my coffee outside to a yard where gray-bearded bohemians with long braids and Hawaiian shirts are scattered about, sipping coffee and chatting amicably. I watch perfectly tanned, self-assured white folks in their late twenties and thirties exit the coffee shop in attire usually seen on house painters and gardeners, but with a twist of hipness, dreadlocks and piercings peeking out from beneath heavy hooded sweatshirts and baseball caps. Everyone seems friendly yet minds their own business.

Jordan pulls up in a rusted-out pickup carrying three of his rat-hunting terriers and his shearing gear. He grabs a coffee and tells me his truck can't be trusted to go long distances, which limits not just his range but also the number of potential shearing jobs he can take. In a good year of working with his terriers, at the winery, and shearing, he

Jordan Reed hugs an Angora goat just before shearing it.

can set aside about $1,500 if he's lucky and tries hard, and it sounds as if he does. But that's not enough to buy a new, reliable ride.

We hop into our respective vehicles and I follow Jordan the few miles to the shearing site, down a road on the outskirts of Sebastopol. On my right is a suburban-looking neighborhood with small bungalows set close together, and to my left are fields that belong to an overgrown ranch with several dilapidated buildings. I wonder how much that land would sell for these days, with the neighborhood across the street fore-shadowing its likely future.

A few moments later, Jordan signals to turn left, onto the apparently abandoned property. There is no way this can be our job site. Two barely discernible tracks pass for a driveway, which is marked by a large tree that Jordan must have known to look for from previous visits. Tall grass and stunted trees scrape the bottom of my car. I cannot see a living thing anywhere in the fields. If there are sheep here, the grass is taller than they are. I'm grateful to Jordan for telling me to bring boots. I imagine all of the things hidden in these acres of ruins: old barbed wire and sharp, rusted farm equipment. I don't know when I last had a tetanus shot. Rattlesnakes. Tapped-out wells to fall into.

Jordan exits his truck and pushes the gate open so we can continue up the driveway. I close it behind me and, not far ahead, Jordan parks. To my right, a bleached wood building tilts on its foundation, which appears to be made of garbage. Jordan tells me another building, a little farther ahead, used to be a hatchery. Three more structures of a once-thriving farmstead ring the end of the driveway near the house, like a cul-de-sac. The elderly woman for whom we'll shear today is the third generation to hold this property, which in her grandparents' and parents' time was a chicken farm.

As we unload our gear, Jordan says, "I went into the hatchery building last year, which is the most stable one. And I noticed it didn't have any power to it. I asked her how they handled hatching before they had power. She told me they had stone incubators and would set them out in the sun to warm them all day, and the stone would hold the heat for the chicks. And we think we know better!" He pulls a wooden sheep crook, just like Little Bo Peep's, out of his truck bed and lightly tosses it down to me. "Here. This will come in handy."

A wisp of a woman, almost invisible in the heat and bright sunlight, rustles in the distance at the far end of the driveway. She is so insubstantial, and the dilapidated ranch so eerie, that I consider I might be seeing a ghost or in the early stages of heat stroke. But the woman is very much real, slowly picking her way toward us along a dilapidated fence, her right hand running along the top beam for balance. I think of splinters. She is clad in a knit navy twinset that may be pajamas, not that it matters, and her long, sparse white hair is tied back in a ponytail. I look past her and notice she has emerged from a house packed to the hilt. Two sliding-glass doors face the pasture, and I can see a wall of stuff packed against the glass, floor to ceiling: a turned-over laundry basket, full of cloth, its open side suctioned against the glass. Every manner of clothing. A mattress. Newspapers. An upturned, upholstered chair. Magazines.

When Jordan sees her, he says, "She wasn't doing that last year." "Walking?" I ask. "Yeah, walking and leaving the house. She was recovering from cancer and totally bedridden. I didn't think she was going to make it. Was surprised when she called me this year, but I didn't expect to see her like this, moving." Jordan removes his hat, throws his arm in the air, waves, and springs forward, quickly walking toward her. Loudly and cheerfully, his voice booms, "How do you do, Miss Alma? You're doing well!" I see him extend his hand for a shake and then take her left elbow. I follow him and introduce myself and, though Miss Alma is little, she has a mighty firm handshake. I grin when I feel it. She smiles and squints in the sun.

I still haven't seen any sheep, but after a few minutes I pick them out in the high grass, can distinguish the tips of their horns from the tips of plants. I see the outlines of dark, sheep-shaped shadows in the shade of a colossal, overgrown tree with branches that nearly touch the ground. All of the sheep and goats are loose in the pasture, and the sheep are Jacobs, so they resemble Robin's flock. At shearing school, our instructors emphasized that we shouldn't chase animals, that we must tell people to pen their animals or we won't shear. "You don't get paid to chase animals! Lost money is lost time," they said. That may be true, but I'd never think of not catching these animals for Miss Alma. What's the alternative? Demand that an elderly cancer survivor—who is going to pay us, no less—run around the pasture instead of us two able-bodied young folks? Not on my watch and certainly not, I know, on Jordan's.

Jordan and I discuss herding strategies with Miss Alma. We will herd the sheep and goats to the far end of the pasture, near the road, down a makeshift chute made of the orange plastic netting often seen at construction sites, and into the small sheep pen up near the house. As I listen to Miss Alma and Jordan discuss this plan, a man in his late forties or so appears and begins pacing, very rapidly, up and down the driveway, so fast that at times he's almost skipping. He is incredibly agitated, rubbing one hand over his head and arm and chain-smoking with the other. He is speaking loudly—to whom I cannot tell—in a constant, breathless stream of words. There is no pause in any of his movements or sound. I follow Miss Alma's lead and ignore him.

Jordan and I check the makeshift chute, making sure it is properly mounted to the fence. Some portable electric fencing and a sheepdog would have come in handy today. We head back into the pasture to gather the animals and, much to my surprise, Miss Alma comes with us, raising her spindly arms and making pffft noises between her tongue and teeth to move the sheep. Her sheer force of will makes up for anything she lacks in mass. Jordan, Miss Alma, and I spread out in a wobbly line across the field, arms extended, a loose wall to keep the sheep moving toward the farther end of the field. Our goal, essentially, is to move the sheep along three sides of a square: down the length of the pasture to a corner; a left turn to walk along another side of the pasture; and then left again at the next corner, up into the chute and through the pen gate.

As we move the sheep along, the agitated man climbs over the fence and launches himself into the field with us, flapping his arms like a marionette, shirttails flying, startling the sheep and threatening to split the flock that we need to stay together. It is not even 8 a.m., it is already very hot, and the ground is so uneven and pitted that I have already rolled my ankles a couple of times. However well meaning he may be, this guy is getting on my nerves. It's no fun to shear an animal all worked up from being chased around a pasture, and the sheep have, clearly, not been kept off feed overnight since they are still grazing. They're full of food, energy, and piss and vinegar.

Almost an hour after our arrival, we manage to get the sheep into the pen. On my way out of it, my baseball cap obscuring sight of anything above the brim, I slam my forehead into the built-for-shorter-generations metal bar over the pen gate. I take a few breaths while holding onto the pen, not quite seeing straight. It's going to be a long day. If I don't keep my attitude in check, I will never get through it in a way I'll be proud of later. I talk myself down. I remind myself that I genuinely do prefer to spend time with elderly people, who are more interesting than most. I focus on being respectful of Miss Alma, on doing a good job for her, on restoring a little dignity to this dilapidated place by neatening up its ruminants. Jordan sets up a folding lawn chair for Miss Alma, to give her a ringside seat for shearing.

We lift the shearing plywood from the back of Jordan's truck and lay it down just outside the pen, in front of Miss Alma's chair. I unfold a clean, canvas tarp and lay it beside the plywood, so Jordan and I can skirt fleeces in front of Miss Alma, and she can examine them without getting up. After light skirting we'll package each fleece up in its own garbage bag and stack the bags up on the other side of the fence. I don't know that Miss Alma will do anything with these fleeces, but we proceed as if she will. Based on her handshake and herding ability today, I have no doubt she might also process, spin, and sell some fleeces.

It's time to catch the first lucky sheep for shearing. Jordan wears a garden glove on one hand, which I only notice after I've grabbed a sheep's horn to catch it and immediately let go: it's like grabbing a dull pair of scissors. I shake my hand and Jordan smiles at me, waves his gloved hand dandily, like a Broadway emcee, and says, "Sheep crook!" He's right. Jordan hooks the crook around the sheep's right rear leg and it stops walking. He places his hand under its jaw and leads it out of the pen, no chasing or horn grabbing necessary.

Miss Alma talks with us while the machines are silenced in between sheep, swapping out combs and cutters and skirting fleeces. She leans forward in her chair, points at me, and says,

It's all right that you're a lady shearer. Anyone ever says anything about that to you, well, one of my girlfriends was a shearer. She competed at the county fair up here. They had separate divisions, the men and lady shearers, but she was competing. I was showing my fleeces, I used to win ribbons and things like that, so I was waiting for the judging on that, and I was sitting right behind the judges' table. I could see everything for the shearing judging, all the times and scores for the shearing competition. And she was best of all of them. She could only win in ladies, but her time and points were higher than all of them, even in the men's. Anyone says anything to you about being a lady shearer, just think about that.

She sits back. I thank her and ask her to tell me about the fleeces and hand-spun yarn that won her all those county fair ribbons. I had not given much thought to being a lady shearer, but I like the moniker.

Shearing proceeds smoothly save for Miss Alma's incessantly chattering son. At any given moment, he is either in the sheep pen, half-heartedly attempting to catch them but really just working them up, or on the shearing plywood, far too close for comfort. He wanders off and returns, over and over again, like a spinning teacup. Jordan says, "Believe it or not, he's better than usual. She said he had an eye surgery recently, which he had to clean up for. They find that stuff in your blood at the doctor's and you've got another set of problems. Looks like it didn't last, though." Jordan ignores him, and I try, but he's so close that I have to keep an eye on him while also trying to control the sheep and shear. I leave my shears running to drown out his never-ending stream of words, but then they get hot. Miss Alma periodically yells at him and he backs off a bit, and eventually Jordan politely asks him to please stay off the shearing plywood.

I'm irritated, but I also feel sorry and embarrassed for him. Jordan and I may be doing work that once belonged to him. He probably grew up and labored on this farm, but whatever's running through his veins does not help him do those things now, though he seems to know he should be, trying in his own way, futile.

Jordan and I trade off shearing all day. We're in full sun and it's well into the nineties by late morning. We keep our already-soaked ball caps on. I should probably eat a little something to keep my blood sugar up, but the idea of food is nauseating. I don't even want much water because it feels like it will only come up when I bend over again to shear. I wear a loose, button-down, cotton shirt for sun protection, and sheep horns keep getting caught in the holes between the buttons, threatening to rip it. It's another valuable lesson: don't shear in button-down shirts, or at least have something decent on underneath if you do.

We shear pretty well, closely and cleanly without any nicks. Jordan shears more sheep faster than I do, but it's a job, not a competition. He shears the rams, of which I'm wary, but I pay close attention to how he handles their more sensitive areas. The most eventful incident of the day is the ram's own fault entirely. While getting his legs after shearing, one ram thrashes against the plywood and knocks the exterior layer of one horn off. The inside looks like smooth, white bone coated in blood, which splatters across the plywood.

Unfazed, Miss Alma waves her hands, points at the plywood, and says, "Pick it up!" She says she wants the outer horn to make a button. I pluck the horn out of the blood, wipe it off on my pants, and hand it to her. As she receives it, she sweetly—but seriously—asks, "Can you just slaughter him?" Jordan and I glance at each other, and with my eyes, I say, "That is not part of our job offering." The ram's self-inflicted injury is far from fatal. She explains, "He's a lot to handle and old anyway." Jordan replies, "I could do it for you, and come back and dress it, but I know a knacker man who will do it better and faster for about $50. I will get you in touch with him."

Miss Alma's not soft by a long stretch.

I shear my first goats, which is not terribly difficult between Jordan and myself. One of us holds the goat while the other shears from the top of its spine down its sides, with no issues. Their fiber, which would otherwise be curly and quite pretty, is unfortunately quite matted. All in all, we shear twelve Jacob sheep and three goats. Jordan and I agree to get some food, and maybe a beer, and sit in a cool dark place for a while before we each drive home. I haven't forgotten about my first (and last) attempt at driving too soon after shearing.

We load up and, as I drive along the road beside Miss Alma's land, a small animal flies into the front seat of my car from the back, landing on the floor of the passenger side in the front seat. I scream and hit the brakes, unable to even see what it is, and nearly startle myself straight into a ditch. It is one of Jordan's dogs, his newest puppy, who must have gotten into my car at some point and taken a nap on the blanket I keep in my back seat. That's what I get for leaving my car windows down all day. Standing on all fours on the passenger-side floor, the dog seems groggy, disoriented, and more startled than I am. I have to laugh. Hopefully the dog's presence kept other creatures from my car.

I honk and flag Jordan down and, when he passes on the right for me to follow, I point at the dog, who is now standing on the front passenger seat, looking expectantly at Jordan through the open window. Jordan laughs and says, "Keep her!" and drives on to the restaurant. The dog looks even more confused but, after I pet her, she turns around in the passenger seat a few times, lies down, and dozes again.

Seated at the bar, in low light, air conditioning, and with tall glasses of ice water in front of us, I ask Jordan, "What do you think will happen to that ranch when she dies?" He doesn't skip a beat. "What always happens. He'll lose it, a fourth-generation ranch, and some rich person will buy it, knock it all down, put a big house on it, maybe subdivide, sell some to a developer. And people will blame the rich person, not him."

NINE

Barn Raising

I first saw sheep shearer Matt Gilbert when he participated in a panel at the initial Fibershed Wool Symposium, the same event that convinced me to attend shearing school. I'd never have guessed that Matt was only in his mid-twenties at the time. He had the serious, competent demeanor of someone at least a decade older and looked transported from an early twentieth-century farm: an ample beard, broad-brimmed hat, wire-rimmed glasses, suspenders, and a tucked-in, button-down shirt. He was earnest and sincere, out of place in our age of sarcasm. Sarah Gilbert, Matt's wife, also seemed wise beyond her years, sharp, resourceful, and an experienced knitter, spinner, pattern designer and maker, and sewer. Together, they were raising and educating Rebekah (six), Felicity (four), and Chloe (two), three smart, capable, unfailingly sweet and polite daughters. The Gilberts are the kind of family that leaves you thinking, "Whatever it is, they're doing it right."

Just before the close of the symposium, Matt stepped up to the wooden podium at the front of the room and announced his and Sarah's plans to start a wool mill. He had been shearing sheep throughout Central and Northern California for nearly fifteen years, since he was thirteen years old. In that time, Matt said he had seen "an awful lot of wool get thrown away, and a lot of people who want local products made out of that wool. But there's no mill that can produce yarn out of the fine fibers that you would like to wear. I want to start one." He hoped to be able to spin yarn finely enough to be woven into fabric. Matt believed Northern California had the potential to become a solid local wool market, with already high unmet demand for wool processing services and a mill's finished products.

When Robin Lynde had described shipping fleeces to Zeilinger Wool, she'd told me, "I'm shipping wool to Michigan because I can't process it here. I did the same last year to the tune of several thousand dollars." Similarly, Julie Rosenfeld, owner of Renaissance Ridge Alpacas in Mount Aukum, California, told Matt she had been approached by a garment design team from San Francisco that wanted to use alpaca fiber, humanely raised within the region, to create truly local garments. Julie would have loved to help them but, without a local mill, she could not provide her alpaca fiber in a processed yarn form that the designers could use. "There are no local mills that produce a good-enough product, consistency-wise. I have had to send fiber off to Virginia to get it milled, which is why I have not had any more made; the cost makes it prohibitive. That is why selling the raw fiber and then having them use whatever mill they like seems to be the more financially logical way."

I found infrastructure problems where I'd expected to find problems of consumer demand and prohibitively expensive local manufacturing costs. There was a market for locally sourced fleece and fiber. Lots of people wanted to buy locally made clothing, California designers wanted to make it for them, and fiber farmers were eager to sell their high-quality raw materials to both audiences. But the local infrastructure to do it wasn't there.

As the most astute entrepreneurs often do, Matt—who also had a career as a certified forester—had identified and hoped to take advantage of these inefficiencies in the supply chain to serve a niche with pent-up demand. He had a market, and as a well-known, experienced shearer married to a creative fiber aficionado, the Gilberts were in a unique position to own and control the entire supply chain. Matt knew firsthand the farmers, fiber producers, ranches, land, livestock management practices, breeds, and wool quality of the sheep he sheared. He directly observed the quality and attributes of the wool he was starting with, during and after each shearing. And he could ensure that wool was skillfully sheared to the highest standard, without second cuts and with the lowest possible amount of waste. With the addition of a wool mill, Matt and Sarah could guarantee that the wool Matt brought home was subsequently skirted, scoured, designed, and spun into a top-notch product, ethically grown, sourced, and processed from start to finish.

Some of Matt's raw materials didn't cost him anything. With so many people throwing wool away because of high processing and shipping costs, Matt had accumulated thousands of pounds for free, the fleeces handed to him with payment for shearing, the shepherd glad to have someone who would take them away so they had one less thing to think about. Free raw material couldn't help but improve the mill's initial margins.

From the podium, Matt described his and Sarah's efforts to get a wool mill going. They had spent most of that year (2012) looking for a suitable commercial facility to rent for mill space, approximately 1,000 to 2,500 square feet in size, with sufficient water (roughly five hundred gallons per day), a way to reuse gray water and get rid of wastewater, 220-volt power, heat and humidity controls (critical in wool processing), and affordable rent. Matt also hoped to be able to install solar panels for a low-impact way to provide hot water and power.

The Gilberts were seeking space in the vicinity of Ukiah, a large town conveniently situated along Highway 101 and several smaller highways, centrally located for a large number of wool growers and their flocks. Instead of spending several thousand dollars in shipping, wool growers could make one annual trip to drop wool off at the mill—or, if Matt sheared for them, send it to the mill for free or for a reasonable fee in Matt's truck. This southern area of Mendocino County was also a short drive from the San Francisco Bay Area, for convenient delivery to urban yarn shops, garment designers, and boutiques.

As Matt spoke, my pink-cheeked, vintage-bespectacled friend Kate Hoag and I knit, like so many other people in the symposium audience. We cast sideways glances at one another and the same idea struck each of us at once: crowdfunding, the practice of funding projects by raising money from a large number of people. Matt was describing a capital-intensive project but had not mentioned a source of that capital. It seemed like an online crowdfunding campaign for a new, local wool mill could be successful. Everyone around us wanted local wool services and products and seemed eager to improve our local wool economy, to say nothing of the much larger community of knitters and spinners not in attendance.

Logistically, crowdfunding was feasible. Matt might have to be out and about shearing or doing forestry work all day, and Sarah might be homeschooling three daughters, designing and sewing their clothes, and everything else, but I had a tech job and spent my entire day online, staring at a screen. I could easily monitor email questions and campaign comments and manage the day-to-day. By the time Matt finished speaking, it was as good as done in my mind, and Kate's. I approached the podium, introduced myself, offered to help with online fundraising, and gave Matt my email and phone number. I am an introvert, so I felt awkward and overeager. But I had Kate as my sidekick and, after a day of stories about the local wool struggle, my emotions were running high. I felt panicked, as if the lovely, precariously positioned yarn world I'd finally found might slip away at any moment. Kate and I felt a shared sense of urgency that some sort of immediate action was required.

As time passed after the symposium, however, I didn't hear from Matt. I thought about the wool mill occasionally, but became preoccupied with work, moving house, changing jobs, helping to care for my grandfather (in the late stages of congestive heart failure and a few months away from death), and shearing school. But when I saw a Fibershed email announcement for the 2013 symposium, I decided to email Matt again, ask how the mill was coming along, and see if I could be of help. This time, he wrote back with a "Great to hear from you."

Matt reported that not much had changed since the symposium several months ago. He and Sarah were still looking for space for the mill, a full year after they'd started their search. They had given up looking for commercial spaces—none of which had what the mill needed and all of which were expensive—and had shifted their search to mixed-use live-work spaces that could house the mill and their family. They planned to make an offer on one such property, for which they had barely enough money. The down payment alone would require all of their savings and 401(k), everything they'd been able to save since paying off student loans a few years prior. The total monthly payment would be lower than a house payment and rent for a commercial space, but there wouldn't be any money left over.

Matt attached a copy of the business plan to his email, and wrote that they'd found some mill equipment to buy, albeit with unfortunate timing since they had no money with which to purchase it. Four industrial-size, midcentury hunks of metal, each one taller than a person and the size of a small room, for sale in eastern Canada: a drum carder, coiler, spinner, and pin drafter. I was eager to read Matt's business plan. Could a wool mill really make financial sense and be sustainable in this day and age? The symposium had shown that there were real problems Matt and his mill could solve and numerous customers at the ready, but I was, perhaps, still influenced by the well-worn story of modern manufacturing: that the capital investment and labor costs required to operate a US-based manufacturing facility are too great, the regulations too many and onerous, and profitability dependent on low-wage labor.

That same year, for instance, the Business Insider website included textile mills in their list titled "10 American Industries That Will Be Destroyed in the Next Decade." As is often the case with mass-media claims, however, the story did not include any substantive information, questions, or thoughtful examination about why this destruction should or would happen, whom or what would benefit and/or suffer for it, or why the foretold destruction might be predominantly beneficial or detrimental.

On the bright side, these unsubstantiated predictions were hardly convincing, so perhaps it *was* a good idea to set up a textile manufacturing facility in a rural area in 2013. I decided to suspend my disbelief and forget, for a moment, what the mainstream hysterics had to say. The world so rarely got to hear from people like Matt and Sarah Gilbert. What did a sheep shearer, native to his county, working on the land with sheep and wool growers for fifteen years, have to say? We know what's wrong with the textile industry, but few people have suggested a better model for what should replace it, and even fewer were willing to work hard to make that new model a reality.

That evening, I settled in with a cup of tea and the forty-four-page business plan for Mendocino Wool & Fiber. The mill would make money by providing processing services, turning people's raw wool into usable products; by distributing and selling its own consumer yarn brand; and by spinning white-label yarns for indie dyers and yarn shops that wanted to sell roving and yarn with their names on the labels. The mill would also pursue an organic certification to offer organic yarn.

All stages of raw wool processing (with the exception of dyeing) would occur on-site. At full capacity, the mill would be capable of running two eight-hour shifts per day, at least five days per week. The quantity of fiber the mill could process within an eight-hour shift would depend on the production specifications, given the raw material and desired end product. Generally speaking, though, six pounds per hour was the anticipated production volume for batting, roving, and combed top products, and five pounds per hour for yarn products. The stated figures allowed downtime for switching between orders and machines. Matt and Sarah would perform all mill labor until the business had sufficient income to pay other employees.

Detailed tables and spreadsheets listed start-up costs under scenarios with either new or used equipment; sample workload by employee, machine, and process; and the price, cost, and revenue per service, by pound of wool, with the estimated market size and future customers for each. It included every cost, down to the pennies per pound for sewer ($.21), soap ($.20), water ($.21), and power ($.10). Mendocino Wool & Fiber was—like all mills in history it seemed—capital intensive to start, thanks to the equipment and facility needs. There was no avoiding the total $250,000 that would be required for industrial equipment and a construction retrofit to make a large garage into a functioning, water and energy conserving wool mill.

But, even by very conservative sales volume and cash flow projections, it looked like the mill could be paid off in a little over ten years and that the business would be cash flow positive early on, even after meeting its loan obligations. Within a year or so after opening, Matt and Sarah might even be able to create jobs for additional workers to run the mill on two shifts, jobs of the sort most needed in rural Northern California: decent paying, no higher education required, with on-the-job training. The business plan included astute decisions that pointed to Matt and Sarah's focus, like the decision to partner with an experienced dyer to offer colored (dyed) yarns without entering the dye business themselves.

I liked the fact that, in not a terribly long time, the mill would belong to the Gilberts, rather than a private equity firm or some such. Unlike the start-up business plans of the more familiar tech industry, no liquidity event—like an initial public offering (IPO) of stock or acquisition by a global corporation—would be required to pay off tens or hundreds of millions of dollars from investors. It would be easy to spend millions of dollars to start a wool mill, but that wasn't required for a mill that could do what its customers and region needed it to do, and the Gilberts knew it. Their business plan showed a clear, conservative, and realistic path to sustainability, profitability, and independent ownership that I found unusual and refreshing.

The business plan convinced me that the mill not only had a lot of promise but could really work. It made sense. I wrote back to Matt, saying as much, and reiterated my offer to help raise money for the Gilberts' endeavor. It somehow seemed irrelevant that Matt, Sarah, and I had met only once in real life for a minute or two. I had the same feeling I had with shearing school: that I was on the right path, that the path would sound insane to anyone else, and that it was probably best not to discuss it too widely.

Just two email messages later, in late September 2013, Sarah, Matt, and I decided to organize an online crowdfunding campaign to launch just one month later, on the day of the November 2013 wool symposium. It seemed critical to leverage that real-world event full of like-minded people to kick things off. I'd spent many hours researching crowdfunding strategies and results and had learned that most successful campaigns raised the majority of their money in the first few days, with donations falling off afterward even if they continued to trickle in. There weren't very many wool-centric events for us to choose from: the wool symposium would be our only big opportunity for a long while.

We had a lot to pull together in a small amount of time. Crowdfunding campaigns are common and may seem formulaic and easy, but they require a lot of work. Running a campaign well is a part-time job or better. We chose Indiegogo as our crowdfunding platform because, unlike others, it allowed the Gilberts to keep whatever money was raised, even if it fell short of the stated target. We had to be specific in our goals, to state exactly what the money raised would be spent on, so donors would have a clear sense of what their funds were helping to obtain. And our target fundraising goals had to be attainable, an amount of money that was genuinely helpful but didn't feel impossible. The total cost to open the mill—$250,000—felt too high, like too much to ask for.

We decided to set the initial goal to $16,000, the down payment needed to buy the four pieces of mill equipment for sale. The drum carder was the most expensive item at $51,500, followed by the spinner at $30,000 and the pin drafter at $10,000. An optional skein winder and cone winder were also available for $16,000 ($8,000 each).

I sent spreadsheets containing wide ranges of donation levels and corresponding perks to Matt, all of which had to add up to the target goal and cover any costs of obtaining perks. We offered cute sheep photos at the $1 donation level. Not only did people tend to give more if a crowdfunding campaign offers perks at very low donation levels, but we also knew a lot of farmers and fiber artists who did not have much cash to spare and wanted to be able to give something. The perk at the $500-plus donation level was a mill tour with a homemade dinner and the agricultural adventure package of shearing with Matt. The Northern California fiber community donated perks to the effort, including handmade soap, naturally dyed skeins of yarn, and high-end machine-knit sweaters. Robin Lynde donated a scarf she'd woven by hand, with yarn she'd hand spun, sourced from her Jacob sheep. Sarah Gilbert offered to make a completely custom, hand-knit sweater out of yarn she'd hand spun.

If anything, Matt seemed to have underestimated the interest in a local wool mill and the level of trust others had in him and in Sarah. I wrote draft after draft of campaign text, we posted perks and photos, established social media accounts, connected bank accounts to Indiegogo, and Matt arranged to get a nicely edited video made by a friend.

Early on the morning of the second annual wool symposium, November 15, 2013, my husband and I awaken at a small Point Reyes inn. I sit up in bed, open my laptop, and deliver a silent, pleading incantation to the rural Internet gods. I flip the Indiegogo switch, launch the campaign, and make an initial donation so no one else hesitates at being the first donor. I am nervous, keyed up, and I haven't even had any coffee yet. Is it too much to ask? Too soon? Too late? We have to use this day to our advantage. There is no better audience or more appropriate event, and it comes only once a year. Ready or not, that day is today.

At the symposium, Matt, Sarah, and I sit in a row as we listen to presentations. I resist the urge to constantly check the campaign from my phone and instead knit my nerves out on a sweater. Distracted, I make so many mistakes that I have to rip the knitting out. After lunch, Rebecca Burgess generously gives Matt time to announce the wool mill campaign. It is momentous to see him walk up to that same wooden podium, exactly one year later, and feel the mill is a little closer.

The campaign raises $385 in the first twenty-four hours. By the end of the symposium weekend, it's $2,380. The next five days are steady, reaching $7,272, nearly 50 percent of our target amount. Kristine Vejar, founder of A Verb for Keeping Warm, a lovely, unique yarn and fabric shop in Oakland, donates to get the first spot in line for wool processing. Kristine, possibly more than anyone else, has sourced local wool to develop her own yarn line for years, visiting farms and even finding and towing baling machines to them. Dozens of friends and family members donate. The support and enthusiasm are humbling and overwhelming.

Late in the afternoon of day six, on Thursday, November 20, I sit at my desk in my downtown San Francisco office during the ten minutes I have free between meetings. I watch the container ships arrive full and leave empty from the Port of Oakland, dreading another pointless meeting like the one I just finished. I steel myself, brew a cup of tea, and log in to see how the wool mill campaign, my welcome distraction, is going.

My stomach drops, and my cheeks flush. Something is wrong. There has been a huge spike of over $6,000 in a matter of hours. We'd hoped to raise $16,000 in sixty days, and—less than a week in—we've already raised over $13,000? Possible but unlikely, since our big initial push has already started to level off. And to have raised as much money in the past few hours as we'd raised in the preceding five days? Even less likely. I've crunched data for many years and well know the myriad reasons that most apparent spikes usually aren't: increase the length of time, adjust for population size or other factors, and most supposed spikes quickly vanish. The simplest explanation is the most likely: a $1,000-level donor got impatient with the donate button and accidentally put multiple credit card charges through, or the crowdfunding platform itself did similarly with all donations from the preceding twenty-four hours or something. Well, crap. Software. I will have to dig into it further after my meeting.

I walk to another conference room, again the first and only person on time. I check my personal email while waiting for others to appear in person and on screen. Bliss: My weekly *Knitter's Review* email newsletter, from Clara Parkes herself, she of *The Knitter's Book of Wool*, and yarn with "crunch." I look forward to *Knitter's Review*—my single best piece of email—every week. It usually contains a review of a new yarn, announcements about knitting retreats, maybe a link to a new book or tool. I can skim it while the meeting organizer drones on with the same "update" he gave last week, enjoying a captive audience and the sound of his own voice.

And there, at the very top, is the explanation for our spike in donations: "Indiegogo: Let's Bring a Mill to Mendocino." I physically jerk and knock tea onto my laptop. "Something exciting is happening in Northern California. Lifelong sheep shearer Matt Gilbert and his wife Sarah are looking to start up a new wool mill in Mendocino. They've set a modest fundraising goal, and I know we can help them reach it."

A few tears escape. Great. Now I am the woman crying in the conference room. Well, screw it. This is huge! Clara Parkes herself had written that?! About them?! I can't email Matt and Sarah quickly enough before flying on to Twitter to thank Clara Parkes in the only, very public, way I know how. Thanks to her, we exceed our initial fundraising goal quickly and, when all is said and done, raise over $28,000 from 517 generous people, netting just over $20,000 after fees.

In the midst of all of this, Matt and Sarah make an offer on that home for both the mill and their family. A few weeks after the conclusion of the mill campaign, Matt writes that he and Sarah expect to be the proud owners of a house, with the right zoning and space to start the mill, on or about the fifteenth of March.

The Gilberts need $50,000 for the mill equipment, of which they've raised $20,000. The best Matt has been able to find for the remaining $30,000 is a business loan with a high interest rate, which won't be available for another three to four weeks, if the Gilberts are even approved. Somehow, with headline interest rates at nearly zero percent, small businesses still have to pay exorbitant rates. Matt posts a message to the wool mill Facebook page: "Anyone want to lend us a portion of that? We'll give you a much better interest rate than you are getting in your savings account now."

Both Kate and I see Matt's message. We put our heads together over beer after work one day. What do we sit in all these ridiculous 6 a.m. and 10 p.m. video conferences *for*? How much good is our money currently doing? Not much, sitting in the bank at historically low interest rates. Indeed, it is more likely doing harm, part of some mutual or hedge fund we haven't chosen, in employer-sponsored 401(k) plans we cannot control, enriching those who need it least: myriad corporate wel-fare recipients. How will we feel if we could have made a difference at a crucial time and didn't? If the mill does not get past critical start-up milestones, there will not be any mill to fund. Put up or shut up.

We agree to loan the mill $15,000 each, a total of $30,000. Matt is willing to do a handshake deal, a foreign concept after years spent with venture capitalists and their term sheets—real, interpersonal trust, the belief that you are as good as your word. I do not feel a need for loan paperwork, per se. The Gilberts will not rip me off. But, it is a lot of money. Like the Gilberts, my husband and I have just spent our savings on the down payment for a house. I believe the mill is a good invest-ment, but in order to risk that $15,000, I need to be able to invest it freely. I have to feel genuinely comfortable without the $15,000 principle and interest on hand, and with the possibility that I may never see any of that money again.

And I am more concerned for the Gilberts. Without paperwork, any-one else who invests in the mill can make up any story they want about what they were owed, or make claims to mill ownership. It would be Matt's word against theirs, and it would cost a lot of time and money to duke it out without documents to reference.

We need documents, but what kind? I dig up paperwork from a $10,000 loan Ian and I made several years ago to local farm, when a CD had expired and interest rates plummeted. Ever since, we receive 7 percent interest in organic fruits and vegetables, which covers most of our fresh grocery costs, and we can get our money back from the farm with thirty days' notice. The loan document is a single, straightforward page and did the trick all these years, so I copy it and make a few edits.

Matt hopes to structure our loans similarly to home loans, amortized over fifteen years (enabling the Gilberts to make payments as if the loan will be paid off in fifteen years) with a balloon payment for the remainder due. I do not need the money paid back in any particular time frame, so we stipulate that in the loan paperwork, too. Matt asks me to determine the loan interest rate, and I pull 3 percent out of the air and advise him to say the word if that is unmanageable. Once we have the document worked out, we send a copy to Kate, so she can request any necessary edits for her $15,000 loan. Matt emails us a Bank of America account number to which we can deposit our checks.

On the crisp, sunny morning of February 27, 2014, Kate and I each stop at Bank of America branches on our respective walks to work and deposit the money to the Gilberts' bank account. Shortly thereafter, Matt sends an email to tell us the mill equipment is on its way. Matt and Sarah closed on their property (in Ukiah, California, just as they'd hoped) in the nick of time, so the mill equipment has a place to land. Exactly one month after the Gilberts move in, the equipment arrives by truck from eastern Canada.

Regrettably, Kate and I have to work the day the mill equipment arrives, but Matt texts photos of it. I cannot believe how large each machine is, much less that there are four of them. A crane lifts each piece of equipment off the semitruck that carried it. Four machines cannot fit in the garage on the Gilbert's property—not as constructed—so a shipping container is left on-site with two pieces of equipment inside. Kate and I long to drive to Ukiah to turn it on and try it out, but the mill has no permit to do so.

Matt gives one month's notice at his forestry job in order to focus on the mill, hopeful he will be able to work as a contract forester when mill work is slow. He and Sarah have three little ones, a brand-new mortgage, and four hulking pieces of industrial machinery and a shipping container in their backyard. The mill feels like a very high-stakes gamble. I hope it will all turn out to be worth it.

TEN

Camaraderie

My next shearing job, in the vicinity of where Jordan and I sheared for Miss Alma, is one that Matt Gilbert asks if I can take for him. I'll be shearing a flock of ten Navajo-Churros, all ewes with lambs. I ask Jordan to come with me. Ten sheep are several more than I've sheared in a day, and I am wary of the breed. Multiple shearers have warned me about Icelandic, Shetland, and Navajo-Churro sheep: "They're built like a box and jumpy. They jump so high, they'll jump right over you. You won't even believe it. It's like they levitate."

This was not the first such thing I'd heard about so-called primitive breeds of sheep with which humans have tampered less, genetically speaking, over time. They are considered more intelligent, less docile, hardier, and stronger than more domesticated breeds. The Navajo-Churro Sheep Association website states, for example, that Navajo lamb easily and often bear twins and triplets, and are excellent mothers who ferociously protect their lambs—exactly what you want in a ewe.

Like Jacob sheep, most Navajo-Churro—ewes included—have horns. They are dual-coated, with a coarser, protective topcoat and a soft undercoat. The rougher topcoat makes Navajo fleeces felt well, and sometimes too easily: fleeces can turn to felt while on the sheep's body. Unlike most breeds, which are sheared annually, Navajo should be sheared every six months.

The Navajo-Churro is a rare breed, the oldest in North America. The first domestic sheep in the Americas arrived over four hundred years ago, brought by Spanish colonists. Spain sent common, coarser sheep—Manchega, Castellana, Lacha, and Churra (the word "churra" or "churro" means "common")—to the New World in the late 1400s and 1500s.[1] In 1598, Don Juan de Oñate brought twenty-nine hundred sheep to Pueblo lands in the American Southwest, the same year he led the Acoma massacre. Oñate and other Spanish colonists killed hundreds of Acoma people, amputated the right feet of at least twenty-four Acoma men, and sentenced Acoma men over twenty-five years old to twenty years of servitude. Spanish ranches subsequently prospered in what are now Texas, New Mexico, and Arizona, with sheep flocks numbering in the thousands.[2] The Navajo-Churro breed may have continued to thrive in the American Southwest, too, if not for the US government.

During US westward expansion in the mid-1800s, the Diné ("the people" in the Navajo language) resisted the intrusion of white settlers on their hunting and homelands. The US government ordered military actions led by Kit Carson and John Carlton to destroy the Navajo economy, crops, orchards, flocks and, more plainly, Diné independence. They intended to starve and freeze the Diné into submission.[3] Carson and 736 men of the First New Mexico Volunteer Regiment carried out their orders to "prosecute a vigorous war upon the men of this tribe until it is considered at these Head Quarters that they have been effectually punished for their long continued atrocities." Carson and his men razed villages, murdered Diné, captured women and children, stole thousands of sheep and goats, and burned the crops they did not steal to feed their own livestock.

During the deep winter of 1864, after tremendous bloodshed, eight thousand to nine thousand Diné people were forced on the Long Walk of three hundred miles to an internment camp at Bosque Redondo, New Mexico, referred to as a reservation but under military control at Fort Sumner. Some escaped capture and hid with their sheep in remote canyons of New Mexico and Arizona, or lived with the Apache people, but many hundreds of Diné people died in overcrowded, miserable conditions at Basque Redondo. Four years later, the Diné signed the US-Navajo Treaty of 1868, which allowed them to return to a much diminished portion of their homeland in Arizona and New Mexico. They began the long walk home in June 1868. Some were issued two sheep per person from Hispanic flocks.[4]

Sadly, this did not end the torment of the Diné people and their sheep by the US government. It continued into the 1930s:

The Navajo were such good weavers and shepherds that their mixed flocks grew to 574,821 sheep by 1930. The large number of sheep, goats, horses, and cattle was considered problematic for the severe drought conditions of the 1930s, so the US government conducted a stock reduction. Some stock was purchased for $1–$1.50 but the reduction progressed so slowly that roughly 30 percent of each household's sheep, goats, and horses were slaughtered by government agents and thrown into arroyos or burned. This terrifying Stock Reduction is still vivid in Navajo memory.[5]

I cannot conceive of watching, hearing, and smelling my own sheep—known since they were lambs, carrying the markings and personalities of their ancestors—being burned alive, their thousands of terrified, screaming voices, powerless to stop it.

To this day, sheep, horses, and cattle that Diné families maintain on Hopi Partitioned Lands (HPL) are often impounded by police. the Hopi Department of Natural Resources claims livestock reductions are necessary due to drought and overgrazing. Even if true, the practice feels like a violation of the rights of Diné people to practice their traditional culture, and part of the shameful legacy of government-mandated livestock reductions. The more I learn about Navajo-Churro sheep, the more I look forward to meeting them. That they exist at all is testament to Diné people who hid sheep from slaughter, and to stewards who have bred flocks back from the brink.

I learn a few important business lessons before I even arrive at the job site, the first of which is that desperation and cooperation are not related. People who claim to be "desperate" to have their sheep sheared will not necessarily be flexible when it comes to scheduling the job. I also learn to be clear about—and stand by—my rates from the get-go.

In speaking with the flock owner by phone (having already scheduled and committed to a shearing date by email), I learn that Matt charges less than I do, even though he is faster and more experienced. And Matt's rate is what the customer expects to pay. Because Matt can shear more sheep, he can schedule multiple jobs in the same vicinity on the same day. This means Matt is paid a ranch call to show up at each place, plus his per-head price for each animal sheared. All in all, Matt might net $500 or more on a day when I may be able to make only $50–$100 for a single ranch call and a few head of sheep. I am disappointed with the lower rate but honor Matt's price. I will make $90 for one full day's work, a net loss with three hours of round-trip driving and fuel and wear and tear on my equipment. I remind myself I am just getting started: this is my first "real" shearing job, I still have a day job that pays plenty, and I need experience before I deserve to be paid well.

Since my visits to Joy's and Miss Alma's, I have "kitted up," as shearers say, meaning I've put my sheep-shearing kit together. Without Jordan's help, I would not have known what to put in it; my online searches for "sheep shearing starter kit" were fruitless. I feel better and more prepared (if more encumbered) with my supplies: a portable shearing handpiece; a few combs and cutters; and a small screwdriver for swapping them out. I have Kool Lube spray to cool hot metal; motor oil to keep blades moving and my handpiece running smoothly; a scrub brush with a metal blade on one end, with which to scrape sodden, wooly gunk off my combs between sheep; and disinfectant wash to prevent cross contamination. I do not want to shear a sheep with an abscess or other contagious condition and pass it on to another sheep or another flock.

I also have worst-case scenario stuff: livestock first-aid items, including wound disinfectant, fly-strike prevention spray (to spray only on severe cuts, to keep flies away and prevent them from laying eggs in the wound), blood-clotting powder, unwaxed dental floss, a curved veterinary needle, an animal ace bandage, and—for me—a clean roll of gauze, Band-Aids, and antibiotic ointment.

Our urban one-car garage is long enough for one of two sufficiently short cars, a Fiat or a Mini Cooper, and we own the latter. Fortunately, with the back seats and the convertible top down, I can load a lot of gear into the car. I throw in an extension cord, the sheep crook Jordan gave me at Miss Alma's, and a roll of garbage bags, for both fleeces and my stinky clothes and shearing slippers. After marinating in my sweat-and-sheep stink with the windows closed and the air conditioner on, I learned to change clothes before a long drive home.

I do not have a piece of shearing plywood, nor did I think (despite my shearing school instructors' lessons) to ask the owner if they do. Instead I've brought a tarp, which I thought I might shear and set fleeces and equipment on. And I make another mistake: for some reason, I do not have Jordan's phone number to coordinate arrival. I'd emailed him the job site address and he confirmed, but I have no way to reach him even if I had cellular reception, which I don't. I arrive at the property and have no choice but to set up and pretend everything is fine.

The house sits just inside a tall front gate, perched atop several acres of sloping land, some of it an apple orchard. I am relieved to see the morning's cool, lingering fog, though I hope the sheep are dry. Mrs. Kelly, who insisted I come on a day when she does not have to work, points out the unpenned (presumably still grazing) sheep in a distant pasture. So much for my instructions to keep them from food and water overnight.

Mr. Kelly moves the sheep to a pen, at which point I count them. Ten sheep have become twelve. The difference between ten and twelve sheep is negligible for most shearers but mammoth for me, the difference between finishing the job and not. My biggest shearing day so far has been five sheep. I do not think I can shear a dozen sheep myself, before nightfall anyway, but will soon find out.

Mr. Kelly points me to the power outlet and then—to my surprise—Mrs. Kelly bids good-bye and leaves for work. Mr. Kelly stays home, but inside the house. It's just me and the sheep. I am amazed at the Kellys' trust in a complete stranger. Matt's word must really count for something. I suppose it figures, though. Shearing days may be new to me but certainly not to them. They have plenty of other work to do and can't stand around watching me all day.

I assess the situation and try to figure out where to set up for shearing. As Jordan's stories of shearing in the wild foretold, it looks like I'll be shearing on a hillside. There is a flatter area on the other side of the sheep pen, near my car, but my extension cord won't reach far enough. I'll need to buy another one, or three. The location of the power outlet creates a lot of distance between the pen and the hillside shearing area, which means I'll expend more energy either dragging the sheep the full distance, or straddling and walking with the sheep, or somehow wrangling the sheep while getting it to walk itself over to the shearing area. This will be an interesting day.

I get started, hoping Jordan will arrive. I enter the pen, and once again, sheep become larger when I find myself beside them. Hefty, almost rectangular ewes run half wild all over the pen, not keen to be separated from their lambs, now a few months old but no less dear for that. As I dart down to grab one sheep's chin, one of the hundred-pound ewes tries to jump right over me. Her front half lands on my head, neck, and shoulders, whereupon she just lays there, each front leg dangling over one of my shoulders, as if she expects a piggyback ride. It is unbelievable and hilarious to see a hoof below each of my ears. I stand up and she stands with me on her hind legs, unfazed by my change in posture.

One at a time, I gently slip each of her front legs off my shoulders, but decide to keep a handle on her: by jumping on top of me, she's volunteered to be sheared first. I flip her in the pen before I realize there is no one to open the pen gate for me, or to close and secure it after me. I am not sure how to do these things with my hands full of sheep. I manage to drag her a few feet and hold her between my legs while I unpeg the gate, then pause. I am not sure how to get her out without the rest of the sheep immediately following us through the open gate—which they assuredly will.

The ewe fights me the whole time, bucking with the same power and force that, moments ago, she used to nearly hurdle me. She will not wait for me to figure out gate logistics. I cannot drag her through a gate with one hand; it is all I can do to move her with two. I am exhausting myself, not knowing what I'm doing.

I let the sheep stand and hold her chin with one hand while I press her against the gate with my hip. Sweating buckets, I think for a moment. The shearing station is about twenty feet away. Dragging every sheep that far will burn me out before I even start shearing. I will walk the sheep over to the shearing area and see if I can avoid the dragging completely, which will be nicer for both of us. I will also bring my sheep crook the next time I go into the pen, to catch these fast, jumpy sheep more easily. I might be on my own all day.

The sheep does not cooperate in the "walking over to the shearing area" plan, but the pressure to maintain my grip is higher than ever. I will not be shearing in a small fenced pen so much as multiple unfenced acres. If the sheep gets away, she can run through a small apple orchard, garden, parking area, and—worst-case scenario—out to the two-lane highway. I'll have to somehow catch an escaped sheep without the aid of Jordan, a herding dog, or an experienced shepherd, and the sheep will be even more riled up and stressed out.

I half walk, half pull the sheep to the power source and tarp, where I've set up my equipment. I pause to catch my breath. The sheep and I are on a slope, so I experiment with how best to situate us. I can't have my backside facing downhill: that makes it too easy for her to pitch me backward. Facing forward, downhill, isn't any better: the sheep sits lower on the slope than I am, harder to reach, and adding several inches to the already long distance I have to bend over. I arrange us sideways, on the most level ground I can find, my left foot farther downhill than my right, but the most stable stance yet.

I tip and flip the sheep and finally get a good look at her, feel her body beneath the wool, and look for bony corners, cysts, skin flaps, wrinkles, anything that I might cut accidentally or that might give me trouble. I spread the wool to see her teats clearly, count how many she has, and get the lay of her land while she breathes beneath me, thoroughly displeased. Other shearers' description of Navajo-Churro as boxy are spot on. Unlike the rotund, fatty Targhee ewes at shearing school; or Robin's longer legged, lithe Jacobs; or Joy's small, almost delicate Shetland, this sheep is stocky. Her bones feel like right angles in some places. She is sharp, strong, and long overdue for a shearing: much of her wool has turned to felt on her body. I wonder how to get my shears beneath it . . . just cut through the surface, I guess, if I can't find a clean spot for the comb to get purchase and started.

The unfenced area and terrifying prospect of sheep escape get me to really lean forward and down on the sheep to keep her in place. I switch my portable handpiece on, start shearing, and everything my shearing teachers said would happen does. The minute I move my feet, the tarp moves beneath them. Just a few moves into my morning, the electrical cord, my feet, and occasionally the sheep's legs are tangled in the tarp. Nothing to be done about it now; just keep shearing.

I finish and walk the sheep back to the pen. She's harder to control now that she is smooth with no wool, but at least she wants to move in this direction to reunite with her flock. I brush off and oil my handpiece, catch and walk another sheep over, and start shearing. As I finish and raise my head to stand, I see Jordan. I hadn't noticed him at all. He smiles and tips his baseball cap, and I'm not sure I've ever been more relieved to see anyone. Jordan has brought a shearing plywood but, because of the slope, we can't stand on it: we slide down it more easily than we do the dirt.

Embarrassingly, after shearing just two sheep, my right hand shakes uncontrollably. I grab my right arm with my left and hold it down by my side, to no avail. My right arm wriggles and spasms. Due to the additional space required for its internal motor, my portable handpiece is wider to grip and heavier to hold than the thinner, lightweight ones at school, powered by external motors. Thank heaven Jordan can take the next sheep. His portable handpiece is a welcome addition, too: we can alternate, let one handpiece cool off while we use the other.

Jordan and I take turns shearing and it goes well. The sheep are not bad shearing once we have them under control. It helps that there's less pressure to shear perfectly: second cuts do not much matter since the fleeces have felted, though we do our best. Early afternoon arrives in no time, and we have two sheep to go before our day is done. I shear my last sheep, with just two or three strokes left, so near the finish line. I am so excited to be done, and doing my best work of the day: almost no second cuts, shearing nice and smooth and close to the skin, with a fairly well-behaved sheep.

At this last thought, perhaps, I relax in a way imperceptible to me but not to the sheep. She decides to prove me wrong. She rears up with all the force she can muster, her hooves propelling her straight up between my knees. I lose balance on the hillside and fly directly backward into a fence post, spine first, handpiece abuzz while the sheep tears down the hill. This only happens, naturally, after Mr. Kelly has come outside to watch Jordan and me shear.

Part of the point of shearing in the New Zealand style we learned is that the fleece stays together, in one piece (imagine a cardigan unzipped). And it does. The entire, white fleece flies behind the sheep like a train on a bridal gown, easily five or six feet long. With just a couple of strokes left, the fleece is attached only at the sheep's back hip, the entire thing sailing from the top of her butt.

I switch the shears off and give chase, my back throbbing from the impact with the fence post. Mortified, I apologize profusely, yelling to Mr. Kelly as I run across the yard and try to herd the sheep toward the shearing area. The sheep approaches a rosemary hedge, about six feet high and ten feet long, and does not even pause before making a flying leap, like a horse going over a jump. She doesn't clear it, though, and—when her belly grazes the top of the hedge—she drops straight down into it, taking out a sheep-width section. After landing at the bottom of the hedge, her legs briefly scramble for purchase before she continues running, taking some of her fleece with her but leaving much of it in the hedge and, increasingly, in pieces around the yard.

"Just kill that one!" Mr. Kelly says, in a heavy Irish lilt, laughing almost too much to get the words out. "Lamb tastes good with rosemary!" I appreciate his sense of humor, though I am not laughing. Chasing animals does not work.

With our crooks, Jordan and I finally catch and finish shearing the errant, rosemary-scented sheep, and Mr. Kelly writes my first official shearing check for $90. I am proud. Even while shearing on a hillside, I haven't nicked or cut a single sheep, half wild and full of corners though they are. I use it to treat Jordan and me to lunch at a popular place called The Barlow that used to be an apple processing plant. It has outdoor seating, and Jordan's dog basks in a sunny spot.

My shearing jobs come through word of mouth, mostly through knitting and spinning friends. It doesn't take long for folks to hear about a twice-certified shearer who will show up for two or three sheep and shear carefully and humanely. I feel safer knowing that people find one another through the grapevine. Interestingly, a lot of women call me: just like I worry about shearing alone in a remote area with a man I've never met before, so these women worry about a strange man showing up in their barn.

I shear two Icelandic sheep in Olema, at a more than one-hundred-year-old dairy in the Point Reyes National Seashore. They have long, beautifully colored fleeces, one that shifts from oatmeal to butterscotch, another every shade from pale, bright winter sky to blue-gray thundercloud. Improbably, I have two shearing jobs in San Francisco proper, both less than two miles from my home: a single, portly Romney wether in a double-lot backyard and two Babydoll Southdown at a fancy, Waldorf-type school.

"Babydoll" may be the biggest breed misnomer going. The name implies something cute and gentle, and nothing could be further from the truth. Gary calls them "pigs with wool," and he is not wrong. They're short and stocky with incredibly muscular legs and a hock like a ham. They're covered in wool, including around their faces, which makes shearing scary: I use hand scissors to trim the wool around their eyes. Their short legs make it easy for them to get their feet on the ground, get leverage, and slip away. A Babydoll will stand up before I even realize what happened.

While wiping down my handpiece before packing up, an apparently affluent, rather arrogant-looking woman, dressed for the Kentucky Derby, pauses on the other side of the fence from the sheep and me. "Where's the new guy?" she asks.

"Which new guy?" I ask. "The sheep shearer," she replies. Somehow, in my overalls, below my motor, removing the comb and cutter from my handpiece, I do not visibly register with her as a shearer, until I wave my hands in front of her face. Beside me, a horrified teacher points at me and says, "She's right here! She's the shearer!" My first experience with sexism in sheep shearing and it comes from a woman in the city, the principal of a school that she no doubt considers a pinnacle of progressivism. Don't that beat all.

I take any job that comes my way just for experience. I am not in a position to be picky: I need to get my numbers and experience up. Drive two hours each way to shear two to four sheep? Sure. I often spend four hours or more in the car to shear two or three sheep at fifteen to twenty minutes apiece, traveling through six or seven counties in a single weekend. They roll on like a song: Alameda, Solano, Yolo, Lake, Napa, Mendocino, Sonoma, Marin, San Francisco, San Mateo.

With the driving, of course, come California's glorious vistas, the mornings I get to see the sun rise and watch its light slowly walk up the east faces of mountains; a black-hooded eagle high in a treetop, humongous even from the ground, waiting and watching us all day, biding its time before it will sail down and take a weak sheep for its meal. Only shearing can bring me to some of the most glorious places in the world, land I'd never set foot on otherwise.

But most jobs of the size I can manage aren't in places like that and do not offer such scenic rewards. Most two- and three-sheep households are within a twenty- to forty-five-minute drive of my house in

San Francisco: Pacifica, Montara, Half Moon Bay, the Los Altos Hills. I like seeing agricultural areas that most people do not know still exist, reminders that not everything, yet, is a bedroom community to Silicon Valley.

I completely failed to consider all of the driving I'd be doing in ever-worsening traffic from the ever-increasing Bay Area population. When I take vacation days from work to shear, I contend with weekday commute traffic if I do not time my jobs exactly right: I have to be out of the city and across the bridges by 6:30 a.m. and cannot hit the bridges back a minute after 2 p.m. or I will sit for hours. Our traffic is, by the latest estimation, officially the worst in the nation, worse even than in Los Angeles.

I shear a handful of sheep in Napa and drive on to shear some Babydoll Southdown in recently incinerated Middletown, in Lake County. The fire Ian McKenzie and I saw while baling has left field after field of melted cars, lone brick chimneys, propane tanks that, miraculously, did not explode. The fire behaved strangely, leaving a small block of burnt, retail shells and, right beside it, an untouched florist shop open for business. Black hills on both sides of the highway show where the fire jumped it.

The third sheep of the day jerks while I'm shearing its neck, and a spurt of blood splatters across my overalls. I can't find a cut on the sheep, but while looking, notice the tip of my left index finger is a hanging flap. I did not cut through my fingernail, which is nice, and at least it's not the sheep. I hold my hand above my head and direct the owner to my veterinary tape. The owner opens an ice-cold bottled water for me, and I rinse my finger with it, roll tape around my finger, and drink the rest of the water. My hand is throbbing but I have to finish the partially sheared sheep and two more, and I do.

The owner tips generously, as folks with the least to spare always do. "I never could have done that myself," he says, handing me a beer. I drink most of it and put the remainder in the cup holder. I know, I know: an open container, but it's almost gone and I'm still on their property. I have slow going before I reach a real road. I find ibuprofen in the glove-box and swallow it with the last of my beer. I drive home, exhausted and aching, my heated seats on to stop my back from freezing up, and the air conditioner on too.

I regret having bowed to peer pressure from Gary and the Gilberts: I have agreed to meet them the next day at the Sonoma County Fair sheep-shearing competition. Shearing another sheep is the last thing my bone-weary body wants to do, but the contest will provide welcome respite to something I hadn't realized shearing would be: lonely. It is mid-June and peak shearing season. I have barely seen my husband or anyone else. I work all day, every day, in an office all week and shearing both weekend days, up at 4 to 5 a.m. and not back until nightfall. And, on the job, it's usually just me and the sheep. Most flock owners do not—or cannot—stand around to watch, lend a hand, or chitchat. I yearn for another job with Jordan, Matt, or anyone, really, not to share work so much as to add levity to a long slog, to have someone with whom to talk and joke around.

The next morning, to my great surprise, I wake up and tell Ian I feel like shearing again. I have evidently lost my mind. It must be the wooly worms John Harper referenced at shearing school. My exhaustion and soreness from the previous day's work tempers my fear, making me more tired than terrified, and yesterday's sheep have dulled the prospect of more. What's one more sheep? Besides, it is the Sonoma County Fair. Despite creeping suburbanization, lengthening commutes, and climbing housing prices, Sonoma County is still pretty rural. I figure at least some people in the stands might be sympathetic to the wily ways of sheep and the occasional nick. I pitch my shearing slippers into the trunk, in case my gumption holds.

I have never seen a shearing contest, not even online. I have no idea what the rules are, how they work, how many sheep each contestant is expected to shear, or exactly when and where the contest is. We can't find any information online, so Ian and I arrive at the fairgrounds early, before 10 a.m. We ask several people where the shearing contest will be held and no one has any idea, so they point us toward the livestock area, saying, "Well, there are some sheep over there."

We wander around, past $60,000 pickup trucks you can win, until we see a shaded area with bleachers and shearing stations, and familiar faces, motors, and drops. John Koehne, John Veatch, and some of the other guys from shearing school are crutching sheep in advance of the contest. We don't have to crutch them? That will save a lot of shearing time! I always burn myself out on the bellies, picking at the wool and taking too long because I worry about the mammary vein and nether regions. The sheep look small, like yearlings, and do not have a lot of wool. The shearing contest feels doable, as long as I don't imagine people in the bleachers.

I pay the $5 entry fee. The woman handling registration says there may not be a heat for women, with so few competitors. She asks if I want to compete in the Open Division: the big time. I recall Matt and Gary's noncompetition shearing, at a couple of minutes per sheep, and the hours I spent shearing half a dozen sheep the day before. I will hold up the entire contest. "I'd really rather not," I answer.

The Gilbert family arrives, their darling daughters playing in the bleachers while Sarah knits up the gorgeous custom sweater—from Cormo yarn she'd hand spun—that someone had won as an Indiegogo campaign perk during the fundraising campaign for the wool mill. Randy is there, kind man of the loose-shoed, wild boar story at shearing school, who called me "little sister." Ian McKenzie from Roswell Wool will compete, as will Robin Lynde's shearer, John Sanchez, from the same Fibershed Wool Symposium panel in which Matt had participated. I am starstruck.

The more expert shearers have volunteered their motors and hung them at the shearing stations. Each shearer will attach their own handpiece to the drop. I do not own a handpiece, but Matt and Gary say I can just borrow theirs.

The announcer—a brusque, weather-beaten, silver-haired man—grabs the mic, welcomes the crowd, and explains how the contest will work. In the Open Division, each man will shear ten sheep each. The top three winners go on to the Open Division final, in which they shear twenty sheep each. Between these two heats, the Ladies and Junior Division (combined to achieve a minimum number of competitors) contest will take place, wherein three of us will shear one sheep each. Our three-person heat includes a twelve-year-old girl, whose father is a well-known sheep shearer; the woman who works the registration table (whom I suspect took pity and has agreed to shear so we could); and me.

The Sonoma shearing contest is popular thanks to its generous prize purse and a structure that ensures all shearers win at least some money. The top prize in the Open Shearing heat is $1,000, with reduced—but not insignificant—awards for subsequent places: $500 for second place, $250 for third, $200 for fourth, and so on to $75 for the seventh through tenth places. The cash awards for the Ladies and Junior Division (for which far fewer sheep are sheared) are $75 for first place, $50 for second, $45 for third, and so on down to $20.

Some of the guys tease me about whether I can handle competing with a little kid, but the idea doesn't bother me in the slightest. Based on what I've witnessed of the "culture" part of agriculture, I fully expect any 4-H kid to have more shearing experience—and to be better at it—than I. It's part of what I like about the livestock world: its children are genuinely competent with solid skills and earned self-confidence as a result. Farm kids do not, as a rule, seem to expect accolades for everyday things.

There are five slots on the shearing board and the first five men take a position. Each shearer has a judge—stopwatch poised and clipboard in lap—who will do nothing but watch that shearer and keep time. In the back, roaming judges evaluate each sheep sheared, counting the number of nicks and amount of wool left. The shearer with the lowest score wins. Judges add points for every twenty seconds spent shearing, for every cut bigger than a thumbnail, and for every bit of wool left on the sheep that is higher than a pencil width.

Each shearer in the Open Division has a friend in the pen beside his slot who, when the competing shearer is ready, hands him the next sheep to save time. I hand sheep to Matt and then, in the two minutes Matt spends shearing, catch the next one and hold it in position so he can reach over and grab it.

Chris Cornett and John Sanchez are neck and neck, the top two shearers in the Open Division, fast and neat. Gary, Matt, Randy, and other fellows from shearing school hold the middle, while John Koehne—a classmate who has not sheared much since school—is slowest but soldiers on, no matter. I am so proud of him for continuing when everyone else is finished, in front of a crowd. All of the other shearers watch him and applaud when he's done.

It is midafternoon and time for the combined Ladies and Junior Division. Gary readies my sheep in the pen as I attach his handpiece to the drop. I mumble a quick prayer: "Dear Lord: Please don't let me kill a sheep today, what with the children looking on. Amen." And it is go time.

Gary Vorderbruggen and Stephany Wilkes at the shearing competition of the Sonoma County Fair.

I start slowly, getting my bearings, while Gary and Ian McKenzie stand over me, screaming at me to level up, saying they know I can do better. While waiting for the contest to start, I thought I would want people on the shearing board with me, but it's hard to focus on shearing over the constant stream of words from the two of them. Or is that part of the challenge? More hazing? I hadn't seen anyone on Gary's board screaming at him.

In the end, I am the slowest and most cautious, per usual, but I don't mind. I finish, I've had a good time doing it, and I have not cut the sheep in public. Gary seems to think I should mind my third-place finish. As I wipe my forehead, he says I need to get my head on straight. John Sanchez overhears and, cleaning his handpiece, says "I don't know....I don't see a lot of wool or any cuts on that sheep. Looks good to me. You got the wool off." He grins at me, shrugs, and wanders away. I'll take it, from the second-place winner that day: John lost, barely, to Chris Cornett.

I can't believe I've sheared in front of a crowd of strangers. I come in last, but win $45 in prize money and my first-ever county fair ribbon, for third place out of three. I shake the twelve-year-old first place winner's hand, tell her to keep it up, and say I only wish I'd started shearing at her age. My winnings more than cover my $5 entry fee. By the standards of my day job, $45 is almost nothing, but I tend to think in $10 increments: $10 is milk and quite a bit of dried beans, $45 is most of the electric bill, and so on.

I carry the spirit of the shearing board for days, the cheering, sharing of handpieces, and good-natured teasing. Addiction to the work is only part of shearing's appeal: the work sets us apart and makes us a community. There are very few shearers in the world, so few people who know how backbreaking and ceaseless and dirty the work is, and fewer still willing to do it, year after year. And their opinions are the only ones worth salt.

Alas, it is a Sunday night, which brings tears to my eyes and wine to my glass. Ian encourages me not to think about it, but dread prevails. Tomorrow at 6 a.m., my day will begin with three consecutive hours of video conference calls. I will not see pasture, herding dogs, or lambs, but a laptop screen filled with a grid of exhausted faces from half a dozen time zones. A weekend's worth of email will flood in from executives, meandering and gutless, full of words that say nothing. I so appreciate the short, direct language of my shearing customers, who unequivocally state their needs: "She's an old ewe. Go easy on her" and "That ram you got there, he's queer as a three-dollar bill. Too bad. He's got a nice fleece on him. Born that way, though. Ain't we all."

With half a workday under my belt and ten more hours to go, I will arrive at the office shortly before the weekly free lunch and all-hands meeting, with so much more food than anyone needs given the sitting we do. Full of calories, needing to move, I will raise my desk to standing, savor my walks through the open-plan office to meetings. About a third of the employees seem to spend at least half the day on social media and, on less-trafficked floors of the office building, I often find people asleep on sofas and floors beneath conference room tables. And people say government should be run like a business.

ELEVEN

Carbon Farmer

Near the T-shaped junction where California, Oregon, and Nevada meet, black capital letters on an imposing yellow highway sign read, WARNING: NO SERVICES NEXT 100 MILES. WINTER TRAVEL NOT ADVISED. They mean it, too. There is no cellular service (better have a CB radio), no water, bathroom, food, gas, or pay phone. If your car breaks down, best be prepared to camp and have a few days' worth of food and water on hand. It will likely be that long before someone finds you, and that is when the weather's fine.

Sometimes referred to as the California Outback, the Surprise Valley lies in the Great Basin, east of the Warner Mountains and Modoc National Forest. About nine miles east of the foot of the Warner, the Nevada border runs through the valley, not even a line in the sand of the pancake-flat plate of alkali dust. Stubby, stunted plants—short, improbable tufts—poke out through cracks. Late afternoon sun spotlights four colors on the valley floor, with no power lines to interrupt: blue sky, black cattle, glimmering gold grass, and white salt plain.

The Warner, I'm told, are the "new mountains," and just over the Nevada border are the "old mountains," the Hays Canyon Range. "Beyond those mountains," says Janet Hill, a nearly lifetime local now in her eighties, "is really nothing. You look over the top of those, and you'd see what nothing really is." It's a lesson the West keeps teaching. Just when I think I've reached a far-off location, the landscape offers something still more remote, just around the next bend or over the next pass.

A lake filled much of the Surprise Valley bottom until a couple of decades ago, enough of one that people could—and did—ice skate on it in the winter. But consecutive years of drought and unrestricted

Alkali flats in Surprise Valley, California, during the month of September.

groundwater usage have drawn down the water table and given the desert greater permanence. There is still a lot of water, but only above ground, hot water springs. My husband and I are staying in a casual hotel with such hot springs, the last place before that desolate hundred miles begins, and the proprietor tells us they pipe in cold water from over a mile away because there isn't any here. They need it to temper the water that is so hot it literally simmers, which we watch at the edge of a duck pond, open water at a low rolling boil. We don't touch it. "That's how we used to do baths," the proprietor tells me. "Fill the tub, let it cool, and get in a lot later."

Though we enjoy them at least once a day, hot springs are not our reason for visiting the Surprise Valley. I am here to visit one particular sheep rancher and carbon farmer. The phrases "carbon farmer" and "climate beneficial garment" had recently entered my lingo, and I met them with skepticism. They struck me as wishful at best and greenwashing at worst. I'd first heard them from John Wick, cofounder of the Marin Carbon Project, a nonprofit organization that works to enhance carbon sequestration in rangeland, farm, and forest soils.[1] The carbon in wool is derived from carbon in the pasture, which was captured by plants from atmospheric carbon dioxide.[2] The plants sheep eat captured carbon, John explained, and sheep convert the carbon they consume to wool: 50 percent of the weight of wool is pure organic carbon.[3] When we purchase a wool garment, we are purchasing carbon sequestered from the atmosphere one or two years earlier.[4] A sweater could, conceivably, be considered a carbon neutral or net carbon negative garment.

Sheep and grazing as key elements of climate change mitigation are a far cry from the usual drumbeat of well-meaning environmental organizations. They seem to universally agree that agriculture is bad for the environment: that it's one of the largest contributors to carbon dioxide emissions on Earth, second only to the oil and gas industry[5]; that grazing sheep and cattle destroy land by overgrazing it, pulverizing plants to death with their hooves, turning soil to dust, and releasing stored carbon into the air; and that livestock contribute enormously to climate change because their anaerobic waste—manure—emits methane, a potent greenhouse gas.

Improperly managed grazing creates a vicious cycle in soil health, too. Tilling the soil oxidizes it (removes hydrogen), which decreases its water holding capacity. This makes soil more easily compacted by animals' hooves, which means water can't penetrate the hard, packed top crust of soil, which means more tillage is required, and tillage releases still more carbon stored in the soil.[6]

John Wick is no right-wing climate change denier or beef industry acolyte—exactly the opposite, in fact. His Nicasio Native Grass Ranch is located in western Marin County, not far north of San Francisco, in what might be the highest concentration of Birkenstock-wearing,[7] baby boomer hippies in the world. John was sunburned, gregarious, and preternaturally optimistic about our ability to back away from the climate change cliff by pulling carbon dioxide out of the atmosphere and storing it where it is most beneficial—in plants, soil, and wool.

When John and Dr. Jeff Creque established the Marin Carbon Project, they initially sought to create a voluntary, local, carbon offset market in which Marin County businesses could choose to offset their carbon footprints by supporting carbon-beneficial on-farm practices. The market could also provide California Environmental Quality Act (CEQA) mitigation opportunities, in which building projects could offset their carbon footprints by implementing climate-beneficial practices, like applying compost to land beside a new building development.

The Marin Carbon Project issued a call for participation in a carbon farm pilot program to the Marin agriculture community. They got sixteen applicants and conducted three pilots, developing a carbon farm plan for each of the three demonstration farms in 2013. As Jeff puts it, "We had one fundamental question: How can we capture more carbon on this landscape? That turned out to be a very functional framework, and one that the farmers and ranchers quickly could understand, and actually got kind of excited about, because it linked directly to their production. Everything they were doing to capture carbon also had production benefit, even if it was only that it was going to increase the water-holding capacity of their soil, which is a big deal."

In drought-stricken California, where rain is insufficient and irrigation comes either from reservoirs or rapidly diminishing ground water, water-holding capacity is a very big deal. In terms of agricultural production, it's a lot of money saved not having to pay for irrigation, to say nothing of less worry and agony during dry years. Benefits like this made the ranchers who participated in the pilot program receptive to carbon farm methods.[8]

Many of us use the word "carbon" as a shorthand synonym for "carbon dioxide," but the two are not the same. Carbon is signified with "C" on the periodic table and is one of Earth's most abundant elements. It exists in pure or nearly pure forms—such as diamonds and graphite—but also combines with other elements to form molecules. Carbon-based molecules are the building blocks of humans, animals, plants, trees, soils, fossil fuels, and greenhouse gases.[9]

There are five main pools of carbon on Earth: (1) the atmosphere; (2) plants and soil; (3) the Earth's mantle, the largest pool, made of carbonate rocks like limestone and chalk in our planet's interior; (4) oceans (surface ocean and deep ocean); and (5) fossil reserves (often classified in the plants and soil category). The carbon cycle describes how carbon and CO_2 are exchanged (cycled) between these.

Carbon dioxide enters the Earth's atmosphere when carbon-based matter (like logs, peat, coal, natural gas, and oil) decomposes or burns. The oil and gas stored inside the Earth were formed by layers of decomposing trees, ferns, and other carbon-based matter over millions of years. When we extract and burn these carbon-rich materials, their carbon combines with oxygen to create carbon dioxide.

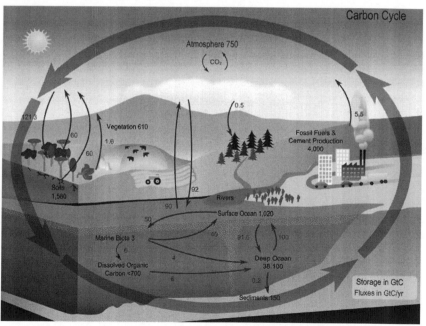

A simplified rendering of the carbon cycle. In any given year, tens of billions of tons of carbon move between the atmosphere, hydrosphere, and geosphere. Human activities add about 5.5 billion tons of carbon dioxide to the atmosphere per year. Credit: NASA Earth Observatory

Carbon dioxide is removed from the atmosphere when it is absorbed by plants[10] and stored in plants and soil. If you farm or like to garden, you know that healthy soils are usually dark. That dark color comes from soil organic matter (SOM), of which carbon is a measurable part. Plants convert carbon dioxide to carbon during photosynthesis,[11] the process by which plants use the sun's energy and chlorophyll (the green color in their leaves) to feed themselves. They convert carbon dioxide, water, and inorganic salts into carbohydrates—"carbo" (carbon) plus "hydro" (water)—to create the plant materials they grow: longer stems, leaves, buds, and so on.

This converted carbon doesn't just stay within the plant, but moves directly into soil through plant roots, the decomposition of leaves, and other processes. Carbon can be stored long term (for decades to centuries or more) in soils and trees, a process known as terrestrial carbon sequestration.[12] That "terrestrial" detail is important: We want to convert carbon dioxide to carbon and put carbon into soils, where it is needed and beneficial. We do not want to put carbon dioxide where it is not needed—into the atmosphere and oceans—and does harm. Every pound of additional carbon sequestered in the soil represents 3.67 pounds of carbon dioxide removed from the atmosphere.[13] This difference in the number of pounds is due to the fact that the oxygen—the dioxide part—remains in the atmosphere, and only the carbon comes into the soil. This is why managing agricultural lands in more carbon-beneficial ways can directly reduce atmospheric carbon dioxide and increase the level of carbon sequestered in soil.

Today, our planet's carbon cycle is out of whack. There is too much carbon dioxide in the atmosphere and oceans, and not enough carbon in the soil and forests. Prior to the Industrial Revolution (1760–1840), the carbon cycle was just about balanced:[14] the amount of carbon dioxide released into the atmosphere each year was roughly the same amount as was annually absorbed by plants and sequestered in trees and soils. Today, by contrast, more carbon dioxide is now being released than the earth's land-based plant life and oceans can naturally reabsorb.[15]

These plain facts make terrestrial carbon sequestration an important and quantitatively promising idea, so much so that soil carbon sequestration initiatives played a part at the Paris Climate Summit in December 2015. There is huge potential for soil carbon sequestration at global scale,[16] with conservative estimates on the order of hundreds of teragrams (one teragram equals one million metric tons) per year in the United States and roughly an order of magnitude (a power of ten) higher globally. And that's a lot. One million metric tons is the equivalent of 147,667 homes' annual electricity usage, or 211,234 passenger vehicles driven for one year.[17]

One of the most promising lessons of Marin Carbon Project research is a sort of snowball effect, that increasing ecosystem carbon also increases the capacity of the system to capture more carbon from the atmosphere. Take, for example, the increased water-holding capacity of soil that results from an initial compost application. The first application of compost leads to more plant growth (more carbon capture), which in turn creates more soil carbon, more water held, more plant growth, and on and on. As Jeff explains it,

> This is a positive feedback system much like—albeit with countervailing effect—the positive feedback currently driving Arctic melting. The more sea ice melts, the more dark water absorbs more solar radiation, and the faster the sea ice melts. Our only hope for reversing runaway positive feedbacks driving climate change is to initiate similar, but opposing, positive feedback processes. We've shown that is possible.

It sounded good, but were there any real, wool-growing ranchers who believed these claims enough to go to the trouble and expense of implementing them on their land? There is at least one. Her name is Lani Estill and, since 2001, she and her family have owned and run the Bare Ranch at the south end of the Surprise Valley. The Bare name, the last name of one Thomas Bare, suits the hardscrabble high desert land that sits just under five thousand feet. Bare and his family entered Surprise Valley in the mid-1800s, among the flood of westward-bound emigrants on the Applegate Trail, blazed in 1846 and intended as the less dangerous southern route of the Oregon Trail.

The Bare family built the first Euro-American cabin at the southern end of the Surprise Valley. Decades of conflict among the Modoc, Paiute, and immigrant people (including the Bares) culminated in the Modoc War of 1872–1873, the outcome giving Bare Ranch its 1873 founding date.

The Bare Ranch is bigger—and busier—than some of the towns we passed through en route to it. Barns and corrals are followed by a set of tidy whitewashed buildings with green peaked roofs and matching trim. These line both sides of a wide gravel driveway, and some are labeled with carved wood signs: Office, Cook House. The Cook House sign includes the ranch's cattle brands, a hand-painted smoking stew pot, carrots, and a spoon. Janet, my local tome, told me, "My mother used to work in that cook house, and it had a sign that read 'Eat lamb. Even the coyotes like it,' or something like that." A large bunkhouse lies to the right, and the Estill home lies farther along on the same side.

This is the home ranch, which occupies about forty-five hundred acres. On the day I meet her, Lani is wearing a shawl hand knit from three undyed colors of her own Rambouillet wool: black, charcoal gray, and white. Her yarn, Lani's Lana (*lana* is Spanish for "wool," as well as a colloquial synonym for "money") is stunning, springy, high twist, fine, and very soft but strong. It suits Lani herself, who is energetic and enthusiastic, with short reddish hair, bright eyes, and shoulders and sun freckles that show she is no stranger to work.

I can see two large flocks of sheep, one of them meat sheep. "That's my daughter's flock of Suffolk-Hampsire crosses," Lani says. "She's away at college, and her flock pays her tuition." I see another flock in the distance, near a sheepherder's trailer, but learn most of the sheep are still in the mountains. The Estill sheep have permits to graze western rangeland managed by the Bureau of Land Management (BLM) in the Warner Mountains. The herders and sheep cover 180 miles round-trip in a summer season: 90 miles out and back, before coming down from the mountains before the end of September.

Western rangeland is mostly composed of grasses and shrubs suitable for grazing. Rangeland is not suitable for other uses: it cannot be turned into a farm, vineyard, or orchard given its rocky ground, high elevations, and aridity. Historically, wild bison, buffalo, elk, and sheep grazed common rangelands. Range grasses took carbon in from the atmosphere; wild herds trampled the grass into the soil, where the carbon was absorbed; new grass sprouted, and the process was repeated over and over again, absorbing more and more carbon. Top-level predators—wolves, mountain lions, and bears—kept animals moving, preventing overgrazing.[18] Today, with wild herds and many predators long gone, western rangelands are managed with prescribed fire and livestock grazing of the sort Lani's sheep provide.

Lani shares a copy of her more than sixty-page carbon farm plan and unrolls a laminated, poster-size map of the home ranch, a mosaic of rectangles and squares of various sizes with ragged edges at ranch boundaries. Notations of a "CF" prefix followed by a number—CF1, CF2, and so on—overlay and denote areas in which carbon farm practices are in place and in progress. The carbon farm practices that will work best on a given ranch are unique to that ranch, and to areas within that ranch, because they must be based on geography, climate, plant life, and water-holding capability. These vary dramatically over forty-five hundred acres. Lani explains, "You have to have your ranch mapped for a whole carbon farm plan in order to do this."

Lani came to carbon farming somewhat circuitously, or rather, carbon farming came to Lani. Rebecca Burgess, founder of Fibershed, had noticed Lani's wool during a wool inventory project. Lani has a reputation clip, meaning her wool is exceptional and sought after. Rebecca had been working with the Marin Carbon Project, and thoughts about Lani's wool and carbon farming came together: Lani produced enough high-quality wool to be able to supply commercial manufacturers. Would they pay Lani more money for climate-beneficial wool, were Lani to implement carbon-centric practices on her ranch?

Lani's interest in carbon farming methods, then, began with wool, and specifically in realizing a higher price for her wool. That was the carrot that got Lani excited and got her family in on the plan. And that's as fine a reason as any. Lani is, after all, a weaver and wool aficionado running a ranch, not a nonprofit organization. Different incentives can lead to the same, beneficial outcome (in this case, carbon sequestration and saving humanity from itself).

The Bare Ranch carbon farm plan (CFP) and map began with a walk that Lani, Rebecca, and Jeff took around the ranch, much like the walk Lani, Rebecca, some attendees of a local Wool Gathering event, and I are about to take today. A CFP begins with a "taking stock," an inventory of natural resource conditions on the ranch, with a focus on finding opportunities for the reduction of greenhouse gas (GHG) emissions and enhanced carbon capture and storage by both plants and soils. Later, this inventory becomes a map, identifying the areas of a particular ranch in which certain carbon farm practices might be applied: what can and should be done, and where. Maps also show

Bales of Lani Estill's
Rambouillet wool
arrive for processing at
Mountain Meadow Wood
Mill in Buffalo, Wyoming.
Photo by Lani Estill.

Lani Estill's Rambouillet wool
combed top at Mountain
Meadow Wool Mill. Photo by
Lani Estill.

existing ranch infrastructure and natural resource conditions, and
envision how the ranch may be expected to look years down the road,
post-implementation.[19]

I had assumed that the Marin Carbon Project (and specifically
Jeff) took soil inventories manually, walking Lani's thousands of

acres, putting soil samples into tubes, and sending them off for testing. That, however, would be incredibly time-consuming, expensive,
and all but impossible to carry out and fund. Fortunately, much of
the soil data on Lani's ranch already existed, thoroughly sampled and
kept up to date by the National Soil Survey, one of the most laudable
efforts of the Natural Resources Conservation Service (NRCS). The
National Soil Survey dates back to 1899[20] and is the largest natural
resource information system in the world. Soil maps and data are
available online for more than 95 percent, soon expected to reach 100
percent, of US counties.

I used the soil survey to see what I could find out about Lani's soil.
By zooming in and selecting parts of a detailed aerial map, I soon found
myself in the area labeled "Surprise Valley-Home Camp Area, California
and Nevada (CA685)." And, just like that, I was able to download a
database's worth of information on the soils on and around the Estill's
ranch. There were sixty-eight tables worth of thematic data alone, with
mind bogglingly discrete areas noted as being "wet clay basin," "saline
meadow," "sodic terrace," and many more. All of the plants found in a
given area of the ranch were noted in the data set as well:

"POSE" | "Poa secunda" | "Sandberg bluegrass";

"DISP" | "Distichlis spicata" | "inland saltgrass";

"SAVE4" | "Sarcobatus vermiculatus" | "black greasewood."

Single-spaced, with one row per line, the plant data alone amounted
to eighteen printed pages. The soil survey is a tremendous resource, one
that would be impossible for Lani, Jeff, or anyone else to create on their
own and keep up to date.

Our walk begins with a visit to about three hundred chickens, an array of breeds and colors, contentedly pecking their way
through hilly green pasture. The chickens are evidence of one of the
Estills' goals for the ranch, which is to increase both plant and animal
biodiversity. The chickens are divided into three groups. Each group
is surrounded by mobile livestock fencing and has access to its own
towable livestock trailer; the Estills have repurposed old, slightly rusted
trailers into excellent mobile chicken housing. These trailers enable even
grazing, can be easily moved when the chickens are ready for fresh pasture, and serve as roosts, cover, and nighttime shelter from predators.

Next, we move toward Bare Creek, which runs the length of the ranch. "In riparian [stream] areas, like this one," Lani says, "we'll put water troughs for cattle in pasture, so they drink water in pasture instead of in the stream. Some of the stream is fenced, but not all of it, so we'll add fencing too. That way they're not getting down in the creek and degrading it further."

The goal of the initial carbon farm walk with Rebecca and Jeff was to identify the Bare Ranch sites most likely to yield significant carbon benefits given specific practices, and—just as importantly—areas for which specific practices may not be particularly productive. The pasture beneath our feet, scattered with nutritious cow pies, is one such place. Compost additions would add little or no value here, on the 11 percent of the ranch mapped as having Cumivar muck soils, with 40 percent carbon. This is the richest, healthiest, carbon-heavy soil on the Bare Ranch, dense yet loamy, and surprisingly light. This is soil the Estills do not want to disturb, because doing so would release the vast stores of carbon already sequestered there. Tilling this soil to grow vegetables would be disastrous, which is why "no till" is one of the carbon farm methods in practice here. Lani notes that this carbon-sink pasture acreage is currently divided into eight areas, but will be further subdivided into twenty for more intensive, even grazing in smaller sections.

On the opposite side of this pasture, between the road and the pasture's far western edge, is another, much smaller stream that Lani calls "the canal." It runs with hot water, much like the hot springs where I'm staying. Livestock will continue to access and drink from this stream, because the fact that the water is hot is important during winter: the water doesn't freeze and provides livestock with minerals. Lani explains:

> The trees on Bare Creek are old willows and cottonwoods and they're falling down, so we need to start planting newer, younger trees, which are a carbon negative, meaning, a positive, as in good, because they absorb carbon dioxide at a faster rate while they're putting on more growth. Then we'll pull the old wood out, chip it, and that goes in the compost pile. That's a perfect fit, because compost is coming from the ranch. It's free and doesn't require fuel to travel.

Compost is also a perfect fit for some areas of Bare Ranch, because much of its soil needs more organic matter than it currently has. When Lani reviewed the Bare Ranch's soils—sagebrush ground—to find places that would most benefit from having compost applied, she found almost no organic matter. Soil Survey maps indicated that some soils contained soil organic matter (SOM) of 3 percent or below. "This is because the land hadn't been grazed," Lani explains. "No manure and trampled plants means no living stuff. The land is underutilized and is suffering for that. It needs more organic matter."

Other Bare Ranch soils are higher in saline than others, due to lake evaporation in Surprise Valley that left salt behind. Sodium does not support plant production and can actually destroy soil structure and make plant growth extremely difficult. High-sodium soils should not be cultivated for this reason or, at least, this aspect of them needs to be understood, so land management and crop choices can be chosen appropriately and not make the situation worse.[21]

The question of methane inevitably arises in regard to livestock, the assumption being that methane emissions (the belches and gas from cows, sheep, and goats) must outweigh any carbon sequestration and similar benefits that their manure might provide. It is worth remembering that bison and other wild herd animals always emitted methane, of course, but left us tens of feet of topsoil and a carbon cycle that was still in balance. Animals didn't throw the carbon cycle out of whack: humans did. Dairy farms and concentrated animal feeding operations (CAFOs, more commonly referred to as feed lots) produce a lot of manure, for example, and this liquid, slurry manure runs off into watersheds or is sent to anaerobic landfills, where it emits large amounts of methane. This same manure could instead be used as compost to increase the carbon sequestration capacity of soil, and this "diverted methane" should be counted, as it is in the Bare Ranch carbon farm plan.

Livestock can help us get the carbon cycle back in balance. Farms that produce too much manure could sell or give it to farms that need it. It is estimated that 4.9 million tons of carbon dioxide could be mitigated annually if compost produced from high-emission waste systems were applied to 1.1 million hectares (just 5 percent) of California's rangeland. Lani sums it up nicely: "Carbon farming is a perfect fit for anyone who generates a lot of manure—a dairy or feed lot. Perfect fit."

Bare Ranch's limiting factor on its own compost production is not manure (they have plenty of sheep, cattle, chicken, and horses) but other carbon matter, like hay and old straw. The Estills obtained a grant, as part of a voluntary sage grouse initiative, to harvest and chip juniper trees that otherwise would have gone to a biomass plant. The grant is part of an impressive effort to proactively conserve sage grouse habitat across the eleven western states where sage grouse still remain. Juniper encroachment threatens such habitat, and removing it has multiple benefits for the sage-steppe ecosystem. Besides providing the Estills with compost, it increases forage for livestock and wildlife, conserves water for other plants, increases plant diversity, and reduces perches for ravens and other predators. It is easier and more effective to save good habitat than to restore it when it's gone.[22]

Next, we walk farther south on the ranch, about fifteen minutes away, to the pivots. If you've ever flown over Great Plains and western states, you may have looked out the airplane window to see perfect green circles on the ground, resembling a checkerboard with circles inside the squares. Those circles are called pivots because, in the center of each circle, there is an actual pivot, a long-armed sprinkler that turns at the center, making the perfect circles we see from the air. Four such pivots sit on the ranch's California-Nevada border. Two grow grass, two grow alfalfa, and one of the four is having compost applied. The Bare Ranch plan also includes the addition of windbreaks, trees that sequester carbon. These help prevent soil from blowing away, which includes both carbon dioxide and nitrous oxide that would then make its way into the atmosphere.

After the ranch inventory and map are completed, the carbon benefits of each practice are quantified, as potentially applied at ranch scale. All of these practices have been rated with the COMET-Planner, also known as COMET-Farm, an online farm planning tool.[23] Ranchers like the Estills can enter their land management practices and acreages. COMET-Farm then estimates the carbon footprint for the farm or ranch operation and allows the rancher to evaluate different options, of their choosing, for reducing GHG emissions and sequestering more carbon. COMET-Farm estimates are considered conservative because carbon farm practices, according to Jeff Creque, tend to be synergistic (meaning that two or more carbon farming practices together create an effect greater than the sum of each practice's individual effects) and the models used in the COMET-Farm tool don't account for synergistic effects.

Finally, with all this in hand, a list of potential carbon farm practices and their climate mitigation benefits can be developed. Carbon farm practices are prioritized based on the needs and goals of the ranch, and high carbon-benefit practices are chosen wherever possible. Economic considerations, like cost and outside sources of funding, may filter the list of options, and funding mechanisms may also be identified, including cap and trade, the California Environmental Quality Act (CEQA), or other greenhouse gas mitigation offset credits; USDA-NRCS and other state and federal programs; and private funding. Then the Estills implement carbon farm projects as funding, technical assistance, and ranch schedules allow. Over time, they will evaluate, update, and alter the Bare Ranch CFP as needed, to meet changing farm objectives and implementation opportunities, using the complete plan as a goal or point of reference.

The funding point raised an obvious question: Who pays for all of this? It seemed unfair that Lani and her family should have to bear all of the cost and effort for treating the land in ways that benefit all of us, and save us from our own demise. She's got businesses to run, animals to tend, and a family to raise and support.

Do carbon credit programs have potential? "Yeah," Lani tells me, "but carbon credits aren't worth anything right now." There is a conservation credit program in Nevada (where part of the Bare Ranch sits), for people who are doing a good job preserving sage grouse habitat, but this particular program is structured in a way that puts all the risk on the rancher. Polluters pay into the program, and ranchers receive the money (credits) upfront. The catch is that recipients of these conservation credits have to sign a thirty-year contract. This would give the Estills a thirty-year obligation, while the polluter could stop polluting and stop paying, leaving Lani and her family holding the bag for thirty years. "No one would sign a thirty-year contract for anything in any other context," she points out. "In that time, other generations take over ranches, things change all the time. It will fail if you get all the money upfront. Even if you have a thirty-year mortgage it doesn't mean you're stuck with your house for that amount of time. You can sell it as your life changes and demands you adjust." She's right. The conservation credits sound like a nice idea, but we shouldn't ask a rancher to do anything we wouldn't be willing to do ourselves.

On the very same afternoon I stood on Lani's ranch, California governor Jerry Brown signed Senate Bill No. 859 (SB 859) into law, officially creating the Healthy Soils Initiative.[24] Initially funded with $7.5 million, the Healthy Soils Initiative is a voluntary program that provides farmers, ranchers, and other organizations with financial incentives to implement carbon-beneficial agricultural practices. The bill includes funding for on-farm demonstration projects, like those the Marin Carbon Project has completed and funded in the past, and for project-related costs like those Lani has incurred, including compost application, cover crops, and reforestation. The Healthy Soils Initiative advisory panel and the California Department of Food and Agriculture will oversee the program, which will be funded primarily with revenue from California's state cap-and-trade program, the Greenhouse Gas Reduction Fund.

Lani hopes to receive funding from the local NRCS to continue their carbon farm project, and she hopes the climate-beneficial tag will bring an even higher price for her wool. Lani's efforts have already gotten her a higher price for her wool—not much higher, about sixty cents per

Rambouillet sheep graze the Bare Ranch in Surprise Valley, California.

Yarn from Lani Estill, Robin Lynde, and other Northern California wool producers at Huston Textile Company in Rancho Cordova, California. The yarn shown
here will be woven into fabric.

pound more, but more than she would have gotten otherwise. Lani says
she is happy if she can get the carbon farm practices paid for and there
is no regulation. "If we can have the feeling of pride, and feel positive
about what we can do, and get a little more product money—for our
wool, yarn, and so on—and the compost should increase fertility and
productivity, those are good reasons to do it even if you don't get paid."

The implications of Lani's work on the ranch are much larger than
her acreage. Her work could make it easier for customers to find and
purchase fabric and clothes that benefit the environment and climate
and, of course, ourselves. In order to produce climate-beneficial clothes,
an industrial manufacturer needs high-quality raw material in sufficiently large quantity. Bare Ranch produces commercial-scale, carbon-
sequestering wool to fulfill this need.

And manufacturers are paying attention. The VF Corporation, par-
ent company to The North Face and others, paid her $2.50 per pound

and bought four thousand pounds of wool, just enough of Lani's total clip to be able to experiment with a carbon-beneficial garment at an industrial scale. They like what they see, and hope to come back and buy her whole clip in the future, but they have a lot of experimenting to do, including testing washing and wearability and determining what products the wool is best suited for. Achieving true carbon-negative or climate-beneficial status is much harder for manufacturers because they must consider the entire garment life cycle, from where it is grown and the practices in place there, to where it is sewn, as well as transportation and emissions between all of these points, and emissions and environmental impacts from the industrial processes themselves. Still, it's a hopeful indication that an industrial manufacturer is sincerely trying to do better and change some things, and that people like Lani could see some kind of monetary reward for their efforts.

Land use currently accounts for about 25 percent of global GHG emissions, but it can be part of an effective climate change mitigation strategy. According to the IPCC, it may not be possible to achieve large enough reductions in energy, transport, and industrial emissions alone to stabilize GHG concentrations at a level commensurate with less than $2°C$ ($3.6°F$) global average temperature increase, without the help of a substantial CO_2 sink from the land use sector.[25] Or, as Lani succinctly puts it, "Agriculture is the only [climate change] solution big enough."

In order to scale, carbon farming requires not just financial support, but outreach and organizational infrastructure to implement carbon-sequestering practices across vast swaths of land with wildly different usage and climate contexts. The NRCS seems best positioned to support ranchers who want to adopt carbon farm practices. Every single state already has National Resource Conservation Districts (NRCDs), some three thousand local conservation districts across the country. Conservation districts are local units of government responsible for the soil and water conservation work within their boundaries. The districts' role is to increase voluntary conservation practices among farmers, ranchers, and other land users. California, for example, has ten resource conservation districts (RCDs), which are best able to understand and address land needs in their areas. The Napa County RCD has vineyards and their associated soil use to think about, while the land in the San

Joaquin—California's produce-producing central valley—has a very different climate and set of concerns.

As Ian and I depart the Bare Ranch, the ground-hugging smudge of smoke from a young wildfire begins to spread across the Warner Mountains. The wind kicks up from the west and, by the time we are ten miles up the road, a hot wisped wall of flame leaps toward the red ball of the setting sun. High desert wildfires are normal but have become more prevalent, unpredictable, and fierce during the recent, years-long drought. There can be no greater testament to the need for Lani's quiet, deliberate, and often thankless work in the valley downwind of the smoke.

Wildfire in the Warner Mountains near Bare Ranch.

TWELVE

Shepherds

Jaime Irwin is one-half of Kaos Sheep Outfit, a contract grazing company. She left her home in Lake County before first light this February morning with her three-year-old daughter, Claire, in snap-up pajamas, asleep in a car seat in the back of a pickup truck. Jaime stopped at Costco to get sandwiches, cookies, and drinks for the Kaos crew that day—shepherds, shearers, wool classers, friends, and kids—while, at the Fetzer-Bonterra vineyard in Mendocino County, her husband Robert Irwin was already setting up a shearing trailer and generator. It was earliest spring in Northern California, not yet hot and dry as it would be for most of the year, mercifully cool with a breeze and abundant shade because the sun had yet to rise over the hills.

A thousand or so of more than five thousand Kaos sheep are currently grazing this organic, biodynamic vineyard (just down the road from shearing school in Hopland), and several hundred of them are penned in the shade of mighty oak trees, a livestock guardian dog lying beside them. Shortly after she arrives at the vineyard, Jaime lifts a half-asleep Claire from the truck and plops her down in a vineyard access road, between the enormous pickup truck and a mobile shearing trailer the size of a small prefab building, hundreds of acres of parallel vine rows stretching on behind it. The trailer contains a tiny, hot pink, plastic chair just for Claire.

Claire wears knee-high Wellington boots over her pajamas, holds a bucket of toy dinosaurs in one hand and her blanket in the other, and seems dazed but unsurprised at waking up in a vineyard. She has spent most of her life in places like this. It's not just the beauty and verdant health of this particular vineyard that says it's managed differently: it's Claire. The Irwins would not set their only daughter down in a pesticide-laden vineyard to play in the dirt all day.

Rangeland, vineyards, and orchards benefit from the presence of sheep and managed grazing, and there are, fortunately, people like the Irwins who want to manage sheep and land. But there's a disconnect. Usually, the people who most want to—and are willing to—do the hard work of running livestock can least afford land, especially in astronomically priced California. But this unjust mismatch creates an opportunity that the Irwins have seized. They've designed a contract grazing business in which a farmer, vineyard, or orchard contracts the Irwins—the graziers—to manage the farmer's land, using the grazier's livestock.

Kaos provides a hybrid of shepherding and contract grazing. The latter usually refers to a farm that rents its excess grazing land to livestock owned by others, or to a livestock manager who rents extra land from farmers in order to feed livestock. But Robert—blond, blue-eyed, and perpetually sunburned; wearing a tucked-in Western shirt, baseball cap, and a big silver belt buckle; and the third generation in an Oregon sheep family—thinks of himself as a shepherd:

> I'm a sheepherder now. I went from being a rancher to a herder. Sheepherding is ancient. In the Bible, in any form of ancient writing, there's sheepherders. And they went nomadically around the world. And before there was people there was buffalo herds and wildebeest herds, and what were they doing? They were herding themselves all around the world. We're doing something that was there whether we were or not. What we're trying to do is to control it.[1]

And business is booming. The Kaos team of sheep, shepherds, livestock guardian dogs, and occasional shearers has more work than it can handle. Its flock is growing, and the Irwins struggle to find and hire experienced, reliable shepherds, a vocation that died out generations ago in most places in the United States. The success of their endeavor has surprised even Robert.

> If you asked me six years ago if I would be where I am today, I would tell you you're a liar. And if I could talk to myself six years ago, I don't know what I'd say. I never thought it would ever be possible to live in a

pickup … and I'm being serious. I lived in a pickup with my wife, hopped out of it, and within a year was running a thousand sheep and managing another thousand sheep for another family, and all of a sudden away we went. The world is a possibility, depending on how you look at it.

I believe him. If anyone had told me I'd be getting up at 4:30 a.m. on a precious Saturday morning to shear sheep for less than free, I would have called them a liar, too.

The hard-won success of Kaos's business is a result of the utterly unglamorous, constant hard work he and Jaime and their team put in every single day, weekends included, and the experiences that would have broken lesser mortals. Every day, from predawn to darkest night, Robert and Jaime drive people and sheep—whether via livestock trailer, on foot through fields, or both—long miles. They lived in their pickup truck, as Robert described, while their sheep grazed for free on some of Napa and Mendocino County's biggest vineyards, whose wines are found on the shelves of every major grocery chain. While Robert was at one vineyard, Jaime—a sleep-deprived, first-time mother—was herding hundreds of sheep with a newborn Claire strapped to her chest. They worked over one hundred hours per week for nothing, barely managing to even pay for their fuel, in order to establish relationships with vineyards.

Robert says, "We're doing that same theory that nature did before we showed up, to kind of control craziness. And that's what Kaos is, I guess. The first year we did this, people said we were crazy. But then when we did it the second year, a lot of the other people started paying attention."[2] Jaime, who has a master's in environmental education, describes herself as "new to the whole sheep industry, and I kind of got thrown in and went for it, and it's been really exciting and it's kind of addictive." She adds, "We really wanted to pursue this, and to pursue this on a commercial level: How can we make this a viable company? It's a very organic process, truly. Five thousand sheep in a thousand-acre vineyard? That's an adventure."[3]

Fortunately, it worked. People now have an interest in keeping Kaos in business. Today, half of Kaos's income comes from wool and lamb sales (selling lamb to processors like Superior Farms), while the other half comes from vineyards and contract grazing. In addition to these services, Robert has a mobile shearing trailer and runs a shearing crew, for shearing both his own flock and those of others. He tows the shearing trailer to wherever wooly sheep are grazing.

At the vineyard that February morning, the Kaos sheep need their annual shearing. It will take three days for four or five people to shear them. Robert had put a shearing crew together and invited me to be part of it. I will be shearing with him, an Irishman named Brian, and two sons of champion shearer Chris Cornett, the same Chris Cornett who had won the shearing contest at the Sonoma County Fair.

By any established shearing standard, I do not qualify to shear on a wagon. A shearer should be able to shear at least one hundred sheep per day before being allowed a spot on a crew. Robert, thankfully, is glad there are shearers who want to help and is happy to give me and other beginning shearers experience. When, embarrassed at my skill level, I told him that I only expected to be able to shear ten to twenty sheep per day, he said, "Then that's ten or twenty I don't have to shear myself."

I arrive at the Bonterra vineyard by 9 a.m. Robert flags me down at the winery entrance and points me toward a dirt road that winds around a pond and over low, almost neon-green, hills. It is, without question, the most idyllic job site I've ever seen.

I pull my shearing equipment out of my back seat and exit, backside first, into two livestock guardian dogs, shoulder to shoulder, noses on my rear. I jump back against the side of my car. I did not see or hear them at any point and have no idea where they even came from. The one dog I noticed on arrival is still lying beside the flock. The two who surprised me are taller than wolves, the tops of their heads at my waist. Livestock guardian dogs have an important job to do, and they have just let me know they are doing it. I stand still for a minute, giving them a chance to get to know me before I make sweet sounds at them and, eventually, after seeing what I believe are slight tail wags, carefully hold out my hands for sniffing and pet them, receiving more-obviously wagging tails in response. Generally, petting guardian dogs isn't a smart practice. They are not pets and most are, deliberately, bonded far more strongly to the flock than to humans. This is why they lay down their lives to defend sheep from predators.

The Kaos sheep graze vineyards and orchards throughout Northern California, including Bonterra, a certified organic and biodynamic vineyard. These days, there is a proliferation of eco-labels associated with food products, and wine bottles are no exception. Put simply, however, organic and biodynamic certifications indicate that Bonterra recognizes that sustainable practices also make good business sense.

Organic farming promotes and enhances biodiversity, biological cycles, and soil biological activity. It is based on minimal use of off-farm inputs (fertilizers and soil supplements) and on management practices that restore, maintain, and enhance ecological harmony.[4] It is regulated by federal law and overseen by the USDA National Organic Program. In the United States, there are two categories of certified organic wines: organic wine without any added sulfites, and wine made with organic grapes (Bonterra included) that has less than 100 ppm of sulfites. In both of these categories, the winery (the production entity) is certified organic as are individual vineyards (the grape vines).[5]

A USDA Organic certification is difficult to achieve, and biodynamic certification even more so. Biodynamic farming meets the organic standard, includes the elimination of synthetic chemicals, and goes even further, stressing self-sufficiency, the reduction of external inputs, plant and animal biodiversity, and enhancement of the soil's structure, health, and nutrient cycles. Biodynamic wines must also be made with certified biodynamic grapes and use only native yeasts.[6]

Rows of grape vines get the lion's share of attention from photographers and wine drinkers, but there's a lot happening on the vineyard floor, too. In commercial orchards and vineyards, the primary purpose of grazing is to manage understory vegetation, and Kaos does so artfully. At the base of grape vines is soil—a vegetation-free strip of land—with grass alleys between rows. In this vegetation-free zone, vine roots can grow without competition from weeds or grass. The mustard plant alleyways between rows serve as a cover crop, fixing nitrogen, conserving water, protecting against erosion, and helping maintain soil structure and organic matter.[7]

As one manager at Bonterra describes it, "The fertility comes from within the farm, which feeds the farm."[8] He continues, "You're looking at the whole farm, rather than just your crop plant. It's looking at what cover crops do you have growing in between, and how do those affect the vine growth? When you mow those cover crops, realizing that you're removing habitat, and therefore that you're changing insect population dynamics, you're changing air flow."

Another says, "It's a different paradigm. We're not feeding the plant, right? We're feeding the soil. When you take care of your soil, the soil automatically takes care of what grows on top." The soil benefits from free, nutrient-rich manure, which makes sheep an important part of land ecology. Their hooves stamp seeds into the ground for roots to take hold, and break up dry soil crusts that rain otherwise cannot permeate. "The sheep come in, they'll deposit fertility, add life to the soil, add life to the farm itself.…They're an organic source for more biodiversity in the soil, more microorganisms that are going to decompose different materials."

The use of sheep, rather than the use of fertilizers and tractors, is key to vineyards obtaining and maintaining organic and biodynamic certifications, but it's not exactly a novel idea. For centuries, sheep and goats have grazed understory vegetation,[9] and it's an obvious win-win. Vegetation needs to be kept in check and sheep need food. Orchard grazing was common practice in North America until the 1950s but fell out of fashion, losing ground to tractors and synthetic pesticides under the industrialized farm paradigm of the twentieth century.

Now sheep seem like a good idea again, and the number of flocks and herds intended solely for vegetation management is growing.[10] Orchard grazing is more common today than in recent decades and is practiced in nearly every state where fruits or nuts are commercially produced. The widest acceptance appears to be in organic orchards.[11] The Bonterra manager is not surprised: "With the market as it is, consumers can drive how companies operate, how farmers farm, right? When the majority of consumers demand an organic product, practices shift."

Vineyard soil must be kept free of weeds, and the grass alleys cannot be allowed to grow out of control. Excessive ground cover not only competes with trees and vines for water and nutrients, especially nitrogen, but it increases wildfire risk during the dry season. Tall vegetation can harbor pathogens, insect pests, and harmful rodents (like mice and voles), and large weeds also block sprinkler heads and disrupt water delivery.[12]

As Robert puts it, "Kaos is in competition with a tractor." He and Jaime want those grass alleys in vineyards to look as if a tractor has mowed them. "The idea that we had is that we want to compete with tractors...because if we want to be in a vineyard, they want a neatly mowed area underneath the vine, between the rows." According to Bonterra, Kaos is winning: "We've seen it. If I look at my tractor hours for under-vine weed control, they've consistently decreased."

Robert points out that sheep also help to naturally control the population of a vineyard pest that has threatened crops and worried California wine growers for years: "The leaf hopper lives on vineyard leaves and they slow down photosynthesis. They get ingested in sheep, come out as manure, and the number of leaf hoppers is down next year."

Both ground cover and sheep must be carefully managed to prevent overgrazing.[13] It's a common myth that sheep can't stand on their hind legs, or won't use their forelegs to raise themselves up into trees and vines to eat fruit. But Robert and others "have watched them do it and there's ample proof on YouTube, so it's best to use a fence." Most shepherds use a combination of herding dogs and electrified, portable fencing to manage and restrict the movement of sheep. This style of fencing is more like netting, with lightweight, plastic poles about three to four feet high to keep it standing. Portable electric fencing and guardian dogs are also predator friendly. They do not harm or kill predators like poisons, traps, and shooting do, but instead deter them with loud barking and intimidation.

Robert moves the Kaos sheep every five to ten days: "Any less than five days and I spend all my money in labor moving fences. Any longer than ten days and my sheep pick up a parasite and re-infest themselves with parasites."[14]

Why would a vineyard or orchard manager call Kaos rather than raise and keep their own flock? Sheep are not a vineyard's primary line of business. It makes economic sense for orchard and vineyard growers to focus on their expertise in growing, blending, and fermenting grapes rather than raising lambs, meat, and wool. The vineyard may need grazing for only part of the year, or a small part of the season, and may not want to pay for a year's worth of feeding and caretaking, to say nothing of lambing and breeding.

Sheep are great marketing, too. People visiting a winery like to see sheep grazing the same vineyard that the wine came from. As Robert points out, the sheep's presence paints a picture of health. People won't enjoy the glass of wine nearly as much if they see people in white hazmat suits walking between the rows, spraying clouds of pesticides, or a coyote in a snare. It's just not the sort of experience you want to accompany your pastoral day out, a $60 bottle of wine, and time with friends and family in an elegantly appointed tasting room. That's why, Robert says, "we use guard dogs, we use electric fencing. If we start getting hit by coyotes we don't shoot and kill the coyote, we move the sheep.... Everything that we do is based on the wine consumer, what they would approve of."

Robert is describing a "triple bottom line" of benefits: benefits to humans (not just our ability to continue living on the planet and to have food and wine to eat, but the health of our businesses and our livelihoods), to the animals themselves (wildlife and sheep), and to the land. He is a consummate businessman who understands that the success of Kaos is not just him and Jaime, but the totality among animals, people, and land that is the business. These things are not opposed to one another: they make one another.

> It's the relationship of Jaime and I, and then our family, the relationship with the dogs, the vineyard people. If the sheep succeed in a vineyard and the vines all die, then my line of income ceases to exist. My feed source no longer exists. If the sheep die in the vineyard, and the vineyard is the only one succeeding, it doesn't work. But for all that to work, the soil's got to be healthy, the water's got to be there, you've got to have a healthy sheep. Every time you do one thing something else happens, and it then becomes a domino effect. The only way a sustainable business is going to be, is if we make money, and they've also got to make money.

Speaking of sheep health, the entire flock needs to be treated, again, for hoof rot (an infection that rots away sheep's hooves and can even eat into their legs) before we start shearing. For the first time in several years, California has had some rain, and sheep standing in damp vineyards makes hoof rot easier to get and harder to control. Jaime thought they'd eradicated it from the flock but then noticed one sheep that had it again. Now the entire flock needs to be treated, because hoof rot spreads easily. Before the sheep can enter the shearing trailer, Jaime builds a long, narrow chute of metal livestock fences and gates and lays down a line of several shallow pans on the ground inside the chute. She adds a little water and disinfectant. Each sheep will step through multiple pans on their way to the shearing trailer, the most efficient way to ensure all of the sheep are treated.

Sarah Gilbert has brought the kids out to play with Claire and to visit with Jaime. It's nice for all of us to have a chance to socialize, because the long hours of driving and being with sheep get lonely. It's fun to have more people around, especially kids. Because it's a shearing day, Felicity Gilbert is wearing a kid-sized shearing gansey that says "McWilliams Shearing," which Ralph McWilliams, owner of a shearing supply company, sent along with Matt's most recent equipment order. I make sure to admire it and take a photo. Rebekah, the Gilbert's eldest, pushes the sheep up the ramp and into the trailer, alternately employing a stick, her foot, two hands, and all of her strength. She is more genuinely more helpful, capable, and competent than numerous colleagues in my San Francisco office.

It's refreshing to step out of my age-segregated world for a day, with kids in day care or school and the elderly in assisted living or nursing homes. I am dazzled by the difference in what "normal" is for Claire Irwin and the Gilbert kids, compared to most of the childhoods I observe these days. I am a big believer in free-range kids, having been raised as one, but this degree of it—running all over a massive vineyard, in and out of the shearing trailer with sheep and sharp equipment all over the place—gives even me pause.

But none of the kids do anything foolish, or get hurt, and I am soon more than assured that they are safe, however busy we adults might be. One of the large guardian dogs vigilantly attends the smallest, newly toddling baby, constantly maintaining a follow distance of about seven feet. When the baby is seated, the dog lies on the ground nearby, never taking his eyes off him. As soon as the baby stands up and starts toddling, the dog stands and takes a few steps forward, maintaining that same distance. The dog must have learned to do this with Claire growing up on-site. It is mesmerizing to watch.

The shearing trailer is a unwieldy, rectangular, plywood structure that looks as if it might fall apart if the wind blows the wrong way (and it rocks back and forth on very windy days). It has five tightly packed shearing stations inside, and the electrical power to run the shearing motors and a few light bulbs is provided by a generator outside. The sheep are herded onto a long, sloping wooden platform that runs into the trailer from the outside, and shepherds—with Rebekah's help—push the sheep, standing nose to tail, to get them to move. The sheep are not eager to walk toward people and the noise of shearing motors.

I'd purchased a real shearing rig—a motor, drop, and handpiece—at the end of the previous season. I was shearing too many sheep for my portable but heavy handpiece to be comfortable in my hand and stay cool for as many sheep as I needed it to. Robert's trailer is the first job on which I'm using my rig, and I don't yet feel worthy of it. I am painfully self-conscious of my shiny, expensive new equipment and the fact that I don't really have the skills to back it up. I'm the least experienced shearer with the nicest stuff, while the better shearers are the opposite: they have more skill and don't have, or perhaps even need, brand-new gear. I only had the money to buy it because I have a day job, the sort of day job nobody else here has. These guys are real shearers, doing crew shearing—real work, all the time—not little hobby shearing jobs with a few sheep here and there. They deserve my equipment and I do not.

Realistically, though, I also don't have the mechanical and machinist skills to buy used shearing equipment and then figure out how to fix it up and ensure it's running properly and safely. So, as my shearing school instructors had recommended, I called Ralph McWilliams in Montana at the end of the previous season and asked him to set me up with a beginner kit. He sent me a three-speed Lister motor, a flexi-drop (rubber tube) that connects the motor to the handpiece, and a handpiece made in Switzerland. Matt Gilbert welded a bracket onto my motor so I could hang it from barn beams. My total outlay was $1,450. I have to shear a lot of sheep to begin to pay that off and make myself worthy of it. Best get to it.

I hang my motor onto a beam beside an extension cord plug, in the last position in the trailer. There's a hierarchy in every shearing shed and it is based on skill, with the best shearer and crew boss at the head of the floor or trailer (the first station), and the slowest shearer—me—at the foot (the last station). Cumulative shearing skill is measured in speed per sheep, quality of shearing, and number sheared in a day. My station doesn't even have a wall where the other stations do. It's just open to the outside, and far easier for the sheep to get away from me by leaping through the large, open space through which it can see other sheep at all times. At least I can feel the breeze.

The sheep stand in a chute that runs the full length of the trailer, which positions them directly in front of the shearing stations inside. There's no pen. To grab a sheep in Robert's trailer, a shearer uses one foot to step onto the wooden lip of a sliding panel, which lowers a section of wall on the slightly elevated platform where the sheep are standing. We must continue to hold the panel down with one foot while grabbing the sheep by the chin and butt, and—in one fell swoop—pulling it down from the platform and flipping it onto the floor. Done correctly, this lands the sheep directly below the motor and in the correct position to be sheared. I was initially relieved at being able to avoid chasing and catching sheep in a pen, but find it surprisingly difficult to hold the door down with one foot, pull the sheep down and flip it, and not let the door fly up, leaving the sheep hanging on it.

After the sheep is sheared, it runs out a little door just below the shearing motor, and down a short platform into the yard, where it happily joins the other sheep. We kick the sheared fleece out a window below the platform the sheep walked in on, where Connie Spinnerholm, a friend of the Irwins and a wool classer, grabs each fleece. It's a big job. With five shearers, fleeces are coming out all the time, from multiple shearing stations. Connie runs up and down the length of the trailer, grabbing fleeces and then grading and sorting them according to quality and style, based on length, strength, crimp, fineness, and more.

The sheep are enormous. The season's rains have created some generous pastures. Some sheep crotches and rumps are so thick with sticky manure and mud that I don't quite understand how I'm going to shear. I can't seem to get the comb through the mud and onto the sheep's skin. The comb just sort of slides through the mud, which quickly builds up on my handpiece. At one point a sheep kicks my handpiece off the drop and it flies out into the yard where the sheared sheep are standing. It most definitely feels like the first day of the season. I feel rusty and humbled and out of shape, like I have no idea what I'm doing. The other guys feel the same way, and we all groan and joke about how it feels to be bent in half again for hours, after the off season when we all swore we were going to work out and didn't. Even so, the other guys are still shearing a lot more sheep than I am.

As the morning passes into afternoon, my strength and energy wane. I have a harder and harder time controlling some of the large sheep, which is critical to do in a trailer with such close quarters. It is flat-out dangerous to have a two-hundred-pound sheep running around, knocking into multiple other sheep and shearers with sharp, powerful equipment. On two occasions, I have to ask one of the other shearers if they can finish shearing a sheep for me. The sheep's bellies are so muddy that I'd wrecked myself shearing them, and on removing one manure tag after another. They don't seem to mind taking on a half-done sheep, at least, with the worst part over, and adding it to their own tallies.

My handpiece feels slow, as if it's not cutting. It's probably just my attitude. "It's a poor craftsman who blames his tools," my grandfather always said. I'm frustrated with how much my body hurts, how lazy I was during the off season, how heavy the sheep are, how slow my ostensibly brand new equipment feels, how ineffective my supposedly sharp combs and cutters seem. I feel like I'm starting from scratch, as if I've forgotten more shearing than I ever learned.

I ask Robert to check my equipment, and it feels slow to him too, so we remove the top of my motor and move the band from the slowest speed to the middle one. I have to laugh. When I'd ordered the equipment, I had asked Ralph McWilliams to please, please make sure the motor was set to the lowest speed. Matt and I had double-checked it when Matt welded my bracket onto my motor. I was so afraid that a fast motor would lead to my cutting sheep that I wanted to make sure it was set to the slowest speed, which was still plenty fast and powerful. I had asked Matt, "How will I know when I need more speed?" He'd said, "You'll just know. It'll feel like your handpiece is sort of dragging. Like your arm is ahead of the handpiece. Hard to explain. But you'll know." Well, that's one thing I've got going for me today: I've leveled up to the middle speed setting.

I don't have a clicker to count every sheep I shear. I didn't expect to shear enough that this would matter but, after just a few sheep, it does. When sweat is pouring off your head and you just keep going, barely pausing before grabbing another sheep, it's easy to lose track. Have I sheared four, or was it just three that took longer than expected? Because all the sheep look the same to me.

I am much slower at swapping out my combs and cutters than the other shearers are. They barely seem to take a minute to do it and they're right back at it, grabbing another sheep. There is no doubt they're here to make money, and money gets made on volume. They'll about kill themselves to shear as many sheep as they can. I can see how a shearing crew might make one feel a bit competitive, though the very idea of competing with these guys is preposterous.

Lunch is a welcome reprieve. I do not know how the other shearers can smoke and eat sandwiches, cookies, and soda, and then bend themselves in half all afternoon without vomiting. I eat oranges, drink water, and play dinosaurs with Claire, who regales me with the names of countless types. I tell her about a field of fossilized dinosaur eggs I learned about on a *Nova* episode, and she is enthralled, more so when I tell her she can go there someday.

We resume shearing, which goes slightly more smoothly than the morning did. As darkness falls, Jaime asks how many sheep I sheared and writes me a check I try to refuse. She also gives me a Kaos calendar with adorable sheep and Claire photos, and a bottle of Kaos Kahlua, which Robert makes for Christmas gifts every year. The Irwins are lovely people, for whom I'll gladly work anytime.

I leave the vineyard at the end of the day, driving slowly on the dirt roads with sheep standing in them, and over portable fencing that rebounds. It is dark, almost impossible to distinguish between the mountaintops and the sky. Lights wink on in the occasional house in the hills, set inside miles and miles of vineyards. My day is done, but the Irwins' is not. Robert, who sheared 130 sheep, has a generator to move and wool to bale, while Jaime has another flock to visit on her way home, and those sheep and fence to move, before doing it all over again the next day. They have miles to go before they sleep. At least sweet Claire has her pajamas.

THIRTEEN

Black Sheep

A little black sheep pokes my palm and knee with her nose, looks up, and holds my gaze, head askance. What is she? The shape of her face reminds me of sketching exercises in art classes that begin with primary shapes, like circles and rectangles: it is sharply triangular, with a short, narrow nose that rises and widens into a bridge between two yellow eyes, set far apart. Two triangular ears are set perpendicular to her head, like handles, level with her eyes. She appears to have an honest-to-God forehead, a clearly delineated if subtle ridge, from which wool bolts vertically like tufts of grass between her ears, a punk rock effect, like a new baby whose hair hasn't learned to lie down yet. She is the size of most lambs, but obviously not one. Her black legs run up to a black belly, which diverges into contoured patterns of white and gray. Her fleece is variegated gray on both of her sides and tail, black across the top of her back and head, and the wool hangs shaggy above her legs.

This ewe is one of the rarest breeds of sheep in California, the Ouessant (pronounced *weh-sahn*). Almost lost to extinction and thought to be the smallest sheep in the world, with rams about eighteen inches tall at the shoulder, this ancient breed hails from Ile d'Ouessant, a tiny island in the English Channel twelve miles off the coast of Brittany, in the northwest corner of France. The original breed existed only on Ile d'Ouessant until the early twentieth century, and its origin remains a mystery. The appearance of sheep on isolated islands is often attributed to Vikings, who carried sheep aboard ships and left them behind, a source of meat, wool, and milk. The Ouessant resemble the Hebridean breed, a short-tailed sheep native to the Hebrides Islands off Scotland's west coast.

Now, voilà. Here were the Ouessant in Northern California, doing critical conservation work. Marie, my wind-kissed, sun hat–bedecked classmate from shearing school, shepherds and stewards this uncommon flock and 378 acres of land on the rocky Sonoma Coast. Marie compared the climate of the Sonoma Coast with that of Ile d'Ouessant and found them strikingly similar: "I actually ran the numbers of average rainfall and temperature. Both places are mesothermal Mediterranean climate classifications. I'm not totally sure if the terrain is similar, to be honest. The best I've seen is pictures. I assume someday I'll go [to Ile d'Ouessant], but that day is not in sight at this time." It's not easy to leave her flock for even a weekend, Marie says. "When I had just seven to fourteen sheep, and no lambs, it would be easy to take two or three days off and not see them for a couple of days at a time, but not anymore."

Breed is not the rarest thing about Marie's flock, nor is the Sonoma Coast's temperate weather the sole feature that suits the Ouessant sheep to it: it's the fact that these sheep eat what other sheep do not and, in so doing, help save native grassland. On a couple of occasions, I've heard Marie tell wool producers and farmers about her flock's remarkable predilections to grazing. "They eat down blackberry brambles, poison oak, and coyote brush," she'll say, which never fails to evince a satisfying, collective gasp. Marie only noticed these omnivorous tendencies after she'd gotten the sheep, in her first few weeks with them. "Coyote grass was growing in a garden where they were mowing cover crop down, and I thought, 'What?! More domesticated sheep don't eat that!' They didn't eat it at the commune, where I used to work, where there was a mix of Corriedale and Romney, and a few Churro." Centuries of minimal shepherding, in which Ouessant sheep roamed the island after the harvest and grazed communally, led to natural selection for hardiness in the Ouessant's native environment.[1]

Coyote brush is the hardscrabble, shrubby chaparral that gives the Northern California coast its distinctive, intoxicating scent of sage, basil, dill, and honey. But this fetching melange is problematic for grasslands. Coyote brush transforms grassland into a wooded area, and grassland is one of the most endangered ecosystems in the United States,[2] which means sheep eating coyote brush is the top priority for coastal land management. Marie explains:

If there aren't grazing animals maintaining the life cycle of these plants by grazing, if nothing eats coyote brush shoots, then—instead of perennial grasses, as there have been for millennia—it grows into more adult brush. That brush blocks out grass, and can burn out of control, and that lays the groundwork for Douglas-fir. Coyote brush and Douglas-fir used to be managed by deer and elk, which were replaced by cattle or, well, nothing, as sheep have fallen out of favor. So the grass is straight up disappearing. The land is turning into a wooded landscape because it's not grazed. If the balance between grassland and woodland falls out of whack, is the coast prepared for that, for woodland where there wasn't? Is the soil prepared for that? Or is it not strong enough, and will it erode as a result?

Marie points to an elongated oval of coyote brush, dead and dry in the center with its entire circumference bright green, very much alive.

This is an example of coyote brush invasion. In the middle of a grassland, the brush sprawls out unchecked and starts dying from the inside. This is why I don't agree that coyote brush developing on the coast is succession, because nothing will succeed it, unless there's a fire that burns all the dead branches away. Coyote brush sprawl is why grazing is critical on the coast. Grassland is the most endangered ecosystem in California.

Coastal grassland is an ecosystem, a temperate grassland plant community native to California and Oregon. It is found along the Pacific Coast, mostly in California, from Los Angeles to Southern Oregon. There is precious little of it, a scant 220,000 acres, down 99 percent from 22 million acres.[3] Certain agriculture practices, exotic species, housing development, and other human-related activities have made California grasslands one of the twenty-one most-endangered ecosystems in the United States, with more than twenty-five grassland species threatened or endangered.[4]

Native grasses are the foundation of many California environments, stream and desert, coast and oak woodland. Over three hundred species of native grasses take diverse forms. Some, like bunchgrass, form mounds and grow in clumps, the space between them increasing the likelihood of their survival. Others, like California onion grass, have very deep roots, indicative of the lengthy, seasonal periods without rain and drought-prone contexts in which they evolved. Those deep roots enable the grass to "drink" water held in the soil, doing more with less. The more water soil holds, the less needs to come from other sources, like irrigation, and the more robust native grass is, providing higher forage value for wildlife and livestock.

Those same deep roots give back to the soil, in a mutually beneficial relationship. Deep roots prevent soil erosion, so when water comes rushing by, the soil stays put, keeping sediment and pollution (from things like fertilizer) out of our waterways. And, when those deep roots eventually die, they leave root channels that help water wend its way farther down into the soil, building and maintaining the soil's water-holding capacity. Native grasslands are busy hubs of multispecies activity, too: there are wildflowers, hundreds of spiders, and birds observed only in native grass habitats, for instance. This indicates that both spiders and birds find insects to eat in native grasses that they do not find among invasive ones.

Marie gets straight to the point:

> If we let the forest take over the grassland in total, a whole host of plants and animals and systems will just be wiped out. Sheep eating coyote brush keeps it in check and keeps the grassland a grassland, as well as performing more general maintenance on grasses that are here, by trimming, fertilizing, leaving compost, and then getting out of there and letting it grow back. If they eat it down, it also saves a person having to come in and hand mitigate.

Things that benefit wildlife—like increased forage value—also tend to benefit domestic livestock.

The flock's work, Marie's managed grazing, and their particular relationship to this land has a name: holistic management. The phrase may have a new-age ring, but it describes a whole-farm management system that harkens back to the way things used to be, managing the relationships between land, grazing animals, and water in ways that mimic nature. Holistic management acknowledges an important, but often overlooked or ignored, truth of ecology and of life in general: you can't change or control one thing in one area without having an impact on something else in another.

Marie rotates the sheep through, moving them to new grazing areas for quick, intense grazing before moving them out. The sheep are present just long enough to graze nonbeneficial plants, reduce the fire risk, and drop life-giving urine and manure. But holistic management is much more than rotational grazing: it's a philosophy and a strategy. It begins with deeper questions, like "Should livestock be in this place at all?" It considers the social, environmental, and economic aspects of grazing so that, by the time Marie is planning the movements of her sheep, she is almost planning backward. Marie starts with what the land needs—its characteristics, the recovery periods that the soil and the species on it require—and grows her plans from this. The land shows Marie how to get the right animals in the right places, for the right reasons, at the right times, for the right behavior (like eating coyote brush and thistles).

Marie shares a recent grazing victory while feeding an alpaca. "I finally got the sheep and cattle grazing right next to each other. The cattle graze brushy areas and trample vegetation down, then the sheep have room to go in and prune areas that were otherwise just rotting. Their small size is helpful. They're not heavy, and it's a very rocky, super compacted landscape, and it doesn't need more compacting." Together, Marie and her Ouessant help keep the Sonoma Coast healthy, and they provide Marie with some income. Hers is not only a real job but an important, ancient one, for the coast, the ranch, and the animals.

When we first met, Marie had been working at the commune in western Sonoma County for a few months and had no immediate plans to get sheep of her own. This is why, when I received an email from Marie in September 2014 asking if I'd like to help her shear seven ewes, I didn't initially grasp that they were hers.

Marie's portable shearing handpiece wasn't working properly. Having spent five days at shearing school with her, I knew she could shear skillfully and well, so I suspected she needed my equipment more than any assistance. No matter. I was not about to turn up my nose at the chance to shear with a friend in a twenty-two-acre apple orchard, just about the only kind of ladies day out I'm interested in having. Marie mentioned the sheep had recently gotten into poison oak, but I'd sheared sheep in that condition before. The only difference this time was advance warning.

I drove to western Sonoma County, between the towns of Sebastopol and Bodega. A sweet little wood-frame, shingled house sat in the middle of a vast, square-shaped, gently sloping property lined with orchard rows. Unlike most farmhouses, which sit at the edges of parcels near the road, this house's central location implied the people who built it worked the orchards themselves. They could reach all of the trees without a long walk to any one place.

Marie doesn't live here, though her sheep do, at least for the moment. The owners point out where I can park, a little way back from the house, beside outbuildings that have power and even a bathroom we can use. Sensing my presence, a distant livestock guardian dog barks loudly. As I unload, Marie walks toward me, waves, and explains, "That's Zita." Marie leads me to seven diminutive sheep grazing a small, fenced segment of apple orchard, with Zita keeping watch. Marie has draped a tarp over some tree branches to create a shelter for Zita. "There was a coyote the other night. Zita would not stop barking until it had left."

"When did you get sheep?!" I asked. "How did you find a place to keep them?"

Marie said it happened accidentally, if fortuitously. "It wasn't a 'finally I'm going to have my own flock' feeling, because it was a surprise to me, the idea that I would have sheep of my own." Marie had been working with sheep for only about eight months and had some very different plans before she got blindsided by the Ouessant.

Marie had hoped to move out of the city and into agriculture. She wasn't interested in raising or promoting food. "Sheep seemed logical because of the wool, and I was interested in animals more than growing plants. Working with the people, sheep, and wool at the commune kind of cemented it. I learned a lot in a short time, and had a plan to travel a lot in order to learn about raising sheep in many places throughout the world. That plan still sounds great to me." She laughed. "I met Robert Irwin and heard him talk about what he was doing, and was completely set. I did not consider myself prepared to run my own sheep. I developed this plan to go work on farms during most of the year, in different parts of the world each time, and then return to Sonoma each harvest season for the crush."

The crush is the grape harvest and the time of year when wine making begins. In Northern California, it's a roughly three-month period of intense, nearly round-the-clock labor, a time when pickers and lots of other folks make as much money as they can, working eighty and more hours per week and earning overtime pay.

The intention was to learn about the wine industry, make connections, and make money to fuel the life of travel. And while I was working at a winery in Sebastopol last fall, I was also farm sitting for Leslie Adkins. When she returned, she had these two Ouessant lambs, who she brought to California from Massachusetts in the back seat of her Prius. She was excited to have Ouessant sheep in California. She thought they would be perfect for vineyards because of their size and pleasant demeanor, so she talked to Karen Seo—the Ouessant breeder in Massachusetts—about sending some of her extra ewes that hadn't sold, that Karen was planning to send to auction anyway, to me instead, as part of a pilot program to try vineyard grazing with Ouessants.

Karen agreed and sold Marie seven Ouessant for little more than auction price, a gift. Marie could not have afforded the usual $500 to $600 per head.

Marie was completely surprised by the swift turn of events, and decided that instead of learning from people all over the world, she would learn by doing. She felt she had beginner's luck on her side.

The reason I felt I could get them is that I had this friend with an acre and a half of vineyard, who was stoked for me to bring them. He said I could start the sheep out there. I had a plan for them to graze there from November to May, and I figured I could find them contract work for the summer and beyond, during that winter and spring. I found the next job for them from people who visited the wool festival at the Valley Ford Mill, and then subsequent places like this mainly by word of mouth, and me checking with people I knew in the area. And so I formed Capella Grazing Project. I named it after the shepherd's star, Capella, because it seemed like the sheep came from the sky, in a heaven-sent sort of way.

The first seven sheep had arrived in November. Not quite one year on, they needed to be sheared.

Our first order of business was to construct a rudimentary shearing pen on a flat spot in the orchard, close enough to run two connected extension cords to the nearest building. Marie hammered four tall stakes into the ground and we dragged livestock fence panels over, making "hinges" out of rope to connect the fence panels to the stakes. Pen complete, we added alfalfa to entice the sheep.

Though Ouessant sheep have a strong flocking instinct, Marie said her sheep tended to scatter quite easily and didn't drive well, probably because they were young (with no older moms to show them how) and inexperienced (born on a farm that did not drive their sheep). Because they are grazing someone else's apple orchard—the owners' bread and butter—we decided to be cautious and build a corridor down which to drive the sheep. It took a while to roll out the flexible, mesh-like fencing, hammer in stakes, and build the chute but, once we did, the sheep ran straight down it and entered the pen in about one minute.

We kept all of the sheep in the pen together and sheared one after the other. I decided to shear right in the middle of a group of sheep, because I suspected the sheep being sheared might be calmer if it weren't struggling to get back to the flock, which would make my job easier. It appeared to work, but then the Ouessant were also good-natured, as Marie had described. They did not struggle and were so small that I found it easier to shear on my knees, the sheep lying on their backs and practically in my lap.

The fog hung on later than usual, providing welcome cloud cover during a hot time of year, and we enjoyed a pleasant, consistent breeze. Itching and blooming, pink patches of rash on my wrists indicated Marie had been right about the poison oak. But, considerately, she'd brought Tecnu, a product that lifts the poison oak oil out of your skin before you wash and spread it around, making everything worse.

The Ouessant fleeces were some of the most beautiful and unusual I'd ever seen and felt, soft, spongy, and springy with excellent crimp, a long staple, and a low luster. Though the fleeces were small, weighing just a couple of pounds each, Marie thought each sheep could produce two fleeces per year that would be more than long enough for hand spinning. The Ouessant has the largest wool yield of all breeds, producing 10 percent of body weight in wool. The colors were glorious. A single staple length from one black sheep began as dark chocolate, wound its way to medium-roast coffee bean, then became caramel. Other fleeces ran from golden tan to creamy white. Captivating. I yearned to see those natural colors spun into yarn and knit into a sweater or scarf but, alas, these fleeces were already spoken for. People from across the United States had heard about the Capella Grazing Project online and called Marie, asking, "Do you have Ouessant sheep? I want to buy your fleece. I will give you $100 for two pounds of wool." Marie said she was shocked. Pleased, certainly, but shocked. Fine wool fleeces typically sell for less than $5 per pound on the commercial market, and $15 per pound is a high price for the hand-spinning market, making $50 per pound extraordinary.

Marie noted that her sheep were not purebred but 63 percent Ouessant and 27 percent Shetland, and still slightly larger than the breed standard. (A breed standard is the description of characteristics, genetic and observable by eye, that are typical of a particular breed, against which individuals are judged.) There are not yet any true purebred Ouessant in the United States, as there hasn't been enough genetic diversity to enable this. Marie explains:

> For Ouessant sheep we—the handful of people breeding them in the Western Hemisphere—have been hitting the limit on how many and at what percentage we can get this breed of sheep without inbreeding problems. We still don't have any purebreds. The low numbers of heritage breeds mean they are already at risk, and lack of genetic diversity just makes it worse, in terms of breed viability.

Establishing a new breed, or increasing the numbers of a rare one, requires genetic diversity, which has not been easy to come by in the United States. Imports of live sheep from certain countries have been banned since 1989 because of concerns about introducing sheep diseases.[5] Some of these countries, like the United Kingdom, are home to many of the sheep breeds people in the United States want to import. Though live sheep imports were banned, semen importation was still allowed.

Karen Seo and her partner, Ray Tomlinson (the man who put the "@" symbol in our email addresses), began to breed Ouessant sheep in 2009. They imported semen from four purebred Ouessant rams in England and artificially inseminated forty Shetland ewes, who produced Ouessant-Shetland crossbred lambs. Unfortunately, in 2010, just as Seo and Tomlinson were getting started, the United States reinstated an import ban on semen as well. For the next six years, Seo and Tomlinson could not import either live sheep or semen to help establish the Ouessant breed in the United States.

Instead, during the ensuing years, Seo and Tomlinson increased the amount of Ouessant blood in their sheep through upbreeding. By November of 2013 they had produced nineteen ewes of three-quarters to seven-eighths Ouessant (the remainder Shetland), which were again artificially inseminated for another round of lambs to be born spring 2014. For future breeding seasons, however, they would need to import semen from new rams to achieve pure Ouessant sheep without inbreeding, which would depend on the ban on the import of sheep semen being lifted. Luckily, it was. The six-year US import embargo on sheep semen from the United Kingdom was lifted in May 2016. American breeders could import sheep semen from a range of British breeds, including Ouessant.[6]

The breed is rather mysterious and unknown, and Marie is still getting to know her predominantly Ouessant sheep:

> They just look at me sometimes and I'll think, "Who are you guys?" I'd been trying to pay attention to how they ate, and moved, and slept together, and I'd pick up on things like the fact that they would all get together and find an area to nest in, sleeping space, and then they'd go to work, a grazing space, and they'd return to sleeping space. They don't just lay down. The smaller the space, the more efficient they were, because if there's no room to sleep, it's all work space. They're confined to an active zone. So I could work with that.

Marie describes herself as observing the sheep from the outside. She's noticed that "the sheep have different roles. Some are more guardian-like. And one, one of them was the queen of all. These were her sheep, and who the hell was I?" Three years passed before the sheep queen even let Marie touch her. "They had a whole hierarchy, like royalty, military, commoners. And there is always one who is doing the opposite of what the rest are doing, asleep when the rest are eating. And that sheep shifts! Different sheep do that, take on that role, but almost never the queen."

Marie and I sheared and trimmed hooves again about six months later. Her flock was grazing at a meadery (that makes, yes, actual mead and other things) in Point Reyes Station, where the annual wool symposium is held. Marie had since gotten Aries, a small black ram, and the ewes were pregnant. Since there was no risk of accidental pregnancy, then, we sheared the ram first and, as we finished shearing the ewes, released them into the same pasture. Fleece removal is a funny thing and often confuses sheep, making it temporarily difficult for them to recognize one another. The ram did not recognize his already impregnated ewes and proceeded to treat them like a fresh crop of ewes who, of course, wanted nothing to do with him.

Marie told me the flock had rejected Zita, the livestock guardian dog I'd met in the orchard. Though that did not make Zita happy, Marie thinks the experience of trying to work the sheep was good for her. She regained energy and mobility. But since the flock wouldn't accept her, Marie returned Zita to the woman who'd sold her. Marie said the former owner barely recognized Zita, who had "perked up like no other" and gone from "being a depressed dog that had a hard time walking, to this bright-eyed dog that would run around the orchard," and still needed two-hour daily walks on top of that. After her return, Zita resided with some goats to keep her spirits and working dog's sense of purpose up.

Nessie, a four-year-old Anatolian Shepherd, is Marie's second livestock guardian dog. This age is not usually the best time to start a new dog with stock, as it is potentially too late in the dog's life, but it's worked out well, according to Marie.

> She's really good. She comes from a working ranch where they use livestock dogs, and use them properly. Nessie is way better prepared, totally bonded with sheep. At first the sheep were scared of her, but now they are like, "Oh yeah, I'm here, this dog is mine, she takes care of me," in a way they never did with Zita. They seem to have a cool feeling about Nessie, as in "I'm a sheep and I just have this dog."

Marie speaks of these dog-sheep observations with reverence. Like the best shepherds, she notices a lot and is genuinely grateful for the opportunity to witness the things she does. "The process of seeing that bonding happen, in front of your face, I could not have read about it."

Marie describes, for example, early observations of a sheep bonding with Nessie.

> This wether, who is indomitable, is like a dog. He goes up to people, even though he was not a bottle lamb. It's just his nature. And he claimed

Nessie as soon as I put her in there, like "You're mine." And Nessie was like, "Who are you?" And now they're best friends, and that introduced the rest of flock to being OK with Nessie. You can't underestimate those interactions.

Marie also noticed that Nessie's arrival has changed the flock's grazing habits, in ways Marie is still in the process of observing. "She'll stand over the sheep…and last night she was standing over one like a protective mom and curled up next to it.…They still bunch up, but Nessie changes their grazing, because Nessie will move them around. She'll walk in a circle around them and push them up to me, or sit in front of wherever they end up resting." With Nessie around, the sheep don't graze in quite as tight a bunch as they used to, and seem more willing to spread out. Marie says this is helpful because it may enable her to put the sheep in bigger areas, where they will graze more efficiently.

When they're in a big area, they zone out from most of it. It's like it's too much for them, so they identify areas. The bigger a space I put them in, the more they identify a few key areas: two eating areas, one sleeping, and they're not even going to bother with the rest. When it's the growing season, I don't want that, because then they don't eat large amounts of a large area. But in a dormant season, a large area is better so they won't overgraze, and it's better for them to rest more, because they're not getting as great of feed, and can then take time to get to know other areas. I shepherd them into other areas to show it to them, and you can see them notice, "Oh hey, we didn't know this was here." And that's in a relatively small area, a quarter of an acre.

For the next couple of years, Marie's managed grazing service worked well. She and the sheep moved every three to four months, staying mobile. When they'd arrived on the Sonoma Coast, Marie thought, "We're just going to lamb and then we're going to go." As the flock grew, however, moving them became more logistically difficult. If Marie wanted to move the whole flock, she had to borrow a livestock trailer. She needed insurance to take more animals around to other properties: sheep might get out and eat a neighbor's garden, or a dog might attack the sheep. In many places, errant and feral dogs are a much greater and more common risk to sheep than coyote, bear, or mountain lion.

Lambing and Marie's holistic perspective pointed to a coastal landscape that kept needing the Ouessant, and to the viability and sustainability of her whole operation. The sheep kept enjoying the ranch, and the ranch folks wanted the sheep to stay. It kept making sense for the land for the sheep to stay, rather than move. Marie herself had rented a studio nearby. So they stayed, even though—just as the Irwins and Kaos had done, to establish a toehold—the sheep were often grazing for free, because it made sense for them and for the landscape. Fortunately for Marie, her work evolved into the paid kind.

Now, aside from renting out a few sheep at a time for grazing (and only to trusted people whom Marie knows will graze them properly), the sheep and Marie hove to the coast, and that's how Marie likes it.

> It's so much easier to have them in one place than move them around. And I want to focus in on this ranch. I want to organize everything around this. If I can give these animals a job grazing orchards and vineyards and doing land management, they have a reason to keep on existing. It keeps me going—new lessons about how important this is, all the reasons there are to keep diversity, and work with a heritage breed, but to develop them in different parts of the world, so that if something happens in France, they're not all gone.

And they're worth it. Heirloom breeds of livestock have the same special qualities that heirloom vegetables do: more robust resistance to diseases and certain climates; stronger offspring; unusual and appealing flavors (for meat) and color, style, and hand (for wool). Marie makes an important distinction, however, about breed diversity and context, that interplay between breed and land.

> Breeds are not exactly like seeds. It's not just about keeping genetics alive, but keeping them alive in a socially appropriate context. . . . You can genetically steward a heritage breed, but if you're not maintaining them in their context, you're not stewarding. They're fine to keep in a backyard, but all the characteristics we want in the primitive breed need to be kept in play. . . . It's so easy to lamb on pasture with them, for example. If I was lambing them in a barn I think that, over time, that would change and lambing would get harder. It's not just keeping up genetics on paper, but keeping up characteristics.

A fortuitous, unplanned series of events brought Marie full circle, back to where she first started with sheep, on the western Sonoma Coast. The land tells Marie what it needs, and it needs her. She pays attention. She listens.

Marie Hoff and Zita in the apple orchard.

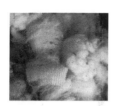

FOURTEEN

Bureaucracy

The Gilbert family moved in to their mixed-use home and wool mill property in the spring of 2013. Several months later, on a dry, hot day in August, a few toys and bicycles lay strewn across the backyard grass, a raw fleece was draped to dry on a fence while laundry dried on the line, and the fruit on a single Gravenstein apple tree looked promising. An awning extended over part of the backyard, attached to a large garage behind a small, nine-space parking lot that fronted a busy road. If the garage door were closed, you'd never suspect it contained two towering pieces of mill equipment—a drum carder and spinner—and thousands of pounds of wool Matt had sheared that season, packed in long jute bags, stacked to the ceiling. The silent equipment and unprocessed wool pointed to everything the Gilberts wanted to make with it, including some income, and could not—at least not legally.

Matt and Sarah had neither a use permit from the city of Ukiah to operate a business on premises and to turn the mill equipment on, nor planning commission approval or a build permit for a remodel. No one could even begin to estimate an opening day for the mill, or when crowdfunding donors would receive the yarn and roving the campaign had promised as perks. Mendocino Wool & Fiber had recently incorporated as an "S corp," which enabled it to do important things like qualify for business loans (which it didn't). It felt like a curse. Bureaucratic hurdles had only multiplied.

Matt had begun working with the City of Ukiah more than a year earlier, in the autumn of 2012—months before he and Sarah had purchased property, and before the crowdfunding campaign had launched—to explore plans for a wool mill, and to ensure the city would allow it before he and Sarah purchased property and equipment. The city had seemed enthusiastic. Like many municipalities in Northern California, Ukiah welcomed business that wasn't based on marijuana or meth production and might offer decent paying jobs that didn't require a college degree.

But verbal expressions of support and the formal process of permitting a mill were two different things. It's not every day that someone attempts to open a wool mill, and conceptually speaking, many people no longer even know what a mill is or does, and thus how best to proceed. A few generations had grown up and passed on since the Ukiah area had had a wool mill nearby.

If nothing else, however, a certain set of things had to happen for any business to operate legally in Ukiah, and for any commercial building to be substantially remodeled. Ukiah's design review board (DRB) had to approve the architect's and structural engineer's proposed designs, to ensure the look and feel of the project was in keeping with that of surrounding properties and of Ukiah at large. Then, the planning commission had to approve the project formally, to allow it to operate within the city, and to give the mill the ability to move forward with final blueprints and a build permit. Following that, various inspections of the construction site would be made as construction proceeded. Permits alone would cost the Gilberts nearly $10,000.

The mill had to morph from a glorified garage into a functional mill. Two walls would be expanded to increase the size of the space, and a foundation laid in the area that was currently an outdoor porch, after its concrete was broken up and carted away. Then there was everything else: the addition of high-voltage power to run the mill equipment; soundproofing to keep neighbors happy; a scouring sink, sewage line upgrades and gray-water infrastructure; solar panels; handicapped access; an ADA-compliant bathroom; fire control; and approval of the mill's intended hours of operation, also with consideration for neighbors. Running two full shifts would mean one shift would start early in the morning and the other would run late into the evening. And that didn't include the installation of the scouring system itself, the feeder that would run wool into the drum carder, and the new motors for the equipment.

Everyone involved agreed these considerations were important. Federal regulations, US construction standards, and things like the federal and California building codes were, after all, the reason that most of our buildings didn't crumble during earthquakes, as they do in many other places. But it wasn't clear why, if certain regulations were so important, it took months for anyone to mention them. Matt, for example, would attend various meetings with the city over a series of months, and no one would mention that he needed something, but would spring it on him later. One example? Handicapped parking.

After more than a year of working closely with the planning department, the first Matt heard about handicapped parking and access was from the architect Matt had engaged to draw plan elevations. Matt told me that he had "carefully read through all of the regulations that city folk had said applied, and—finding no specifications saying we needed handicapped parking—assumed we didn't." After the architect's query, Matt emailed a head planner at the City of Ukiah to ask, and the planner told Matt, "Yes, you do need one handicapped, van-accessible parking spot, and there needs to be a handicapped accessible walkway into the mill building."

That was news. One year earlier, Matt had emailed a preliminary mill site map—parking lot included—to two city employees, one of whom was a planner. Handicapped access and parking were not included on this map, and no one at the city mentioned it. A few weeks later, a city planner had detailed the parking requirements for the mill and made no mention of handicapped parking. Months later, as the mill's crowdfunding campaign reached its successful conclusion, Matt mailed six copies of the mill site map along with a completed application to the city, with no provision for handicapped parking. No one at the city mentioned any issues with either the application or the site map.

More than five months after this, in April 2014 correspondence about the mill, the planning department asked Matt to resubmit his site map and application. Even that request had nothing to do with handicapped parking but, they said, had been requested to "make sure that the parking spaces and the back space actually functions." Three months later, in July, Matt met with a newly hired city planner, showed her an updated, even more precise map of the parking area and—months into site discussions by this point in time—begged for feedback. She said everything seemed to be in good shape and in order, but that she would have to check the regulations and make sure that she wasn't forgetting anything. She promised to get back to Matt soon but, more than one month later, Matt still hadn't heard from her.

Matt said, "It has been a frustrating journey through the city bureaucracy, and I don't know how to figure out what all the criteria are that the city has, so I am unable, it would seem, to design a project that fills those criteria." When I related all of this in conversation to my mother in England, she said, "There's an entire television program about that here, you know, about how ridiculous it all is. It's called *The Planning Commission*." I believed it.

The months stretched on from summer into the autumn of 2014, with the mill making no significant forward progress with the city. The latest, newest set of delays stemmed from the DRB and its five members, who needed to approve the look and feel of the project before it could move on to planning commission approval. The DRB seemed, in general, most concerned with things that were least important, things not at all critical to getting the mill up and running but easier to understand: the parking lot layout, roof lines, signage styles and typefaces, and paint colors. It was primarily the DRB that had managed to delay mill progress for nearly one full year over trivial issues, and seemed neither to feel a sense of urgency nor care about getting the mill running. Then again, they were not out of time or money with a young family to support, like the Gilberts were.

The DRB made a big deal, for example, over the trees that would provide attractive cover over a chain-link fence that existed on the property at the time of purchase and, prior to mill discussions, had received no attention from the city at all. The DRB members engaged in unhurried, lengthy conversations on beautifying the site with trees, a site that would soon be torn up with construction activity. Though we did not say so, neither the Gilberts nor I could see the point of planting young trees with the potential for debris to fall on them when walls would be bumped out and a new roof put on. Trees in five-gallon planters would be too small, the DRB said, so the Gilberts would need to plant trees in fifteen-gallon containers.

Matt, a certified forester who probably knew more about trees than anyone in the vicinity, bit his tongue. The DRB took myriad "issues" like this seriously, and they had a formal role and power. After all of this, however, the DRB backtracked, saying that trees would take too long to grow anyway, to not bother planting them at all, and that the Gilberts would need to do "something different" in the meantime, to find some other sort of camouflage for a shipping container holding two pieces of mill equipment. Perhaps they might install a wooden fence and do a couple of other, as yet unspecified, things to make that corner of the property (barely visible from the road) prettier.

One city planner had also visited the property, essentially unaltered since the Gilberts had purchased it one year earlier, and wanted them to clean up and beautify the lot before anything else happened. Immediately next door to the mill, by contrast, was a parking lot full of old cars; across the street, an overgrown, trash-strewn lot; and, a few lots away, a long unsold house steadily slouching toward dereliction. The mill had definitely been singled out for beautification.

Most preposterous of all, though, was the DRB's unexpected proposal that the mill pay for and provide a parklet, where "people could bring a bag lunch and eat it," apparently thinking people would come to eat lunch at an unopened business. In case you've not seen one, parklets are little platforms placed in what used to be single parking spaces, for people to sit on. They're usually placed in dense urban areas in front of restaurants and coffee shops, to provide additional outdoor, sidewalk-like seating. Other parklets are covered in fake turf or real grass with a few benches placed on top, to make them feel more park-like.

Lest historic mills come to mind—those vast, multistoried brick or stone buildings beside a river, with a water wheel—remember that Mendocino Wool & Fiber is a large garage on a high-traffic four-lane road almost immediately beside a freeway entrance, with Highway 101 whizzing along immediately across the street, behind a dilapidated diner, inexpensive motel, post office, and Department of Motor Vehicle (DMV) branch. Massive trucks drive up and down the busy road all day long, en route to the freeway entrance. Who would want to sit on a parklet eating a sandwich with dirt, dust, and diesel flying in their faces and up their noses? And that's without considering the potential liability issues for the mill, for any accidents involving the parklet.

By this point, I was willing to concede that the antigovernment people who railed against regulation had a point, although I also believed their vitriol should have been directed at the local level rather than the federal. Matt told me that he learned it's not unusual for a permit to take a year to be approved. "I'm beginning to realize," he shared, "why urban sprawl is such an issue. You can actually get things done outside of town. I wanted to be in town so no one needed to commute, and because I've seen the woodlands and wild lands be really damaged in subtle ways from so many people living in them. I didn't want to add to that. So much for good intentions."

All of our spirits had reached a low point. The Gilberts were coming up on one year since announcing their fundraising effort. The November wool symposium was just one month away, and the mill no closer to opening. Matt would be able to give an update on the mill at the symposium, but not the news he wanted, exactly two years after his initial announcement.

Earlier that year, Matt had quit his full-time forestry job to focus on opening the mill. He'd supported his family of five by shearing over three thousand sheep that season. Now, with shearing season over until early spring, Matt was considering a full-time forestry job in distant Del Norte County to earn money. This would leave Sarah with three children to manage on her own. Plus, Sarah was pregnant (the only bright spot in all of this) and the Gilberts' fourth baby was due in May 2015.

In addition to city bureaucracy, the funding that the Economic Development and Financing Corporation (EDFC), a local nonprofit and lender, had promised was a long way from materializing. The EDFC was not even close to beginning to raise funds on behalf of the mill. Even if the planning commission allowed the mill project to move forward, the funding wasn't there. For the first time, there was a very real, distinct possibility that the mill might never open, that small town bureaucrats might actually kill Matt's lifelong dream.

We felt desperate. Christmas was coming and, with it, the fact that another year would end without the mill in operation. The Gilberts felt pressure from every conceivable place: shearing customers asked if they could "send their wool up the road" and Matt had to say no. A great deal of local wool sat in barns, unprocessed, lost income for the mill and for wool growers. Crowdfunding donors sympathized, but understandably asked when the mill would be able to make their perks. The days were short and dark and the drought ground on, with every prediction of rain evaporating. Matt and Sarah's finances were not where they'd planned. They could pay their mortgage and that was about it.

One night, Matt, Sarah, the girls, and I were sitting in the Gilberts' living room, tense, wracking our brains to think of one more thing, anything we could try. I said, "I guess slow money is slow." We laughed so hard we cried.

I sourly resented the businesses that the state and city ignored, especially in this particular region of Northern California. Dangerous, illegal marijuana growing operations abounded on other properties and even in state parks, where growers (some of whom were affiliated with murdering, torturing Mexican drug cartels) diverted wild streams during drought and wildfire. Every single day, the marijuana growers earned money, but not the Gilberts, who lost money every hour the mill wasn't open.

And, at virtually the same time, Chipotle wanted to open in Ukiah. They met with nowhere near the degree of scrutiny the mill received. The *Ukiah Daily Journal* reported, for example, that the city council and planners did not even consider Chipotle formula fast food, which enabled Chipotle to circumvent zoning restrictions and open in Ukiah's downtown core. It felt like the city was putting the mill and the Gilberts through the wringer just because they could, because Mendocino Wool & Fiber was not a large, well-known brand or corporate behemoth with a lot of money and attorneys behind it.

We had no choice but to double down. We knew that it was when things seem most hopeless, and you're most tired, that you must keep going, that there are critical times to not give up. Matt spoke with a woman who owned a couple of businesses in the area to see if he could get advice on what it took to get those open. He and Sarah rechecked spreadsheets, financial assumptions and models, and kept the business plan up to date.

I called in Tim, my father-in-law, an experienced architect serving on the planning commission in a small town in nearby Napa County, to see if he could help us. He spoke with Matt by phone for a few hours about the parking lot and handicap accessibility, and whipped up an ADA-compliant bathroom for the building plan. He also advised us to make friends with city council members, as they ultimately decide what projects to approve and may even put pressure on the planning commission to get the project moving.

We engaged the fiber community in a letter-writing campaign to the

City of Ukiah head planner, to create a sense of urgency. Matt, Sarah, and the girls made adorable felted wool and embroidered Christmas ornaments to send to crowdfunding donors whose perks remained unfulfilled, and thanked them for their patience.

Fortuitously, the planner so concerned with beautification of the mill site quit her job in December ("A Christmas miracle," I said), but Matt built a beautiful wood facade on the shipping container anyway, with a peaked roof that made it look like a burnished small shed, and a nice-looking fence. The mill property looked immaculate.

We strategized like crazy, considered every possible way to get more income going, from offering shearing lessons to agritourism. We wrote a loan application to the National Livestock Producers Association (NLPA) Sheep & Goat Fund. I called the USDA to explore grant funding opportunities there. And we did not let up.

On January 31, 2015, we held a mill workday to skirt fleeces and try to lift our flagging spirits, to restore the faith of friends and supporters, and to feel a little less alone. We had to do something, and dealing with the pile of several hundred fleeces was something we could do. Matt's three daughters ran around the yard, the chickens pecked around in their chicken house, my software engineer husband was doing a mighty fine job learning to skirt fleeces, Matt's apple tree had been pruned, Sarah showed a brand-new baby would be afoot in a few months, and the sun was setting on a glorious late afternoon. It was the kind of day that makes people move to California.

My husband took a video of Matt and me hand cranking the drum carder, which we could do without a permit from the City of Ukiah. Alison Kent, a member of Robin's Farm Club, came to the mill to help skirt fleeces. She brought a Targhee fleece she'd scoured from Hopland, from the flock of sheep on which I learned to shear. Someone at school had definitely sheared it, and it might have been me. Matt and I carded the fleece, so that Alison could then spin, dye, and weave the wool into a scarf, a raffle prize for an inaugural Barn to Yarn event at the Extension Center in which we'd all volunteered to participate. Matt would do shearing demos, I would teach wool classing, and Alison would spin, establishing a community spinning circle.

As I directed the fleece out of the Matt-powered carder and into the basket, it dawned on me that I had been there, hands-on, for almost every step of the process. The few people around me controlled an entire supply chain, and I was standing in the middle of it. No harm had come to any person, animal, or the environment at any point. I recalled a passage author Barbara Kingsolver had written in her book *Animal, Vegetable, Miracle*:

> A lot of human hobbies, from knitting sweaters to building model airplanes, are probably rooted in the same human desire to control an entire process of manufacture. Karl Marx called it the antidote to alienation. Modern business psychologists generally agree, noting that workers will build a better a car when they participate in the whole assembly rather than just slapping on one bolt, over and over, all the tedious livelong day.

I'd found an antidote to alienation, and it had started, strange as it seemed, with caring about where my clothes came from (or my yarn, anyway), "the carbohydrates and proteins we wear," as Rebecca Burgess put it, not only those we eat. Who knew? Perhaps becoming a less energy dependent, more independent nation could start with a good sweater. The mill had to happen. It had to.

Late January became March. Sarah was due in six weeks. Matt had begun another shearing season with nearly four thousand sheep ahead of him; he was trying to earn as much as he could and not be too long on the road with the baby coming anytime. Another DRB meeting was scheduled. I blew out my hair, put on makeup and jewelry for once, and donned a long dress, cowboy boots that made me look more confident than I felt, and a long, handwoven, poncho-style shawl made by Robin Lynde.

The shawl was a comfort but also, for the DRB, an illustration of the sort of 100 percent local garments the mill wanted to help create. I hoped to give the DRB the impression that I was some rich Bay Area lady wondering just what the hell was going on with the money she'd invested in her hobby wool mill. I didn't think they'd fall for it, but I at least wanted them to know that Matt and Sarah were not walking through this process alone, that a lot of people had a stake in the mill. I wanted every member of the DRB to feel at least a little bit of the external pressure that the Gilberts had to experience.

I drove two hours north to the city hall building in Ukiah and met Matt and Sarah in the lobby. Matt carried copies of architectural plans, photos, and more documents. We entered a small conference room, signed in, and the meeting began. I introduced myself as an investor, a bit of an exaggeration even if it was technically true.

The style of the false front of the mill building quickly became a flashpoint for the DRB. Matt had proposed a western-style facade, very much in keeping with multiple other, western-style false fronts in Ukiah. One local mill supporter, Leslie Smyth, had even driven around town and taken photos of every western facade she saw, to show how many there were. Some DRB members found the western style attractive while another said it wasn't appropriate in "urban Ukiah," a town of fifteen thousand.

The general consensus, if such it could be called, was that the mill building should either match the house or look quite different. Subsequent to this, a nearly hour-long discussion ensued about exactly how dissimilar the two buildings needed to be. Matt, increasingly perplexed, asked the DRB if they had looked at the color palette and other materials he had provided, which could facilitate similarity or difference. Every DRB member said no, they had not looked at them. They disagreed with the mill's proposed aesthetics without knowing what they were.

Next, the DRB members spent nearly forty-five minutes discussing possible paint colors and the style and placement of the sign that would face the street. The existence and position of bicycle parking was discussed at length. Who was going to bicycle hundreds of pounds of wool to a mill? Veins throbbed in my forehead and temples. I wanted to pitch the table over and scream, "None of this will matter if this business can't even open. The Gilberts here don't even have permission to turn the machinery on and you're talking paint colors and the typeface style on a sign? Every single day the mill's not open is one more day of lost money!" But I didn't. I kept my mouth shut and Sarah and I exchanged glances while my blood pressure continued to rise.

Then, the DRB covered the same territory all over again: facade styles, the style of the sign. Two DRB members criticized the paint color in a photo, and Matt reminded them that the color shown was the color of the existing building (an actual photo), and the DRB and the planning commission could choose the future color from paint samples, if they wished.

One man, whom I'd dubbed Mr. Hold Out after the first hour, refused to budge on the roofline. He didn't want a western facade but could not say what he did want. The closest he got was "Maybe more peaked?" I finally pushed the facade plans—a large paper showing three facade styles, architecturally rendered—across the table, handed him a pencil, told him to draw the roof line he wanted to see, and that it would be so, as long as the mill could open. Matt reminded Mr. Hold Out that whatever roofline he drew had to be tall enough to serve as a fire wall, yet not so tall as to be unsafe in high winds or in an earthquake, per the building code. There's a lot more to a roof line than meets the eye. Mr. Hold Out set the pencil down.

After nearly two hours, the DRB said that the mill plans were still not sufficient to go before the Ukiah Planning Commission, but also said that the plans didn't need to go before the DRB again. Where should they go, then? Fortunately, two heroes—one DRB member and one planner—began to make their stand. The planner reminded everyone that the DRB could make a recommendation, but that ultimately the planning commission would decide everything, anyway. That reminder seemed sufficient to clarify their thinking. The DRB gave the mill plans conditional approval, with a few edits, which meant the mill could move forward to its planning commission hearing. I nearly wept on the table.

The date for the planning commission public hearing was set to the following month but, soon after, delayed to May. Matt and Sarah were disappointed with the delay but I was elated: the May meeting fell smack in the middle of shearing school week and would be held in Ukiah, where many of the shearers stayed. I thought we might be able to rally a barn full of students and fill the planning commission hearing with supportive sheep shearers, perhaps before taking showers, in angry mob style, banging on a podium and asking why they can't send the wool they shear at Hopland, twelve miles up the road. In my dreams, anyway.

The day before the Ukiah Planning Commission's public hearing soon arrived. It would determine, once and for all, whether Mendocino Wool & Fiber would be able to legally operate in the city and build out the site as planned. The city planner who would present the mill's case before the planning commission sent an email to Matt and me that morning and noted that she would not have any letters of support to present, as none were received ahead of the meeting. I was furious.

I recalled the letter-writing campaign of just six months prior, in which we'd asked mill supporters to voice their support and try to create a sense of urgency when Matt was struggling through meeting after meeting with the DRB. There was simply no way letters of support hadn't been received. I immediately replied to the email and told the city planner about this. I asked if all previous letters of support would be included and listed how many letters they should have on hand, minimally. Since I doubted anyone would seriously look for these letters, I also fired off an email blitz to rally all of the fiber folks who had previously written letters. I asked them to please find and email them, immediately, to this planner.

Even this far along, could nothing go as planned? I tried not to ascribe malice to what was probably just incompetence. The letters sent to the head planner may have never left his email box, but after months of the tiniest things holding up the project—from potted trees to parklets—it was difficult not to be paranoid. If someone wanted to doom the mill project, conveniently having no letters of community support would help make that point. It didn't bode well. Or was I reading too much into it?

The next day, I sheared sheep all day and departed the barn half an hour early to clean up and drive to the planning commission hearing. As I left, a local shearer said he'd walk out with me. As we exited the barn, he whispered, "I don't know if you heard, but you know that lady on the planning commission, the one who tried to stop everything? She always said 'My job is to keep Ukiah exactly the way I found it,' and stuff like that?" I nodded. He further lowered his voice. "Well…she died!" We stared at each other, my eyes popping out of my head. It felt like a blessing, and I immediately felt guilty for even having the thought. I could not delight in anyone's death, especially a well-intentioned person I had never met, but I also couldn't help but marvel at the timing. I only hoped the deceased's colleagues wouldn't honor her memory by saying "no" to everything that came before them that night.

I showered, put on clean clothes, drove straight to the Gilberts, and threw three days' worth of rank shearing clothes into their washing machine. Bless them for sharing it. They scrambled to get themselves and brand-new baby Gregory ready for the meeting, and the three girls ready for church, all of whom were a bit sulky about going to vespers instead of the meeting. Rebekah told Matt that his beard was "maybe still...a little too long." I am not sure Chloe managed to get underwear on before pulling up her jeans, but oh well, at least she wasn't wearing a dress.

Sarah looked gorgeous in a royal blue wool shift dress, belt, heels, and yellow print scarf, as if she could not possibly have had a baby just six weeks ago. Matt's shirt was blue so they were color coordinated. Sarah had dressed Gregory in a onesie with a tie printed on it. Oh yes, every single one of us—infant included—would look trustworthy and dress professionally. I had to believe that Baby Gregory's first outing would mark a truly momentous occasion, the one in which his family's business was approved.

We arrived early. Fiber folk filtered in to the seats. Cara Randall, a woman I'd just met at shearing school that week—and who had also spent the day bent over sheep—entered, sat down, pulled out her knitting, and winked at me. Debby Bradford, of the Navajo-Churro project, and Peggy Agnew and Nancy Finn, with award-winning fiber flocks, gave thumbs-ups and smiles as they took their seats. John Harper, shearing school instructor, filed in, too. The support was palpable and humbling. After opening the meeting and observing a moment of silence for the recently deceased commission member, the public comment period for the mill began.

John Harper spoke eloquently on behalf of Matt, the need for a mill, and the many ways in which the Extension Center would benefit from having the school's wool processed just up the road and possibly selling a truly local Mendocino product, rather than being forced to sell raw wool for export. Leslie Smyth entered with an oxygen machine and walker, and—in regard to the earlier, protracted discussions on handicapped access—assured everyone that she already moved through the wool mill parking lot just fine, and that it was unlikely the mill would have visitors in worse condition than she. The planner assigned to represent the mill at the hearing described the letters and calls of support she had received, as well as one against. She also mentioned the open issue the DRB put forward, of the facade shape, and passed architectural renderings around.

The planning commission reviewed these and then one planner asked, "Matt, since this is going to be on your property, which one do you like best?" It was all I could do not to laugh aloud. After all those meetings about signage styles and paint colors, now it was "whatever Matt wants?" Fine! So be it.

Finally, it was time for the commission to take a formal vote. I exhaled and bent my head forward, almost to my knees. One yes. Another one. Matt and I glanced down the aisle sideways at each other. Maybe? Not there yet. I looked back at my knees. Another yes. My dirty fingernails left half-moon marks in my palms. And then, the last yes. Unanimous approval. A few tears of relief escaped, and hugs, handshakes, happy and tearful faces all around. Finally. My rejoicing felt tempered, because I couldn't quite believe such a major milestone had been crossed.

We enjoyed a cider at the Gilberts to celebrate. The mill could legally operate. Now to find the quarter million dollars to build it.

Felicity and Rebekah Gilbert in the mill during its early stages.

FIFTEEN

Local Color

I am hardly the only human being to adore color. The muted red, warm pink, sunset shade of quince flowers, the nearly florescent orange of California poppies that cameras never quite capture, and the dusky gray-green of blue spruce trees make my heart sing. Our natural attraction to color makes it particularly painful when we learn that synthetic dyes are one of the most toxic, ecologically disastrous aspects of the textile industry. Their creation requires destructive mining and the heavy input of nonrenewable, poisonous resources. Four hundred pounds of coal tar are needed to produce just one ounce of dye powder.

Dye runoff is the single-largest source of water pollution in China.[1] Even a very small amount of dye contaminates water, interfering with light penetration, reducing photosynthesis in aquatic plants, and destroying aquatic ecosystems.[2] This water also pollutes crops when contaminated water is applied.[3] Dyes can be toxic, carcinogenic, and mutagenic—a serious hazard to human health—and are difficult to remove from water because most synthetic dyes do not biologically degrade. According to the World Bank, 17 to 20 percent of industrial water pollution comes from textile dyeing and treatment. Of toxic chemicals in our water, seventy-two come solely from textile dyeing, thirty of which cannot be removed.[4]

Despite this, I just sort of assumed that we were effectively stuck with chemical, synthetic dyes. I knew nothing about natural dyes but, somewhere along the way, formed a belief about them anyway: they created weak colors that didn't last, fading quickly between wash cycles and in sunlight. I did not recall the numerous, ancient—and thus obviously naturally dyed—textiles I'd seen in museums, several thousand years old and richly colored inside their glass cases. They outlasted one human lifetime after another, and many more fashion seasons than that.

Soon, my baseless beliefs would be tested firsthand. I had agreed to attend a natural dye class with Kate, mostly because the class would be held on an idyllic Napa ranch and I would get to spend a Saturday outdoors in her company. But I felt hesitant and like a bit of a pill for a few reasons. The dye class would use mycopigments, myco as in mycology, as in mushrooms. Mycopigments are color molecules found in fungi and lichens. Kate and I would, through natural dye processes and chemistry, extract colors from mushrooms and dye things with them. I anticipated the mushrooms would look and feel slimy, and hoped I would not have to touch them.

In my six years in California, I had also grown wary—and weary—of what I referred to as "California woo." Living in California changed people. I feared that, one minute, I'd be dyeing yarn with mushrooms and, shortly thereafter, find myself clad in animal skins, felting wool into wall panels for a yurt, and harvesting kelp to make soup broth. A natural dye class was simply the next in a series of West Coast steps that led straight to a belief in the powers of crystals and the existence of chem trails.

Nevertheless, potluck items in the back seat, I drive Kate and myself to Napa. We head west on an urban, then suburban, road and beyond. The road narrows, curves, and becomes poorly maintained, with big chunks of patched blacktop shaking the car as views of pasture and hills open up. This is what more of Napa used to look like, before the Walmart, international conglomerate wine tasting rooms, tract housing, and traffic.

We pass through a gate, and barks herald the arrival of a handful of livestock guardian dogs in the road, ready to attack the hood of my car. Sheep are definitely afoot, then. We roll up our windows and crawl along, not wanting to hit the dogs that refuse to move from the front and both sides of the car. One dog's angry, large-jawed face tries to bite my car window, leaving slobber and muddy paw prints streaked all over it and the car doors.

A sheep rancher and fiber artist named Mary Pettis-Sarley has volunteered her ranch as a class site, and we find a cozy cluster of barnlike buildings nestled into a slope that rises gradually to the west. We slowly drive past her house on the left and, on the right, outdoor livestock pens and a barn. Sheep and goats graze while several brand-new baby goats perch on small rocks just slightly larger than they are. We veer left, on a single-track drive behind the house, past a big oak and on to another set of outbuildings, long and single-story this time, and slightly higher on the slope.

One building has a large, flat stone terrace with grapes woven through a large arbor, commanding views east over gently sloping green hills and a couple dozen sheep. The porch is attached to a building much like a single-story ranch house and reminiscent of a small, early twentieth-century hospital inside. Two rows of antique metal beds hold freshly scoured, white fleeces, air drying where mattresses would normally be. Bags of fleeces are piled like laundry bags along the edges of the floor, waiting to be washed. More fleeces fill shelves along the wall, some of which also bear dye plant seedlings.

A dozen or so women, ranging in age from twenty-five to sixty-five, are arrayed around dyeing stations, steaming stockpots mounted on gas burners. Behind them, a clothesline hangs between posts, and a few picnic tables and chairs are arranged in the middle of the porch.

The mushrooms look more disgusting than I could have fathomed. Gallon-sized Ziploc bags slump, holding what look like moldy cow pies, dark, cloudy liquid filling the corners. Nothing in the bags looks like an attractive color, or any color at all. Everything we dye will come out brown or black, apparently.

Things get down to earth, so to speak, when class begins. The instructors introduce the mushrooms with which we'll dye. They tell us where in California the mushrooms were found, and at what time of year; why they grow in the soil, environment, and climate they do (some need a certain tree, for example); and how to harvest them responsibly. Wielding a small pocket knife, our instructor Dustin Kahn—cute, petite, and freckled, wearing a felted vest, shoulder-length brown bobbed hair—shows us how to cut the tops and take only what we need, leaving the mushroom, roots, and mycelium in the ground to make more mushrooms and keep the soil healthy.

The mushrooms are poisonous to eat and we have to wear gloves when handling them, but they are safe to dye with. The instructors advise us to keep the Ziploc bags away from our faces when we open them to avoid inhaling spores. We each receive a smock, a small amount of white wool yarn, and one square of undyed, beige silk. We'll be able to see how the effects of the same dyes vary depending on the material to which they are applied and the preparation of that material beforehand.

The mushrooms are deposited into the pots of boiling water and simmer away as we turn our attention to five-gallon, stainless steel vats of prepared mordants. A mordant is, as Rebecca Burgess describes in her book, *Harvesting Color*, "a translator that speaks both the language of the fiber and the language of the dye. It functions as a chemical bridge, binding to both the dye and the fabric more effectively than either can bind to the other."[5] Mordants help color adhere to fiber but also affect the final color outcome.

Some mordants are metallic, using tin, copper, and chromium, which—though naturally occurring—can be toxic to humans in tiny concentrations. Our mordants, instead, are local Pacific seawater, alum, and iron; the latter explains the rusty pieces of metal I see in jars, oxidizing in water and turning it orange. Alum, pure potassium aluminum sulfate, is a mineral salt that generates good color accuracy with plant pigments.

We dip yarn into each mordant, applying different mordants to yarn samples destined for the same dye pot, to observe the different color outcomes caused by a change in mordant alone. Next, we dip the mordanted yarn into the mushroom dye with tongs and let it soak for a while. Given the appearance (and smell) of the mushrooms in the pot, I expect the yarn is going to stink. Who will want to knit with that?

Somehow, after twenty to thirty minutes in the pot, the mordants and moldering mushrooms have combined to create sage and olive greens, periwinkle blue, a bluish dark gray like the ocean on a stormy day, a deep rose pink bordering on pale red, lavender, and deep gold. "Absolute witchcraft!" I say to Kate as we behold our first dye samples, dripping and steaming at the ends of our tongs. "Who figured this out in the first place? What human discovered that a nasty looking mushroom and seawater could make rose pink? Was it an accident?" No matter. It was a beautiful one.

We rinse our yarn in afterbaths, which also function as color modifiers. Vinegar, an acid, can create strength and variation in color and increase the adherence of some dyes. Even plain old tap water can function as a color modifier, because the blend of minerals and the pH balance of water varies greatly. After this, we clip our dyed samples to the clothesline to dry. I find it a meditative, pleasantly repetitive process, and in this way, dyeing reminds me of knitting: dip, soak, wait. Dip, soak, wait, hang to dry. Repeat. I relax into the sedate flow of things, chat with Kate, and snack on brownies while staring at cattle in the distance.

After our yarn dries we cut and write out sample cards and tie our dyed yarns through punched holes beside the mordant and dye combinations we've documented. From the labels, I can see that lobster mushrooms create a tangerine orange color with no mordant in a dye bath with neutral pH, while adding a little ash water (an alkali) shifts the dye color to hot pink or magenta.[6] The red-capped cort creates brilliant red, orange, and violet, and an iron mordant shifts those colors to violet-purple and rose pink. I like the western jack-o'-lantern, a California treat coveted by dyers the world over, so named because it glows in the dark when it's fresh. It has produced two of my favorite colors of the day: a dark violet without any mordant and a dark olive green atop iron mordant.[7]

Later that evening, as I run my fingers through my marvelous yarn samples, I consider that natural dyes seem fine and well for personal craft use. I feel inspired to dye items of my own at home. But what about factories? Could natural dyes scale to industrial levels of fabric and clothing production? Were there enough dye plants, mushrooms, and cochineal insects in the world for this? Did natural dye houses or dye plant farms even exist?

After some online research and several phone calls, I found Donna Hardy of Charleston, South Carolina, founder and owner of Sea Island Indigo. She personally occupies several spots in the natural dye supply chain: indigo grower; rare seed saver and propagator; natural dyer; teacher, historian, and researcher; and visionary with a plan to produce tons of indigo and establish a facility to store, process, and perform contract dyeing with indigo. When we spoke, she seemed surprised to find herself wearing so many hats. When I asked how she got started, she said, "A long, long time ago, I bought a book on herb gardening…and in it was a chapter on how to grow a dye garden. And I had never thought about where the color on your clothes comes from. And that's what started it all." She laughs.

Crazy, huh? So I said, well I'm gonna learn how to grow dye plants, so I've gotta have something to dye. So I found these women up in the mountains, up in north Georgia, and they were foraging for dye plants, and one woman was raising Shetland sheep, and another woman was raising Romney. I learned how to spin, and then I learned how to knit, and then I learned how to weave.

We both laugh at that. The fiber arts, apparently, present a slippery slope: learn to knit or spin and, next thing you know, you're sowing an indigo crop and shearing sheep.

Not only could natural dyes scale, Donna said, but the growth and manufacture of natural indigo dye had, prior to the Revolutionary War, accounted for fully 35 percent of the South Carolina economy.

> Over one million pounds of indigo extract was being shipped yearly from the port of Charleston to England. It was a huge industry here. Before the Revolutionary War, Ossabaw Island [a tiny barrier island off the coast of Georgia] was a huge indigo plantation. In fact, it was so productive that after the war, the warehouse on the dock of Ossabaw was raided and two thousand pounds of extract were stolen.

The fact that two thousand pounds of natural dye extract were available to steal points to the scale of indigo production required to produce such a quantity.

In 1744, Eliza Lucas—or rather, the people enslaved by her family—successfully cultivated, processed, and exported indigo from her father's plantation outside Charleston, South Carolina. This shipment of Carolina Indigo to England caused quite a stir in London, and the British government immediately offered a bonus of six pence per pound on indigo exports from the colonies. Colonial exports soared from Eliza's six pounds in 1744 to five thousand pounds the next year.[8] Indigo dye dates back farther than this, however: The ancient dyeing tradition is over a thousand years old, indeed twice that. In 2017, six-thousand-year-old indigo-dyed cotton textiles were discovered in a coastal area of Peru, the oldest known examples of cloth dyeing in the world.[9]

Even though Donna knew that indigo had once been produced near her home, she had never given much thought to using indigo in her natural dyeing. That changed during a visit to Seattle, where Donna periodically traveled from Georgia in order to study with natural dye pioneer Michelle Wipplinger. It wasn't until Michelle said that indigo used to be grown commercially that something clicked for Donna. She thought, "If they did it then, why can't we do it now? I'm going to grow indigo."

Donna wanted to grow indigo, but it was too cold in the mountains of north Georgia to do so. Donna had been driving down to Charleston, South Carolina, every other month or so to visit archives. She was on the hunt for instructions, sometimes in sources dating back to the 1700s, for how to grow indigo commercially in the southeastern United States, as well as information on the indigo varieties grown. Eventually, Donna says, she decided to "move to Charleston and start growing indigo."

Donna had no land and no firsthand farming background. She ordered indigo seeds from Mexico because, as she'd been assured numerous times, none of the Carolina indigo had survived. "I closed up my cabin in the mountains and started looking for a little plot of land," she says. No matter how hard she looked, she could not find one. Frustrated, Donna thought, "I'm going to throw the seeds in the marsh already and be done with it!"

One day the farmer from whom she bought goat milk and yogurt told Donna she could grow the indigo on the farm. She offered Donna an area beside a barn for planting and plenty of goat compost besides. Even though Donna later realized she'd sown her seeds a little too soon, in temperatures too cold, the indigo sprouted in about a month and grew right over Donna's head. It grew more than ten feet tall, an extraordinary height even by indigo standards.

Donna's extensive research on indigo varieties historically used in the region continued. (If you remember learning the Linnaean system of biological classification in school, singing that descending order chant of "Kingdom, phylum, class, order, family, genus, species," you may find it helpful now.) Among natural dye hobbyists, indigo plants are colloquially described as "Japanese and non-Japanese varieties," a shorthand to describe types of indigo that do or do not grow well in cooler, milder climates. Varieties native to Japan tend to grow well in mild climates, like mine in the San Francisco Bay Area, while varieties native to Asia (India) and Central and South America tend to require warmer temperatures, like those in the southeastern United States, in order to thrive.

But these two types of indigo are far more divergent than this: they don't even share a genus. Over in the Fabaceae family, *Indigofera* is a plant genus with over 750 species. Several of these species are used to produce indigo dye, and *Indigofera tinctoria* (indigenous to Asia) and *Indigofera suffruticosa* (from the Americas) are two of the most popular. The Japanese varieties—*Persicaria tinctoria*, commonly referred to as both Chinese Indigo and Japanese Indigo—hail from an entirely different family, the buckwheat family Polygonaceae. Japanese varieties became more common in the United States after World War II, but Donna wanted to know how to grow the varieties grown in the southeastern United States—from India and Central and South America—long before World War II.

As noted earlier, Donna had sourced indigo seeds from Mexico, because she'd been told no regional indigo had survived for over 270 years. But it had. On the north end of Ossabaw Island, on the site of that former colonial indigo plantation, some mighty well-adapted indigo was growing wild, hanging out and hanging on in the seaside, saline air. Unlike most indigo, it also lives through frost and self-seeds. Ossabaw Island is a twenty-minute boat ride from the coast of Georgia that, mercifully, does not have a bridge to it and has never been developed. Today, it is managed by the Department of Natural Resources (DNR) and the Ossabaw Island Foundation, and the folks who worked there gave Donna indigo seeds that they'd collected and saved. Jackpot.

Technically, the seeds Donna had ordered from Mexico and the seeds from Ossabaw were both *Indigofera suffruticosa*, but they produced distinct, and peculiar, dye outcomes. As Donna explains it, "Like with azaleas, you might get one with small leaves and white flowers, and one with large leaves and pink flowers." Seeds of the same species won't necessarily produce the same plants and may sire distinct varieties. After dyeing with "the Ossabaw variety" for a while, Donna has come to suspect that it may be subspecies of sorts. "There used to be a variety of *Indigofera* called *guatemalensis*, from Guatemala, and it has a more red base to it. It's a warmer, red-based blue, not yellow-based or cool, not purple, but a warm and vibrant blue. And the Dominique Cardon natural dye book says it's not a variety, but a subspecies." Donna thinks the Ossabaw indigo may be *guatemalensis*, because the blue it produces is "just incredible."

Dr. Brian Ward, research scientist and organic vegetable specialist in the Department of Plant and Environmental Sciences at Clemson University's Coastal Research and Education Center (CREC), says that—though laboratory tests have not been funded or completed—the Ossabaw indigo is more likely a new phenotype of *Indigofera suffructicosa*. Historical records indicate that the Ossabaw indigo originated in South America. Over its 250 years on the island, it has likely undergone a phenomenon known as phenotypic plasticity, which means it has changed to fit its new environment.

"My goal," Donna shares, "is to bring this indigo—of our history, of our heritage—back into production, so we have a domestic source of indigo, so our blue jeans are dyed with domestic indigo, back to true American indigo. It's been here longer than people of European descent have been here." And though her initial crop exceeded all expectations, that "back into production" goal creates a much greater challenge: it means growing Ossabaw Island indigo at a sufficiently large scale to be able to make and sell dye extracts to, and/or serve as a natural dye contractor for, commercial-scale manufacturers.

Donna has picked up some helpful allies along the way, one of whom is Glenn Roberts, founder of Anson Mills. (You may have seen him on episodes of the PBS program *A Chef's Life*, featuring chef Vivian Howard in eastern North Carolina.) Glenn has resurrected the Carolina Gold variety of rice and several nearly extinct varieties of Southern mill corn. Much like Donna, he conducted extensive historical research to find and reinvigorate heirloom seed stocks.

Glenn was interested in seeing Donna's first ten-foot-high indigo crop and, after he had, he took Donna to the CREC's Organic Research Farm, which conducts field trials of a multitude of crops, including Carolina Gold rice, Sea Island cotton, and tea. It also helps farmers transition to organic methods. Importantly for Donna, the research farm also investigates specialty niche crops for repatriation and inclusion into vegetable rotations, including Ossabaw Island indigo. *Indigofera* is a legume and nitrogen fixer, which makes it an intriguing cover crop candidate to improve soil.

Indigofera has other benefits, too. In the coastal region where the Ossabaw indigo grows, sea levels have already risen and continue to rise. This means salt reaches coastal land and plants that it previously did not, which has folks looking for more salt-tolerant crops. Indigo that has evolved on a barrier island beside the sea and survived countless storms and hurricanes over 250 years seems an excellent candidate for helping us adapt to climate change. In addition, spent dye leaves can be used as compost to improve soil health.

The CREC work is critical because, in order to produce indigo at scale, everyone involved first has to get a handle on how best to grow Ossabaw indigo, and they haven't yet. "Even the state botanical garden had a hard time growing indigo," Donna says. Donna has yet to find anything in her historical research that is helpful in regard to commercial crop practices, so the CREC has to figure it out through hands-on trial and error.

Even if Donna could uncover the colonial-era commercial cultivation practices for Carolina indigo, they may not neatly extend to our modern context. Historic farming methods depended on—and thus implicitly assume the availability of—a massive work force of unpaid, enslaved people to manually tend and harvest plants. Indigo seeds, for example, were covered with boiling water for one minute to speed germination. Today, that might be fine for a few plants at home, but not necessarily for a farmer who has to pay people for such painstaking, time-sensitive labor. Indigo also requires very warm soil, which means plants start out well in a greenhouse, but their long roots make transport to larger areas tough and labor intensive.

It's tempting to think we can simply transfer our former labor reliance on human slaves to machinery, but that too is more easily said than done. Sea Island cotton plants, for example, grow so tall that no combine in existence can harvest them (it's still harvested by hand today). Bringing back a particular type of heirloom cotton, then, means we need to either pay for more expensive human labor to tend and harvest it or create a new machine that can do it, neither of which is easy or affordable.

Donna understands, though, that we have to do something, because what we're doing isn't working.

> We're brainwashed that synthetic is better. What we're doing in these countries where we set up these dye facilities ... the effluent coming out of the factories is poisoning the water, the drinking water of the people who live in these countries. They don't have clean drinking water. It's killing

the fish in the rivers. Natural indigo, the plant, has low toxicity, but synthetic indigo is a petroleum-based product, and it's pretty toxic. It's toxic to the people that make it, it's toxic to the people that dye with it, it's toxic for the people downstream of it, and if you think about this, you wear a pair of jeans. And what's the largest organ in your body? It's your skin. You're going to absorb those toxins through your skin.

Lest this seem like an exaggeration, I have a long, painful story about a months-long "bra burn" I got after wearing a bra for just a few hours that I failed to wash beforehand. It required biopsies and steroids, and the doctors suspected formaldehyde was the culprit.

Dyeing with natural indigo is quite different from the way in which Kate and I dyed with mycopigments and mordants in class. Indigo comes in many forms (fresh or dried leaves, a powdered extract, or composted material). The indigo is added to water to create a dye bath, traditionally referred to as the vat. An indigo vat has special requirements that go beyond those of mushrooms simmering in water: it must be alkaline, have a pH between 10 and 11, and all of the oxygen must be removed, because oxygen reduces the effectiveness of indigo dye.[10]

Oxygen is reduced and eventually removed through the use of chemicals, fructose, or bacteria. When bacteria is used, it is known as the fermentation technique of dyeing, and the fermenting vat can stink, strongly. Because indigo forms a physical bond with the fiber, not a chemical bond, dye mordants aren't needed: they do not help indigo chemically bond to fiber or increase colorfastness.

Donna has big hopes about how we and the textile industry can begin to change our habits, materials, assumptions, effluents, and employment. She envisions a multipurpose facility, one that would include a natural dye house; research, teaching, and indigo processing and storage areas; and a gallery and studio space for artist-in-residence programs, a functional space open to the public and tourists. Indigo cultivation and farming are central to this vision. Donna would like to see at least five or so acres of land with different farmers on them, for example, who would be able to provide indigo seeds. She wants to be able to pay people to grow indigo.

Donna knows natural dyes can scale and last. They are already produced in concentrated extract form for industrial machinery by companies like Botanical Colors in Seattle. It is currently possible to dye hundreds of pieces of fabric at a time.[11] It makes so much sense for Donna to create a central indigo vat and keep it going, using it repeatedly, and composting its contents when it's done. She describes that it was once common for people in Japan (with its *Persicaria tinctoria* varieties of indigo) to bring their clothes to a community dye vat once per year to freshen up their appearance.

As Donna colorfully puts it, "Before 1856, it was dyed with a plant, animal, mineral, or bug." Those textiles, still rich in color, have outlasted many generations, and natural dyes perform comparably to synthetic dyes in both washing and lightfast tests.[12] "Any dye, whether synthetic or natural, that is improperly applied will run, streak, rub off, or fade," Donna adds.

She has done a lot of heavy lifting, setting a chain of beneficial events in motion. To reduce the ecological and health damage synthetic dyes do on a global scale, though, it is neither pragmatic nor fair to put all of the responsibility on individuals like Donna, or to expect everyone to do our own dyeing at home. Though it may seem paradoxical, ease and convenience have a place in sustainable fashion, in that it can and should be easier and cheaper for people to do the right thing, in much the same way that energy efficient appliances and the pervasiveness of LEDs, Energy Star ratings, and low-flow toilets create far greater change than all of us trying to remember to turn florescent lightbulbs off. Likewise, we should be able to easily purchase naturally dyed clothing, which brands like Patagonia are at least beginning to offer.

Before Donna's natural indigo dye house can exist, however, we need enough plants to make the dye, and for that, to understand how to cultivate them at scale. The latter depends on learning about how the Ossabaw indigo behaves and thrives as a crop. Donna's vision is being carried forward, with more space and support, through the nonprofit she established (the International Center for Indigo Culture), and at the CREC Organic Research Farm. The farm began growing the Ossabaw Island indigo variety on one acre in 2015 and has grown it for three seasons so far. The first crop was planted organically in 2015, conventionally in 2016 and, in 2017, as an intercrop with sunflowers. After the sunflowers die and deteriorate, the indigo comes in and thrives till first frost. Conditions at the CREC site are similar to those on Ossabaw, though Ossabaw has slightly warmer temperatures. The CREC seeds indigo in mid- to late May at the earliest, either by broadcast or drilled seed methods.

What have three seasons and one acre at the CREC demonstrated about the Ossabaw indigo? A lot of things, according to Brian Ward. Heat treating the indigo seed in boiling water for about one minute increases the speed and rate of germination, but seeds germinate without it. The indigo likes well-drained, sandy loam soils, and can be harvested by hand or with a combine. The indigo does not reach the ten-foot height Donna achieved at her goat-manure-rich test site, but grows three to four feet high. In wet years, the Ossabaw indigo does not seem to produce nitrogen nodules (root nodules associated with nitrogen-fixing bacteria) very well, nor does it harbor disease or pest insects, but, instead, predators like ants and parasitic wasps. It competes well with weeds, is tolerant of preplant herbicides, and is drought tolerant and very hardy, surviving extremes like a weed.

Importantly, Brian and the CREC team have also come to understand challenges of commercial Ossabaw indigo cultivation, such as potential difficulties growing commercially under organic standards, considering weed mitigation and management cost against the expected price the crop might bring on the market. Experiments with intercropping, single herbicide applications, broadcast seeding, and letting the indigo become competitive with weeds have, so far, been part of figuring out how to make indigo succeed. At even larger scale, Brian says, the need for starter fertilizer, proper inoculants, and herbicides may need to be tested, as well as whether or not the plant volunteers from seed, making indigo a potential weed for successive crops. Further research is needed on whether or not the indigo may be a vector of disease, nematodes, and pest or beneficial insects.

In addition to cultivation lessons are those on how best to harvest the dye. Repeated harvesting with a tea combine may be a possibility, which is of special design and would allow multiple harvests per season. There may even be historical precedent for this method, as tea harvesters were used in the southern United States on tea plantations.

Closer to home, Fibershed was making strides on the cultivation and processing of that other indigo variety, *Persicaria tinctoria* (syn. *Polygonum tinctorium*) that thrives in Northern California and many other parts of North America. It's not a legume, like the Ossabaw indigo, but a member of the buckwheat family. *Polygonum tinctorium* has multiple varieties, such as "senbon," with red flowers and rounded leaves, and "kojoko," with white flowers and pointed leaves.[13]

I can't help but wonder if the farming effort required to grow more natural dyes might make it unsustainable, but then, the effort required would be driven by how much we consume. If we insist on buying multiple new pairs of jeans every year, changing the dye source alone cannot undo or offset all of the damage of that decision. Today, plant-based natural indigo makes up less than 1 percent of the indigo dye currently produced worldwide. If the world's total annual production of indigo dye was sourced from plants, rather than synthetics and other sources, it would require two million acres of cultivated land, roughly equivalent to the area of a square that is fifty-six miles per side.[14] And even naturally sourced indigo presents problems as an industrial-scale dye, not just in terms of the large amounts of land and water required to grow it, but the production of highly alkaline and dye-laden wastewater.

By contrast, the ideal indigo dye system envisioned by Fibershed has a closed loop, which moves from soil to dye to textiles and back to soil, and experiments are under way. As of early 2018, four Northern California farming operations are growing *Polygonum tinctorium*, all organically and some biodynamically, with others developing no-till organic methods as part of carbon farming strategies. Together, these farms can accumulate the critical quantity of dried indigo leaves needed for a successful compost pile.[15] When it comes to indigo, a compost pile is part of one type of dye extraction method.

The goal of dye extraction is pigment, with as great a purity and potency as possible. Extracting indican (blue) dye from indigo leaves with natural methods can happen in one of two ways, through either a water or sukumo extraction process. During water extraction, plants are submerged in water, then heated and/or fermented. This pulls the indigo precursor—the indican—out of the plant cells and into the solution. Indican's reaction with water causes it to split into two other compounds, indoxyl and a sugar. The spent plant material is separated and set aside, and the remaining, indoxyl-laden liquid is alkalized (given a basic pH) then oxidized (usually through aeration). This creates indigotin, an insoluble, dark, crystalline blue compound that is filtered, optionally rinsed, and dried to produce indigo powder. Once dry, this indigo pigment is compact, predictable, and shelf stable, with a higher indigo-tin purity than dye extracted through the sukumo method.

The sukumo method concentrates the indigo pigment by composting, rather than extracting, it. First, the indigo plants are harvested and dried. The dried leaves are separated and piled on a "compost pad," a constructed, multilayered floor that allows for good moisture drainage. The base layer of the floor is leveled rocks, then individual layers of sand, rice hulls, more sand, and clay, which is wet after it is spread. Once the floor sets, at least 450 pounds of dried indigo leaves are placed on it, the minimum required to create effective heat-retention and composting action. Piles can, in practice, weigh many thousands of pounds. Straw mats cover the indigo leaves, and it begins to decompose. The layered materials allow the indigo to breathe just enough to prevent rot.[16]

For one hundred days, the compost pile is carefully turned and mixed. Water and various amendments keep the compost pile biologically active, and over time, this process reduces the mass and volume of the leaves by roughly 75 percent, concentrating the indigo.

Both indigo powder (from the water-extraction method) and concentrated sukumo are chemically reduced in a dye bath, which converts them into a green-colored, water-soluble form known as leuco-indigo. This saturates textiles when they are dipped into the vat and, when they are removed and exposed to atmospheric oxygen, the leuco-indigo once again oxidizes to water-insoluble indigotin. The indigo pigment adheres to the fibers.

Fibershed studied both the water and sukumo extraction systems for technical and economic feasibility, and concluded that the sukumo system could produce about three times the quantity of pure indigo pigment—thirty-five times the dyeing capacity[17]—as water extraction, and much less expensively, too. The break-even price for indigo pigment from water extraction is about twenty-two times that of the compost process: $190 per pound for 40 percent pure pigment, compared with a significantly lower $7 per pound for indigo compost. The work is ongoing, but it's encouraging to see work on natural dyes at scale, and on the entire dye supply chain, not just on how they are sourced and applied.

A year and a half after Fibershed began growing and harvesting fresh indigo, composting it on a special clay floor for four months, and drying it into sukumo, Lani Estill starts an indigo vat with it at Warner

Mountain Weavers in the Surprise Valley, just up the road from her family's ranch. She adds potash liquid, bran mash, and lime to the sukumo in the vat, hoping to see some life in it after about ten days or so. She texts: "Going to stir it now. Feed cats, stir indigo. Twice a day." The vat begins to ferment and stink, and Rebecca reports this can last for the duration. Lani says they will put a bigger exhaust fan in the dye kitchen. Lani and Bonnie Chase, founder of Warner Mountain Weavers and Lani's business partner, record temperatures, how many pounds of fiber they dye, and how long the vat lasts. When folks in the community hear Lani has a dye vat going, they come to the store just to see it. Maybe that idea of dipping faded clothes or undyed yarn into a community vat, Japanese style, is not so far-fetched after all. New materials sprout new practices.

Sukumo indigo vat at Warner Mountain Weavers in Cedarville, California.

SIXTEEN

Slow Money

After nearly two years spent jumping over bureaucratic hurdles, Mendocino Wool & Fiber had achieved hard-won approval from the City of Ukiah Planning Commission to operate a wool mill. But it still needed money in order to turn a glorified garage and equipment that hadn't run in years into a functional mill. The building footprint had to be expanded and a foundation poured. The bathroom had to be installed, the scouring system built, and the sewage line upgraded. Wool is sensitive to static and humidity, so HVAC installation was paramount, as was high-voltage power for the equipment. To do all of this, and more, with proper permits, and in accordance with the earthquake- and wildfire-minded California Building Code, the Gilberts would need at least $250,000.

Small businesses in need of start-up capital typically have several ways to get it, and Mendocino Wool & Fiber was no exception. They could try to obtain small business loans from a bank or credit union; donations and loans from supportive people they know; donations from crowdfunding campaigns; and/or grants from municipal, federal, or private foundations. Each funding option had its pros and cons.

Because new, small businesses are considered particularly risky, bank loans carry a high interest rate (13.5 percent), even at a time when savings accounts earned almost no interest. A bank loan turned out not to be an option for the mill, anyway. The bank declined to lend, saying the venture was too risky, Matt and Sarah too unproven, collateral insufficient, and the capital investment too large.

Suitable grant programs took time to find and, when found, the mill did not always qualify as a recipient. Some grants, for example, were only for commodity producers: if the mill had also had a flock of sheep, or belonged to a co-op of wool producers, it would have qualified for certain types of USDA grants. But it did not, so it did not. Matt applied for a loan from the National Livestock Producers Association (NLPA) sheep and goat fund, but—during that particular application cycle—the sheep and goat fund didn't have enough funds.

And, though supportive people (like Kate, the mill's crowdfunders, and me) might be interested in investing in the mill, most people had no corresponding mechanism with which they could actually move their money off Wall Street and into businesses on their nearest Main Street. There was no way for someone to say, "I want 50 percent of my portfolio to be invested in small businesses in Northern California, where I live" and easily make it so.

Why? Largely because of US Securities and Exchange Commission (SEC) regulations, some of which date back to 1933 and are the result of the 1929 stock market crash and subsequent Great Depression. In order to invest in a small (implicitly riskier, according to the SEC) or new, unestablished business, a person or organization has to be what the SEC calls an "accredited investor." The full definition is lengthy and somewhat complex, but in short, an accredited investor can be a bank, insurance company, or nonprofit, but not an individual who isn't already wealthy. An individual must be a millionaire at least once over, and that's without including one's house in calculations of total net worth.[1]

If someone has at least a million dollars to their name, not counting their house(s), they can invest in whatever they want and the SEC won't try (or at least, is not required to try) to protect them from their own foolishness. That person is free to go ahead and lose as much money as they like, investing in stuff that's completely unvetted by anybody. If someone does not have at least million dollars, they're out of luck.

The spirit of the law is to protect people who can't afford it from being snookered and losing their life's savings (and possibly becoming dependent on social programs as a result) on less established, sound, or rigorous investments. Securities law believes it knows how to evaluate large, established corporations and more typical investments, setting aside, for the moment, all of those highly rated hedge funds and established investment firms that bilked their clients and caused the recent depression of 2007–2013. There are no equivalent mechanisms to evaluate small business quality. The easier "solution" is to bar non-wealthy folks from investing in small businesses, rather than find ways to evaluate and communicate the risk of investing in small businesses.

For their part, small businesses are not allowed to offer shares publicly, as large corporations do in initial public offerings (IPOs) of stock. If a small business wants to market its shares to the general public in order to raise capital, it either needs to go through a public listing process with the SEC, or all of its potential share buyers need to be accredited investors. The business must be able to find enough accredited investors to purchase all the shares it wants to sell. The people running that small business had better know, or have access to, a lot of millionaires.

Federal securities law felt a bit heavy-handed for a family-owned wool mill in a small city, yet the mill and its investors, incorporated in and citizens of the United States, were governed by it. But high interest rates and arcane regulations weren't the only reasons that the usual methods of raising capital didn't feel like the right fit for the mill. At a more basic level, there was a major mismatch between typical economic models and Mendocino Wool & Fiber, what it was trying to do, and what its supporters valued. Regulations embodied traditional business expectations and economic models, which did not take certain variables and values into consideration, much like the way modern textile production didn't take certain variables and values into consideration.

Most economists don't put a value on diversity of business, range of true consumer choice, availability of local infrastructure, or things they call "externalities" (polluted water and air; labor abuses; carbon emissions) because they do not want to count them. The two most efficient deliverers of goods in the United States (and possibly the world) at the time of this writing, for instance, are Walmart and Amazon. From an economic point of view these are the best retailers, all others exist in their shadows, and there is nothing particularly problematic about that. Barring monopoly and antitrust issues, most economic models put no value in having, say, a more urban, physical retail environment in dense neighborhoods. As a result, almost no one makes an economic argument for people to be able to invest in smaller, possibly less efficient, conceivably riskier businesses simply because people want those businesses to exist.

Let's say my neighbors and I were given two investment choices, in which we could make either 2 percent by investing in a local hardware store, or 3 percent by investing in Walmart. If we chose the local hardware store, opting to make a little less because we have motivations besides financial ones (sometimes we just really need to be able to walk a few blocks for one or two small things, without getting into the car in the Bay Area's nightmarish traffic), economists would say we were crazy. Economics doesn't take these kinds of human preferences into account, yet insists "the market" is a reflection of our choices, choices—like investing in a mill—that we don't actually have. A lot of people would choose to invest in the local hardware store or a wool mill if it were viable, even if it were not optimal.

Traditional economic and financial systems do not—and cannot—reflect these values because they do not include the people or the types of businesses who hold them. This fundamental disconnect between where people want to put their money and businesses that need money has driven the emergence of alternative models of raising capital and investing, many of them inspired by the philosophy of Slow Money.

The core tenets of Slow Money, to name just a few, hold that there is such a thing as companies that are too big, and finance that is too complex; that the twenty-first century will be the era of nurture capital, built around principles of carrying capacity, care of the commons, sense of place, and diversity; and that we must learn to invest as if food, farms, and fertility mattered, and connect investors to the places where they live. The success of investment models built on these ideals—like community supported agriculture (CSA) and microloans—has been helped along by online crowdfunding and social media tools, and indicates that people are hungry for alternative ways to grow their savings and communities.

It was in this daunting, yet enthusiastic, context that the Ukiah-based nonprofit Economic Development & Financing Corporation (EDFC) set out to create an ambitious direct public offering (DPO) in what they dubbed a social impact investment fund. A DPO is a type of crowdfunding called investment crowdfunding. This is a generic term that describes any offer and/or sale of an investment opportunity to the public, and in which anyone (both wealthy people and not) can invest. The entity raising the funds (EDFC) would offer the investment directly, without the middleman that an investment bank would use.[2]

In structuring and offering the DPO, EDFC acknowledged that it had been difficult for people to invest locally, that investors faced strict standards, and that social entrepreneurs struggled to access capital. The fact that EDFC wanted to connect entrepreneurs like the Gilberts with lots of folks like Kate and me, and that it might manage to do so both legally and on a large scale, was innovative and clever.

If they pulled it off, EDFC would create the first community-based DPO opportunity of its kind in the state of California. The DPO would embody the best things about Slow Money and similar movements: investing in a small business would be affordable and easy, with all the risk mitigation to make it safe for non-wealthy individuals; it would have all the right considerations for values, while providing the wool mill with capital on terms that would make money for investors. And it would do so without sacrificing the health of the business, community, environment, investors, and employees.

The idea of a DPO itself was not new. They've been around for a while. But some critical differences made this particular DPO unique, namely the fact that it was not being launched by a single business (like the mill itself) and was open to nonaccredited investors. Any California resident could invest a minimum of $1,000 up to a maximum of $2,500. Qualified investors could make larger investments, up to 10 percent of their net worth. Each investor would get a Social Impact Investment Note, similar to a stock certificate. EDFC advised that investors be able to afford to hold the investment for six years and base their decision to invest on the amount they were willing to lose.

The notes would pay 2 percent per year, simple interest, after two years, with principal returned at the end of six years. The mill loan interest paid by the Gilberts, in other words, would pay DPO investors a dividend of 2 percent after two years, which was the time allotted for the mill to become established and start earning money. A $10,000 investment, for example, would pay an investor $200 per year. For the first two years, while the mill got going, these payments would accrue ($400), and would then be paid out over the remaining four years, making the interest payments $200 per year.[3]

Conveniently, EDFC itself met the criteria of being an accredited investor. It was a certified nonprofit and community development financial institution.[4] It served as an intermediary lending partner to the USDA, providing financing to people who couldn't otherwise get it, primarily to small businesses. It also provided gap financing, incubated rural economic development projects and districts to diversify the economy, and coordinated economic development activity for Mendocino County. Since beginning operations in 1995, EDFC had built up an extensive history of local lending to small businesses, having disbursed—by 2013—forty-one loans totaling $2,792,715. Mendocino Wool & Fiber was hoping to obtain one of these business loans at a reasonable interest rate.

But even for EDFC, the idea of a community investment fund was new. Like other types of investment funds—mutual and money market funds, for example—an investment fund is a pool (because people pool money together to create it) of capital that belongs to numerous investors (to all of the individual and institutional investors who participate). The investment fund is used to collectively purchase securities while ensuring investors retain ownership and control of their own shares. A fund can be broad, like index funds that track companies that trade on the S&P 500, or it can be more narrowly focused, like a community investment fund that would initially invest in only a wool mill. With most investment funds, individual investors do not make decisions about how the fund's capital will be invested, and the DPO was no different: EDFC would decide how assets would be allocated and would continue to act as a fund manager. Down the road, EDFC hoped to support like-minded endeavors, like local meat processing and sustainable fishing businesses, from the same fund.

Further, the DPO was not created to provide loans to just any business, but explicitly to those deemed to be sustainable, and of social and community benefit, in addition to having sound business plans. EDFC had determined that Mendocino Wool & Fiber provided social and community benefit because many residents of Mendocino County kept sheep on their property to maintain agricultural use designations and zoning. Shearing cost money, and the wool producers could not derive any value from that cost. With the mill running, by contrast, the Gilberts would aggregate wool and other fibers, which were normally taken to the dump or sold for pennies on the dollar, and turn them into a value-added product within the region. Adding value to a natural resource in town, and providing economic benefit to the people who produced that resource, would be a nice departure from the usual way of things. Typically, natural resources (especially lumber from Mendocino County's rich redwood country) were extracted from the community in which they were produced and benefited not the producer, but people further down the line, in other places.

For the initial DPO, EDFC would direct funds raised to the Mendocino Wool & Fiber Mill in the form of a loan. If the DPO turned out to be successful, EDFC would offer more local investment opportunities for other businesses, via the same fund—a sort of revolving loan fund.[5] Over time, this revolving loan fund would build local infrastructure by the people, for the people, infrastructure that was not completely privatized.

The DPO sought to mitigate investment risk by matching investments with grant funding and portfolio insurance. This risk mitigation, beneficial for investors, might also translate to more delays in the mill obtaining its loan money, however. Even if the DPO hit its funding target, EDFC would still have to find and write grants to obtain that "backstop money" to prevent people from losing their investments. Those cycles could be very long, indeed, which created the possibility that the DPO might raise enough money, but be unable to disburse funds to the Gilberts right away, putting mill start-up on hold once more.

The Gilberts had hoped to have a loan in hand from EDFC by August 2014, but the DPO wasn't anywhere near ready. It was perhaps just as well, given how long it took for the mill to obtain city approval to operate in Ukiah. Six months later, though, on March 10, 2015, the DPO was approved and legal, and EDFC representative John Kuhry immediately got started fundraising. As a complete beta project, no one knew what to expect: Would the DPO actually reach its target investment? The $250,000 goal was substantial.

Like the idea of a Northern California wool mill itself, the DPO felt like a bit of a throwback, a barn raising more than anything else, with a palpable, mid-1800s-era spirit of "Wool mill opening up and shares available!" John Kuhry is the DPO front man, stumping for the wool mill and hoofing it to every conceivable venue and audience. John, sometimes accompanied by Sarah and Matt, speaks at community happy hours and dinners, at libraries and grange halls, to newspapers, public radio stations and podcasts, to church groups, Rotary Clubs, meetings of Slow Money chapters, and a Bioneers conference. I am exhausted just thinking of all the places he goes and the amount of speaking he does.

I was floored by how different fundraising was for technology start-ups, how my previous experience didn't apply, and by the onus of proof not only on Matt and Sarah, but on EDFC as well. I was astonished at the sheer amount of time they had to put into fundraising, because I was not prepared for the mill to have any difficulty in raising money. When I'd read Matt's business plan and his target of $250,000, I thought, "He needs less than a million dollars? Less than half a million? Great. This is kid stuff." That amount of money was literally nothing to well-heeled technology investors ($250,000 is perhaps two full-time salaries at most start-ups), yet it was everything for the mill, the foundation of a sustainable business, a family, and a community. Silicon Valley was chasing good money with bad: no investor or board had ever applied this amount of rigor to any company I had ever worked for.

This contrast troubled me not only because it was unfair, but because it signified a misallocation of capital driven by cultural values. Granted, the potential investor payoff for the wool mill was smaller than for some tech companies, but bias played a part. Let's face it: in the United States, we no longer think of manufacturing as something that people do. Saying "we're going to put some money together and start a factory" doesn't much happen anymore. If Matt and Sarah were, by contrast, in Shenzen, China, and wanted to start a wool mill, lenders might be circumspect but probably would not be openly hostile to the idea.

Putting capital in the hands of people who can use it effectively is, ostensibly, the fundamental purpose of capitalism. Indeed, misallocation of capital is one of the chief criticisms of communism—central planning doesn't allocate funds correctly. But, in the case of the mill, American capitalism was failing to be capitalist in its most essential way. This angered but also motivated me to promote the DPO in my techie-heavy social circles until I was blue in the face.

A few months after the DPO launched, money started to trickle in. John Kuhry reported that the DPO had $32,000 in hand and a total of $77,500 committed. He also had good news: members of the EDFC board of directors had been approved to invest some of their own money. Matt and Sarah spent several busy days helping EDFC ramp up publicity for the DPO. A professional video was made, featuring the Gilberts, their adorable children, and their very compelling story.

In September, we promoted the DPO to our crowdfunding donors, who had funded the down payment on the equipment, telling them how to get involved if they were California residents. By October, Matt figured the DPO was bringing in an average of $1,344 per day, which was not too shabby a pace: if sustained, the DPO would hit its $250,000 goal before the New Year.

The Gilberts continued the DPO road show with John, telling people about the mill and why Mendocino County needed it. We were all relieved that the DPO was running during the sheep shearing off-season rather than at its peak, which provides a major portion of Matt's earnings. John said he would start to prepare the loan paperwork when the DPO reached $225,000.

I invest in the DPO. I pester friends to invest, especially those I know have some extra money lying around, and love getting away to the wines and coast of Mendocino County. John, Matt, Sarah, and I attend another Fibershed Wool Symposium, where John and a colleague man a table in the busy entryway, talking to anyone who's remotely curious. Rebecca Burgess makes an announcement about the DPO, and members of Robin's Farm Club invest. One woman even invests $10,000.

The New Year rolls around and the mill has, more than six months into fundraising, not met its target. It is getting closer, though. As the February investment deadline looms, activity ramps up, substantially and rapidly. The deadline seems to create the necessary motivation, a now-or-never moment of decision. One person contacts to John to invest $50,000 in the DPO, pushing it well past the $250,000 mark and into $300,000 territory. By the close of the DPO, the social impact investment fund has raised $356,000. Of this, approximately $280,000 will find its way into loan paperwork to the Gilberts.

Then, after such promising community momentum, everything seemed to return to snail's pace. John reported that EDFC didn't want to release the loan paperwork and funds yet, because a grant EDFC had expected to get—one that would serve as a backstop to DPO investors losing money—did not come through. This meant EDFC would have to find other sources of grant money, apply for, and win them before the Gilberts could have the loan in hand and get the mill going.

I knew EDFC meant well, but felt perturbed. It wasn't that everyone wasn't incredibly grateful. Certainly, we were. But EDFC had raised $100,000 over and above the $250,000 target, and had done so on the basis of Matt and Sarah's story, their personal trustworthiness, and on Matt's reputation as a humane, skilled shearer and native son of Mendocino County. With $100,000 extra in hand, why couldn't the Gilberts have at least some of the money up front, so that they could get started building the mill while EDFC went out and raised the backstop money it needed?

Matt and I scheduled a conference call with John and asked for exactly that. Specifically, we requested a minimum of $100,000 to start, as $256,000 had been raised in addition to that, more than double the money that would be needed to bail out investors if the mill were to improbably fail in its earliest days. Matt tries to design scenarios in which the most critical construction work can begin with a diminished amount of money. He removes a French comb from the equipment list, assumes he can do more labor himself, and more. John is understanding, says the request is reasonable, and says he's willing to make a recommendation to the EDFC board that they loan the mill at least some money, as soon as possible.

The EDFC board is scheduled to meet on a weekday afternoon in mid-February. Matt, working hours away on a forestry contract, could not attend, nor could I. Sarah had to go it alone with kids in tow. I was on tenterhooks. And then, around 2 p.m., the phone rang: "I'm standing in the parking lot," Sarah said. "You won't believe this. I can hardly believe it. They're giving us all of it. All of it." And, just like that, the mill was fully funded.

Months later, in July, Matt received the loan check. More than a year had passed between the mill receiving planning commission approval and their having EDFC loan money in hand. Slow money is slow. But it had happened. Matt had once said to me, "Mendocino's motto, 'Wine, Waves, and Wilderness,' needs another W: wool. I want the sign to say 'Wine, Waves, Wilderness, and Wool' when I drive across the Mendocino County line." It just might. Mendocino County was getting a wool mill.

A few months later, without warning, I receive a check in the mail. It's my mill loan money back, with interest. It makes me feel blue, because it marks the end of a very special time. I console myself by deciding that this is money that needs to be out in the world, circulating, supporting fiber businesses. It will stay with me for a while, but only until it finds a new home.

Matt Gilbert with the mill equipment in Ukiah, California.

SEVENTEEN

Flock

Robin shears early each year, so her Februrary shearing date signals that the season is about to get busy. The off-season—during which I am supposed to stay in shape, but tend to knit, spin, and catch up on projects around the house—will return in July or August.

Joy, my first-ever shearing customer, is also the first person scheduled for the upcoming season. She will have top scheduling priority for as long as she wants me to shear for her, given what she put up with in my earliest days. Hers is a lovely, uneventful job as usual, everything set up in advance of my arrival, with clean, well-behaved sheep and a generous breakfast prepared by Joy's husband, Jon. Every year, I say that I do not expect them to feed me, just because they have in the past, and every year, they do.

Next on the roster, in the Bay Area suburb of Pinole, I have a particularly poignant shearing job. One year ago, a little ram lamb almost hadn't made it: Mr. Lonelyhearts, rejected by his mother, alone beneath a heat lamp in his red sweater, revived by Robin. Now named Bruce, he lives with Rachel, another Jacob sheep, at the home of Roy and Gynna Clemes. Unlike virtually all other sheep, Bruce does not run away when I approach the fence to set up my gear, and he lets me scratch him before shearing.

I flip Bruce over to shear him, pet his face, and tell him he sure has come a long way from a soup pot in the kitchen sink. I know they say sheep don't remember people, and I'm not convinced either way, but I have never had a sheep let me scratch his nose before and after shearing.

My calendar grows crowded. Every weekend, both days are booked solid with one shearing job or another. I take paid vacation days from my day job in order to take more shearing jobs on weekdays. Through word of mouth alone, I get more requests and refer work to Jordan, Matt, and other classmates that I can't take on myself. Just as I hit my stride, things go off-kilter.

At one job, I recall Jordan's words of wisdom. During a difficult shearing moment, Jordan once said, "Sometimes, a sheep lets you know how it's going to be sheared." Sometimes, for instance, you have to shear a three-hundred-pound ram on one side and roll him to the other, because you cannot handle either his weight or temperament well enough to shear him in traditional, proper position. Sometimes, you shear a tiny sheep on your knees because it's too far of a reach otherwise. And sometimes, a two-hundred-pound Jacob wether reverts, as he ages, to the ram behavior that was his birthright, stomping a front hoof the minute anyone approaches his pen, charging people and animals. I will shear him after a morning of lambing at Robin's, so his owner can have wizened Mr. Wether's last, gorgeous fleece before the butcher escorts him from this mortal coil. Just one sheep. No big deal.

Soaked with sour, acidic afterbirth, blood, urine, manure, and sweat, I leave Robin's and drive a few miles down the road. Mr. Wether does indeed stomp and snort like he's ready to run the streets of Pamplona, so I sit beside him on the other side of the pen fence while I set up my portable shearing handpiece. Sometimes, sheep calm down as they become accustomed to me. It's worth trying. After a short while, I climb into the pen and grab a segment of livestock gate, carrying it before me like a shield in case he charges. I'll use it to create a mini pen inside the larger one.

"Shearing" is a generous term for what ensues. I manage to tip and flip Mr. Wether three times, but awkwardly, using all of my power to do it. Turning his jaw over his shoulder does not induce him to sit or do anything besides stiffen. He is so round that, with my left hand holding his jaw, I can barely reach my right arm around to his right front foreleg. When I do, I am practically lying on his back, my torso and left cheek embedded in his wool, my head directly in back of his horns. This is not a smart place to be: Mr. Wether has only to tilt his head back to send a long Jacob horn into my eye.

Eventually, I flip Mr. Wether three more times and muscle him into proper position once, where—at long last—he settles. I shear his belly wool off and observe what I am dealing with: long, thick wool, lanolin gummy with dirt, more like soft wax than loose oil. Dust sandblasts my face as my shears kick it up from Mr. Wether's fleece. "Free dermabrasion," I quip. I regret not having eye protection.

My portable shears barely make headway, leaving track marks in the wool and a centimeter and more of wool on the sheep's body. I push the handpiece just to get it to move. Normally, I "let the shears float," as Gary instructed, guiding them as the motor propels, but it doesn't work. From this day forward, I will bring my full-sized motor and drop along, even for one or two sheep. I could use that motor's power right now.

I apply copious amounts of oil to the handpiece, combs, and cutter, to no avail. I only have thirteen- and twenty-tooth combs with me, and would try a nine-tooth one if I had it. Fewer teeth means more space between them, so the comb grabs more wool. I decide to adjust the comb and cutter, the only other thing I know to do. Regretfully, I have to let go of Mr. Wether while I do so: I need both hands on my equipment. I lower the comb to set the cutter farther forward, so it will cut the wool sooner than later. This increases the risk of cutting the sheep but ultimately, it does not matter. I absolutely bury the tip of the comb in the wool, right against the sheep's skin, and the shears still slog along and leave wool in their wake.

Mr. Wether is not keen on being flipped again after his brief taste of upright freedom, so his owner suggests I shear him on a halter, which has worked well in the past. I have never sheared a sheep this way, but adapt what I remember from shearing a few goats on milking stands. I begin at the top of his tail and head straight up his spine, shearing toward his neck. Next, I shear in horizontal stripes down each side, and downward to clean up Mr. Wether's neck and the tops of his legs. Who knew it would be trickier to shear a sheep standing than turned over? Once you have to break with bodily memory, no prior experience really exists. On the bright side, the amount of wool left on Mr. Wether means the rest of his flock still recognizes him upon his return, and he appears to have stopped charging them.

From arrival to finish, I spend over two hours shearing one sheep. A fine performance. I want to disappear in shame. The owner does, at least, seem genuinely happy to have Mr. Wether's fleece and a clean, calmer animal. I refuse payment, the best I can think to do for the "service" I've provided. When I reach my car, I realize that—for the first time in years—I have forgotten clean clothes. I am livid, my brain a string of invectives: a whole day of lambing and shearing, and I have to sit in fetid, soiled clothes for at least two more hours, in traffic on I-80, the only highway back from the mountains, choked with weekenders and brake lights.

I turn on the heated seat for my back muscles, tap my own brakes, and wonder what I am playing at. I am maybe, sort of, a shearer. I have sheared several dozen sheep that weigh as much or more than I do, but not this much more. I want, so much, the upper body strength of a two-hundred-pound man who has sheared for fifteen to twenty years. I've been working on it, lifting weights, doing yoga and push-ups, but Mr. Wether proves how distant and elusive my goals are. My size and weight are no excuse, though: I should make up for both with technique, finesse, a better understanding of physics. Maybe I need a martial arts training, the kind that focuses on resistance, using your own weight and that of your opponent.

I tell myself to buck up and be grateful, that this is exactly what I wanted. My willingness to do anything to get shearing jobs has worked. Gratitude mitigates some exhaustion but does not make it sustainable. Some hours are so much longer than others.

Two months later, it's a Saturday in mid-May. Matt Gilbert has a two-day shearing job at the farm of Sally Fox in the Capay Valley, and Ian and I are headed out to help, a way to banish Ian's residual work stress and help a friend. I will move sheep, remove devil's claws from their wool (a sharp plant the size of an adult hand with pointy ends that stick in wool like armor, causing shearing strife), and hand the sheep to Matt. Ian will retrieve fleeces from the floor and run them over to the skirting table, where a small group of folks remove vegetable matter and cut burrs out with scissors. Sally has a lot of helpers, because she is active and well-known in fiber circles for her organic, biodynamic operation of wool, colored cotton, Sonora wheat, and carbon-centric soil practices. Shearing-school classmates are on hand to help out, for free, just to be part of it. Kristine Vejar and her team from

Verb will help skirt fleeces and get their first look at the local wool that will become Pioneer yarn.

Like me, Matt has sheared sheep all week. We have no fresh energy, only bodies in agony upon waking. Matt has a new baby at home, a cold, and over 130 sheep to shear. As the day wears on, Matt asks if I want to shear a few times. I say no. I do not want to shear a Merino sheep, because I do not believe I'm ready to.

Technically, the label "Merino" designates a family of fine wool sheep breeds, not just one. For centuries, Merino sheep—which produce the finest wool—were considered so valuable that exporting them from Spain was a crime punishable by death. All Merino sheep belonged to either the King of Spain or to his royal relations throughout Europe and were selectively given as special diplomatic gifts to other rulers in Europe. Before the War of 1812 between the United States and Britain, a British embargo on wool and wool clothing exports created a "Merino Craze." Diplomat William Jarvis, appointed by Thomas Jefferson as US Consul in Portugal, imported approximately thirty-five hundred Merino sheep to the US between 1809 and 1811, through Portugal.[1]

Bred for so long to produce so much wool, Merino today exhibit the consequences of human-centric choices. Their dense wool grows long, pulling on their thin, delicate skin. Merino also have excess skin, the greater the area on which to grow wool. This includes a big wrinkle down their necks that is difficult not to cut, one reason Merino warrant a distinct shearing pattern. I have never sheared one and have no plans or desire to do so.

Matt crosses the seventy-sheep mark and asks, again, if I want to shear. It is blisteringly hot, the hottest part of the day, and he looks so tired. I feel obligated to shear a few so Matt can take a break, and ensure the job still finishes on time. No one else can serve as relief shearer, and I have my equipment. If I can help and choose not to, isn't that patently wrong? None of this, of course, mitigates my Merino terror in the slightest.

I take pity. Nervous, I set up my equipment and tie on my shearing slippers. Sally announces, "Oh, Stephany's going to shear!" Observers gather round, all fiber ladies, my fellow knitters and spinners. I flip a sheep, position it, take deep breaths, and tug my handpiece on. I remind myself of what Robert Irwin has said, trying to find courage: "Sometimes you've just got to go for it. Shear like you mean it." I do, and on the first stroke, which runs from the sheep's brisket down the belly, I nick a vein. I yell for Matt, who immediately sees what has happened. "I'm not doing this," I say and hand him the sheep and my handpiece.

"It's not that bad," he says, stopping up the cut with a sheared piece of wool while he finishes shearing. Drops of bright, almost orange-red blood pepper our plywood. I think I may pass out, with the blood, in this heat, but I did this. I have to try to fix it. I run to my car for the supplies that, in three years, I have never opened and hoped not to: unwaxed dental floss, blood-stop powder, and a curved, sterile veterinary needle. Matt finishes shearing the sheep and lays her on her side, so we can get a good look at the cut. We kneel on loose soil beside the shearing floor, one of us on either side of the sheep.

We can see past the blood-soaked wool, and the cut is not a large one, shorter than a thumbnail. I nicked the vein's surface, but it is, mercifully, otherwise intact. I pile clotting powder on and we watch, bated breath, bent over the sheep, faces inches from the sheep's body. The blood clots somewhat but not enough: We see drops of breakthrough bleeding. "We have to stitch it," I say. Matt nods.

A small crowd presses in on us, and I can scarcely breathe. Sally is totally calm, and gracious besides. She asks what she can do to help us and, thankfully, tells the onlookers, "Okay, okay, let's give them some space. They do not need all of us staring at them right now." And, to set an example, even though it's her sheep we're working on, she walks away. Everyone follows.

I hold the sheep down and pinch the wound together, while Matt—more experienced and, I can tell, feeling responsible—baseball stitches it together. "I'm sorry, girl," I whisper. "I am so sorry." She breathes heavily but shows no other signs of stress: no jaw grinding, no attempts to escape. The bleeding slows. When Matt finishes the stitches, I apply clotting powder on top. We watch for all of it to work and, when it does, lift our hands. The sheep stands, shakes it off, and trots out to pasture, rejoining the flock.

Matt and I are covered in blood: hands, wrists, forearms, the tails of our shirts and tops of our pants. Post-emergency, stress hormones surge. Light-headed, I waver as I stand. My husband reaches out, rubs both of my shoulders, and says he now knows what it is for color to fall from someone's face. I hear his words but cannot speak: if I open my mouth, I think I will throw up, cry, or both.

Sally approaches, and I apologize over and over. If a vet is needed, I will pay for all of it. If, God forbid, the sheep dies, I will buy another one, no matter what a Merino costs. She just shakes her head. Sally has brought Matt and I jars of cold orange juice and says she's going to watch to make sure I drink mine. Rubbing my arm, she asks what she can do for me. I would feel better if she screamed at me, better still if she hit me, because that is what I deserve.

Matt and I empty our juice jars. He returns to shearing, I to picking out devil's claws and throwing sheep. Cara Randall, whom I met at shearing school a couple of weeks ago, and her partner, Cricket Frerking, are especially sweet to me for the rest of the day. I wipe tears away with grimy gloves, hand Matt a sheep, and ready another. I must keep working but fear the sheep will bleed out in pasture. Distracted, I keep looking out to the adjacent field, trying to find her, willing her not to be lying on her side in the dust. Blood smeared across her belly, so I can tell which sheep it is. But, when my eyes find her, nothing is dripping out of her. She is standing up and grazing like normal.

At the end of the day, Sally tells every worker that she maintains an open tab at a bar and restaurant down the road, one that "makes its own barbecue sauce and has a heck of a beer list." Even if she can't go out to eat herself, Sally ensures all of her helpers have as much food and beer as they want, on her dime. I am tempted until she says that she and her daughter will join the rest of us. I do not want to face them and everyone else at dinner. I want to crawl into a pit in the woods. I change clothes for our drive home.

Ian and I bid everyone farewell, and Sally says "No! Oh, no! I really want you to come. You both worked all day!" I figure I should do whatever she wants. I owe her that much. Ian and I are admittedly starving after ten hours of work on an excruciatingly hot day.

The restaurant has plenty of outdoor seating, always key since no one wants to stink up a place. Our large group takes up two long picnic tables pushed together. Tough, competent, bright Alexis, from shearing school, is sitting at the table behind us with her husband and some friends. I say a weak hello but dread the fact she'll overhear conversation about what happened. Now she'll know, and maybe word will get around. No one will hire me again.

Worse, Sally sits down right beside me, on my left. She can tell I'm still upset. When our beers arrive, she turns to me and says, for the whole table to hear, "Look, accidents happen. Bad things happen when you absolutely don't mean for them to. I know. Believe me, I know." And right there, in front of everyone, she—famous steward of the fabulous Merino flock—tells us what happened when she got her first sheep.

> I paid for six, so I could incorporate sheep into this farm that I wanted to go biodynamic with, which requires livestock. Six sheep seemed fine to learn on. But when I went to pick them up, the people managing the ranch informed me, in tears, that all the sheep not taken that afternoon were going to slaughter the next day. So they shoved thirty of their favorite sheep into my horse trailer. Thirty sheep in a two-horse slant trailer! Then, in a matter of just three days, all the ewes started having lambs. I had no idea I was buying pregnant ewes.

That admission widens eyes over beer pints. Sally once could not recognize a pregnant sheep?

> In a few days, it seemed like I had dead lambs everywhere. I had four rejected lambs in the trailer with me, that I was trying to bottle feed. I was not sure how to do it and I utterly failed. They all died. There were many stillborn lambs that I found as well. The ewes were lambing on pasture, and I'd heard sheep were hardy, that you don't want to interfere with birth too much, so I left them there. And a lot of the lambs died.

Sally locks eyes with me, left hand resting on her full pint glass. "Merino are terrible mothers, it turns out. And I had no idea. Why would you think that about a sheep? I had a field of dead lambs. We all have accidents. We all make mistakes. I've made big ones."

The next day, though it is Sunday evening and I am aware of my rudeness, I am also distraught. I call Ralph McWilliams in Montana, who sold me my drop and handpiece. Near tears, I tell him about the Merino the previous day, that I've never done anything like this before and it absolutely cannot happen again. I've made Ralph into an emergency shearing call center because I do not know who else I can call.

"All right, well, now that's an accident," he says, level. "Now, tell me what kind of combs you have." I do. We discuss technique, comb width, bevel, and splay. "Ah," Ralph says. "What you've got there could be a bit much, especially for fine wool sheep. Don't need that for them." He suggests a good, general purpose comb, 10mm narrower, medium bevel, no splay. When my combs arrive, I practice setting them up on my handpiece over, and over, and over.

Monday morning, I am back in the office, my work wardrobe more limited by the month. My shoulders no longer fit very well in my tailored shirts. They fit everywhere else, and some places better, just not in the shoulders. Sunburnt, exhausted, still dehydrated, I ease into the day with excess coffee and community kitchen cereal, one of few employees present at 9:30 a.m.

I review bug fixes all morning, making sure new code behaves as it should, unable to care as much about it as the land, animals, and families I'd met over the weekend. The wrongheaded waste of mainstream economic values contrasts with a world in which nothing—neither water, nor food scraps, and certainly not time—is wasted. Here, I feel surrounded with the wasted physical energy of young, capable people set into chairs: wasted brain energy, intelligent people with advanced degrees tweaking pixels on mobile ads rather than addressing climate change, energy independence, or doing some anti-terrorism hacking.

I am paid so much for doing what is comparably so little, all of it ephemeral. In a year or two, the mobile device the company has spent years and millions of dollars to build will be obsolete, as if it never existed. Irrelevance hides in the word "iteration," a positive sheen to iterating work away, rather than building a foundation for future beings. None of us are creating a foundation for the health of a flock, soil, or people.

I bike seven miles home, most of it uphill, my favorite part of the day as frustration subsides in physical effort. I have a too-brief conversation with my husband and shove food into my face before an evening of calls with the Taipei office begins at 7 p.m., where it is 11 a.m. the following day.

My 10 p.m. meeting begins with a male colleague in California passing off my work as his. Despite the fact that I am present, he points people to a technical document I wrote, every word obviously mine per the document history viewable by all. He had less than nothing to do with it. My screen alights with instant messages from other colleagues, all of whom are men, in the same meeting: "Isn't that your stuff?" they ask. "Yes," I type back. "And why are you asking me, not him?"

I point out that the work is mine and ask why he's showing it as part of his weekly progress report. He has the gall to say, "Don't interrupt me," as if his behavior were not the problem, so much as the fact that I am asking about it. No one else, including the people who sent me private messages, chimes in with supportive statements like "Yeah, that work is hers." This is in stark contrast to my respectful shearing customers. They are so good to me, better than I deserve. They never fail to thank me, tip me, feed me, or send thank-you emails and happy sheep photos. A gal can get used to that sort of treatment. I am.

Recently, a fairly senior fellow announced he is leaving the company. He is intelligent, diplomatic, professional, decent, and hardworking, so his absence will be felt. In his last week of work, he tells my boss that every man on our team makes $70,000 to $100,000 more per year than we do. We are the only women on our team.

I don't know what it is about this specific, numerical bit of information, but as soon as I hear it, a switch flips. I am done, well and truly done. That gap is an astronomical loss of savings, security, economic opportunity. Every five years, each man has $500,000 more in his pockets than I, millions of dollars more over the course of his career. The gulf has grown too wide.

I confront the human resources department, though I know it is foolhardy, an exercise in futility: HR exists to help and defend the company, never employees. We agree, at least, that I have a better track record on the job than anyone else, seniority, advanced degrees, and the company is grateful that I am doing the jobs of what used to be four people, in addition to the one for which I was originally hired, all without a raise.

I point out that I have spent 2.5 calendar years on my current project but, in terms of actual hours (which I assiduously log), it's actually over 3.5 working years. I have completed an extra year of work for free, enabled by the absolute racket that is salaried employment. Unfazed, HR says they've frozen even regularly scheduled, paltry cost-of-living adjustments, company wide, and so of course cannot entertain anything else, including "level setting."

In twenty years of doing this work, it has only gotten worse. This, of course, I knew. But someone else quantifying just how much less I am worth, and management standing by it, pushes me. If I must make $100,000 less per year, then I may as well make it in a lot less time, with a lot less grief, out in the great wide open.

Memorial Day weekend rolls around one week later. I have scheduled several shearing jobs, but have also decided to give myself one real, very necessary holiday on Memorial Day itself. Rather than take two shearing jobs on the holiday, I scheduled them for the following day, preferring to take another vacation day away from work instead.

The weekend kicks off with a job in the Napa Valley, a short drive from Tim's house, where Ian and I will stay that weekend. It's my third consecutive year shearing this particular flock. I arrive to find the elderly gentleman of the household jogging down the long, sloping driveway, waving his arms. I roll my window down and he leans on my car door, out of breath. "Some things is changed since last year," he says, removing his ball cap to wipe his brow.

"I see that!" I reply. "The place looks great. New livestock area, fencing, more space for the sheep—"

He cuts me off. "No, some things around back. But I can explain!" He waves me on and walks up the drive as I slowly follow behind. I park in back of the house and notice him looking rather sheepish, hands in his pockets, standing beside a picnic table. On it sit a small US flag and Confederate flag, side by side. My customer explains that some "city people" recently purchased the rural property next door as a part-time residence. They promptly commenced complaining about the "noise" from my customer's tiny flock of usually silent sheep, which they claim they can magically hear even while inside their house, half an acre or so away.

"So," my customer continues, "I thought about how best to piss off some people from San Francisco. Memorial Day coming, I got a Confederate flag and put that up, but only where they can see it. And my friend's a policeman, so I had him bring me one of his targets from practice, and I put that up behind the flag." So he had. A bullet-riddled outline was posted to the tree behind the picnic tables bearing the flags. "So they's the only ones that can see it, but then you were coming, and we all realized 'That gal from San Francisco's going to pull around back and see it!' so I came down the driveway and told you."

At this consideration, I laugh so much I give myself hiccups. I contribute some additional suggestions during shearing breaks: "Garden signs about using GMO seeds will go over well. Maybe attach a hose to a wine barrel and put a 'glyphosate' sign on it."

My shearing life has grown too big to fit with a traditional job. Working seven days a week for six months no longer works. Depleted, I spend my Memorial Day holiday planted in a chair on Tim's front porch, accompanied by a carafe of coffee. Circulating between the chair, hammock, and kitchen mark the height of my exertion.

I have a video chat with Terri Shoemaker, an old friend and former colleague from our days working in food banking in Chicago. A few months ago, Terri and her husband left their jobs to do their own thing, and I ask for her advice about the same. We discuss finances and logistics frankly, the nitty-gritty of how she and her husband are making it work: health insurance, taxes, finding contract work, managing context switching, and working at home.

I tell Terri I feel guilty: leaving my job at this juncture was not part of the plan. Ian left his job just two weeks ago, and I am supposed to keep the stable salary and health insurance while he transitions to self-employment, consider my leap later. It feels like a bait and switch, even if Ian himself doesn't feel this way. Indeed, happily ensconced on the greener side of the fence, he encourages me to quit: "There are all these things I want to do, like go on a road trip, that I don't want to do alone."

He reminds me we have savings and, given our anti-consumerist tendencies and affinity for home cooking and haircuts, really do not spend much money. We do not have kids, which reduces our costs, but I also consider the Gilberts. "There's six of them," I say to Ian, "and they live life on their own terms." In one conversation about food costs, Sarah told me they spend less than the food stamp allowance for the entire family.

I summarize spreadsheet calculations and spending trends with Terri. Shearing alone covers our food bills and utilities, and that is on a part-time basis. The difference we'd have to make up with other work (or more shearing work), shrinks, becomes doable. And, for the first time in our lives, we have an affordable alternative to $1,800/month COBRA health insurance (which lasts only one year, anyway): the Covered California state exchange, created as part of the Affordable Care Act (ACA). I look at the site and find a $635/month plan. Three months of Covered California or one month of COBRA? No contest.

Terri has multiple sclerosis and, from one day to the next, does not know when it will get worse. "My advice? Shear as many sheep as you can, while your body can do it," she says. "Get in as many good shearing years as you can." That, above all else, hits home. Given our situation and discussion, Terri can't understand why I wouldn't leave. She thinks I need to pick a day to give notice, and makes me commit to her that I will. "Okay," I say. "I'll do it tomorrow." June 11 will be my last day in the office and, Lord willing, any office. Having choices is the greatest luxury there is. If I finally have the ability to make a different choice, yet don't, then I am permitting my own suffering.

The day after Memorial Day, I drive winding Highway 29 after a hot day of shearing. I mentally construct the portable shearing rig I plan to make that evening in the garage, a copy of one Jordan designed and uses. Many shearing sites have no place to which I can mount my shearing motor, which has a bracket designed to hang on a typical two-by-four beam or post. I often lose an hour jerry-rigging risky setups, lashing my motor to round, rotted, and wiggling fence posts, or setting it on a flock owner's truck bed, the sheep sliding beneath the tailgate.

Jordan solved this problem by screwing two two-by-four boards together lengthwise, one slightly offset from the other. This creates a long, solid post that, with cinch straps, can be secured to just about anything at the correct height. The motor can be mounted to the end of the board. Building a similar rig will reduce my setup time, increase safety for all involved, and enable me to shear more comfortably, in proper position.

I pull into the short gravel driveway of Tim's 1920s, pale gray, white-trimmed bungalow and step onto the front porch. Ian reads a book while Tim naps in the hammock, right in front of a long redwood board, bound to the corner porch post with a red cinch strap. "You made it?" I ask, as it dawns on me. "You made my rig!" Ian smiles, retrieves the motor from the car, and hangs it. "Now you can relax after dinner, not work in the garage," he says. Our voices awaken Tim, who smiles.

The craftsmanship and clever details make it obvious an architect and engineer collaborated. Rather than use two full boards, Ian and Tim constructed a three-sided box from a wooden wine crate. Screwed to the top end of the board, the box creates a fitted nook in which my bracket rests perfectly. They've also made a bottom board to accompany the top

Sheep make their way toward Robert Irwin's shearing trailer at Sears Point Raceway.

one, with black tension dials to secure both boards together if needed. I am so touched by their perfect, thoughtful gift.

The following week, I am shearing in Robert's trailer at the Sonoma Raceway, still known as Sears Point to locals, the name of the land mass that bears its 2.5 miles of hilly track. At the edge of San Pablo Bay, over the sound of distant NASCAR engines, sheep reduce wildfire risk as they graze the raceway's 720 grassy acres. It is strange to see the San Francisco skyline from my spot in the shearing trailer, fog flowing through the Golden Gate toward Berkeley and El Cerrito. Peruvian shepherds use rattle paddles to move the sheep toward the trailer and push their tails to get them to walk up the ramp into the chute. There is no Porta-Potty, so I have to pee in the eucalyptus grove, but I don't mind. Most woods are cleaner than the average public restroom, anyway.

I learn to just keep going, to not stop and rest, to grab another sheep. Resting too long between sheep makes shearing harder, not easier: you get cold and lose your flow. I'm getting better. I can tell. I'm shearing cleanly and close, proceeding nick-free, finishing faster than I used to, leaving less wool in my usual spots, preventing the sheep from escaping more often than not. I grab another sheep, and another.

On the second day at the raceway, something clicks: my hand becomes one with my handpiece. It is difficult to explain, but mesmerizing and dangerous: I catch myself forgetting that this very sharp, furiously fast handpiece is not my hand, that I need to keep my distance. Later, I tell my husband how beautiful "she" really is: at some point that day, the handpiece became "she," like a ship or a plane, though I refrain from actually naming her. I ask that my handpiece be buried with me.

Robert turns a rock 'n' roll station on, sings along to Bruce Springsteen, and we all bop our butts to the beat while bent over sheep. I shear two sheep during Led Zeppelin's "Kashmir," which, granted, is almost nine minutes long, and the sheep have no belly wool to remove, but that's still four minutes per sheep, a personal best. "Don't get too excited," Robert says. "We're only making a few bucks a head. Don't quit your day job." "I already did," I reply. "My last day at work is less than one week away."

Robert pulls his handpiece off, sends a sheep out the chute, and looks at me, hard. Biting the inside of his cheek, he crosses his arms and shakes his head. "This?!" I say. "This is what I get from the man who lived in his truck to be able to work with sheep, and his wife, too?"

"I can't argue with that," Robert says. Then he points his finger at me and says, "You don't come from sheep, but you have sheep in your veins. The majority of the industry would say you have to be born in it, but I think you're born with it whether you're born with the sheep or not."

Two Years Later

Mid-February, 2017, eastbound on Interstate 80, I am two hours late with hours to go, the first time I will arrive late to a shearing job, provided I arrive at all. This drive, to Winnemucca, Nevada—basin and range, rock hounding, rodeo, and opal mines—usually takes six hours, but all bets are off in the snow and rain that has broken California's long drought. Snow has piled too high for many ski lifts to run, and rain has deposited vast flash lakes smack-dab in the middle of desert. Kayakers paddle across the Black Rock Desert where Burning Man is held.

An hour ago, approaching Sacramento, I crossed the silvery brown chop of the flooded Yolo Bypass, filled nearly to spilling, waves licking the guardrails. The bypass is 16,538 feet long and more than twice as wide as the Mississippi River at its widest point (7,600 feet) in New Orleans. The water has wreaked havoc on my shearing schedule, soaking sheep that did not reach barns in time, creating one rain date after another.

I ascend the Sierra foothills and floodplain becomes woodland. Narrow ribbons of forest hint at once-thick stands of sycamore, walnut, alder, and oak trees, now restricted to patches between reservoirs, lakes, and levees. I cannot see past water management infrastructure to what were rivers, wetlands, vernal pools. The road rises, and I see foothill pine, no inkling of the blizzard a few thousand feet above.

The Coast Range and Sierra Nevadas push moisture-laden air, fresh from the Pacific Ocean, upward. Their west-facing slopes are wet, pounded with rain and snow they push higher, while the east side of the ridgeline lies in rain shadow, dry and arid. The higher the altitude to which the mountains can force the air, the greater the precipitation. And that is exactly what is happening: the temperature on my dashboard drops as elevation rises, another inch of snow on the hood with each passing minute. Delicate flurries at 5,200 feet become worrisome at 6,000.

The light dims, sun vanishes, and clouds rest on treetops. It's quiet. My ears pop. The pressure change is not only from elevation; it's barometric, the storm you feel in your bones. A digital Caltrans sign flashes orange letters: CHANGEABLE WEATHER AHEAD — CHAINS. Roadside motels, too, sport neon signs that say CHAINS in addition to VACANCY. I pull into one rare, open, and plowed gas station to put brand-new, expensive snow chains on my front tires.

Local economies have sprouted beside chain checkpoints, impromptu service stations busy with men in snowsuits, flanked by hand-stenciled sandwich board signs: Chains On/Off—$15. Semis—$25. I wish I'd known. I'd gladly trade $15 to have saved forty-five minutes on icy ground, slashing my chapped hands inside my tight wheel well. At least they'll be covered in lanolin the rest of the week.

I feel anxious, impatient in the chain-check line. The storm bears down in the rearview mirror, flecks of white snow backed by dark, charcoal sky. Waved through, I proceed up the steep eastern approach to Donner Pass, 7,227 feet elevation, one lane open in each direction. As I crest the ridgeline the situation reverses: the temperature climbs as elevation signs show lower numbers, though snowfall remains heavy.

I'm still driving on ice when, after a paltry few miles of use, one snow chain snaps, a thwack, thwack, thwack with each rotation. I pull into an RV park before the chain wraps itself around the axle, an ideal spot given its gas station, restroom, and solid building that sells cocoa and chili. If necessary, I can sleep here. I have a tent, two sleeping bags, ample woolen goods, extra water, some food. A few weeks ago, headed to backcountry snowshoeing, some friends teased me about these excessive preparations. "You will never need all of that," they laughed. "I-80 never closes." I can see the other side of I-80 and the Caltrans sign that says it is closed westbound. But I can still go east, if I can leave.

I pull on my rain pants and lie down on the ground to inspect the chain. The short, broken end got sucked into the wheel's center bore, through a hole in the plate. I mess with it, further cutting my hands, but can't free it. If I remove the tire, the broken chain will drop out of the hole. I practically excavate the car but cannot find a jack. "Run-flat tires," Ian texts. "There isn't any of that stuff in there." Modern short-sightedness strikes again.

"It's gonna be a while," says the local tow service. "Truckee is completely shut down. Nobody's going anywhere. Even the train's not running. Avalanche risk."

I text Sarah Gilbert who, with the rest of her family, reached Winnemucca yesterday and is currently working at the eleven acres of Cole and Katie Estill, Lani Estill's son and his wife. It will be a work party, a field trip, if only I can get there. Sarah offers to retrieve me in the Gilberts' 4x4 truck, from three hours east. "No! Stay!" I type back. "Do not drive into this." This is my fault, bringing a Mini Cooper convertible into the Sierra in winter, and I prefer to keep it my problem.

I scrambled a small crew together after three scheduled shearers called Cole to say they couldn't make it from California, for reasons now abundantly clear. Discussing the job by phone, Cole said, sternly, "I don't want anyone who's rough on my ewes." We have not yet met, but I've seen photos of him corkscrewing through the air, boot heels higher than his head, fringed turquoise chaps sailing. Cole is a true buckaroo, the 2015 champion of the Silver State Stampede, the oldest rodeo in Nevada and a classic. Competitors ride in their everyday working stock saddles. The Stampede features saddle bronc riding, what it means to "ride the rough string," saddle horses that buck every time they are saddled.

I buy a hot cocoa and thaw inside the shop, cheered by the very conditions that may strand me. The weather has a certain rightness: California needs snow, which is our drinking water. The weather takes its own time and upset and cussing do not change it. Like a trailer in mud, I'll be stuck or I won't, for however long.

The tow guy calls. "Where exactly are you again?" I describe the RV park. "I just pulled away from there. I'll turn around." Minutes later, he removes my wheel, the chain falls out, and I pay and tip him nearly all the cash I have. Because of this roadside savior, I am not stuck in Truckee for the sixty-one inches of snow that fall in the next thirty-six hours.

I descend to Nevada flatland with its ragged rock, racing streams, and dry pavement, nary a flurry, the desert oblivious to the paralyzing storm in the low notch in the mountains behind me. A handful of distant wild mustangs trot into the foothills, clouds of breath hanging in the air.

Segments of this stretch of I-80 were once the Oregon and California Trails. "Hubris," the wind whispers through rusted, Nevada-shaped, historic markers of wagon train routes. "Hubris."

I arrive in Winnemucca five hours late, well after 3 p.m., the shearing nearly done for the day. Cole and Katie's property sits on the edge of town, tidy, pointy-tipped acreage beside scrub sage, mountains to the west and south, and some shorter ones to the north, giving Winnemucca its own basin. I park in front of a livestock gate that marks a tree-lined, two-track, muddy driveway. It separates a several-thousand-square-foot barn and holding paddocks on the left from a cute, single-story, early 1960s house with a big tree in the fenced front yard on the right. It's a pretty patch.

A couple of hundred sheep huddle toward the barn and their flock mates inside. I unchain the gate and, alert to herding and guardian dogs, walk toward the telltale sound of a wool baler and into welcome reunion. Inside the barn, Sarah Gilbert, Lani Estill, and Ian McKenzie rapidly skirt fleeces at a long, slatted table. "You made it!" Sarah says, giving me a hug. "Finally decided to show up to work, eh?" Ian winks, dropping fleeces into a pile in front of the baling machine. He rotates between the skirting table, the wool piles, and the baling machine, sharing fleece observations as lessons: which of these fleeces are tender, and how to tell; which fleeces are finer than the rest and why that may be.

Below the skirting table, Gregory, eighteen months old, tiptoes on accumulated wool that has drifted down from above. He reaches toward the table slats, giggling and trying to catch second cuts before they land. Two older boys, about seven or eight years old, run and hurl themselves into wool piles, divided by wood pallets stood on end. Who can blame them? Each pile marks a different wool grade given by Ian McKenzie: the largest pile is the main line; others hold shorter, longer, finer, or coarser wool, relative to the main line.

Two shorter beings hit me with thigh-level hugs from behind, nearly knocking me off my feet: Felicity and Chloe Gilbert. "My favorites! Are you working hard?" They nod, solemn. "Well, I am working hard," Felicity, older by two years, says. With a pointed, sidelong glance at Chloe, she adds, "Other people are climbing on wool bales and getting shoe marks on them, even though mom said not to. Rebekah is reading or something."

"I'm right here!" Rebekah hollers. Her head pops up from inside a wool bag, where she stomps wool with her feet, a copy of *Black Beauty* peeking out. "Hi! Are you okay?" Felicity returns to her perch on a pen gate over the sheep, her cowboy boots gently prodding sheep tails toward the shearing floor. "She won't let me move the sheep!" Chloe explains, in her defense. "Do you like my boots? Are you going to eat dinner with us? Are you cold? I'm a little cold, but not too cold."

I pinch wool staples from the skirting table and tug at them. It's white, crimpy, springy, gorgeous Rambouillet, very fine, with a micron count in the high teens or low twenties. It's not too long but long enough for mill equipment, at least three inches. Not bad, considering Cole sheared less than a year ago. "Cole sure grows nice wool," I say to Lani. "He does," she says, laughing. "Some of it might be finer than mine!"

In the center of the barn, livestock gates form an oval sheep pen occupied by several dozen ewes. The right side of it flows into Felicity's chute, where sheep stand nose to tail, single file. The shearing floor setup is unusual but clever and resourceful, optimized for what the barn layout allows. John Thomsen, whom I met at shearing school, shears at a station separate from the rest, alongside the sheep chute. The rest of the shearers—Matt Gilbert; my shearing instructor, Gary Vorderbruggen; and a few guys I don't recognize—have stations along three sides of a narrow, rectangular shearing floor. Matt's station is on the long left side of the rectangle, near John at the end of the sheep chute. Cole's neighbor from across the road occupies the short end of the rectangle, nearest Matt, while Gary and two more guys share the long side opposite Matt. The last short side is open, human entrance and sheep exit. Tight quarters: the shearing floor is full, with very little space between shearers. It's easy to knock into a sheep, shearer, or handpiece if you don't mind your surroundings.

Wiping his head with a towel, Gary hobbles off the floor, his free arm outstretched for a hug. "Ah, I love this gal! My ankle's acting up. You okay? How's your car? I'm only shearing today, can't stay all week. Hope I can get back home." We hug.

"Car's okay. Lucky you live in Auburn, you might make that with 4WD. How are Trudi and Ely?" Trudi is Gary's daughter, and Ely is Gary's baby granddaughter. I see a tear in his eye at the sound of their names: "Aww heck, you know. Perfect," he says. "Perfect and beautiful."

Rambouillet sheep exiting the barn after shearing at Cole Estill's ranch in Winnemucca, Nevada.

It's easy to guess who Cole is, weathered brown cowboy hat, blue eyes, and impressively groomed red handlebar mustache. He acknowledges me with a nod and quick tip of his hat, says "Cole," shakes my hand, and is off and running to the next job to be done.

I guide sheep off the shearing floor, run fleeces to the skirting table, and sweep. Shearing is not the only skilled labor in a wool shed: wool handling, too, is a competition-level event. Picking up a fleece properly, in seconds, requires a precise style, as does throwing it onto the skirting table. As each shearer finishes, I run up to the fleece, the neck area landing against my ankles. First, I need to find the hind legs of the fleece, almost always hidden beneath the rest of the wool and farthest from my feet. While squatting on my ankles, I spread the fleece out to detangle it, but not much: the fleece must stay in one piece, and I have to gather it quickly. Five other fleeces are coming off at the same time, and you never want to hear a shearer call "Wool away!" because you're slow.

Once I find the hind legs, I reach for them, remove the dirtiest shank wool, and leave it on the floor to be swept away. My thumbs and index fingers pinch the center back section and—accumulating wool in my hands the whole time, never letting go—three fingers on each hand (middle, ring, and pinkie) hold the sides in as I roll the fleece toward me. Just before rising from my crouched position, I swoop my arms over the sides of the fleece, wrapping and lifting it as one big ball, a grand version of putting the seam beneath a loaf of bread I'm baking, rounding the smooth side of the bread out. A properly lifted fleece looks similar, the shape of a domed, sourdough boule.

I run the fleece to the skirting table and fling it out from the bottom, flicking my wrists forward and upward at the same time, without letting go. I carried the fleece sheared (skin) side up but, properly unfurled, all eight to fifteen pounds flip to land sheared side down, enabling any second cuts to fall through the skirting table slats to the floor. I finish holding the first part of the fleece I grabbed—the rear legs—now in front of me, not farthest away.

Six fleeces hit the floor every few minutes, sometimes simultaneously. I crouch, toss dirty shank wool aside, pinch the center back and hind legs in, roll, swoop, pick up, run, hurl and unfurl, run back, crouch, and grab again. It keeps me warm.

Gregory likes to help me throw fleeces. Sarah lifts him and he lays his hands on the fleece, watching my every move to throw his arms into the air exactly when I do, dissolving into pure baby glee when the five- and six-foot-long fleeces fly forward. At one point, racing back and forth, I forget to include him in a fleece toss. Gregory is crushed: a tear slips out and he walks away, glaring. I apologize but he crosses his arms, turns his back, and looks over his left shoulder, just once, before turning away again. "He really means it!" I say to Sarah. "Oh, he is the master of holding a grudge," she replies. "He absolutely breaks your heart."

It's dark when I get my first look at Winnemucca's Americana charm, a few sagging gold rush relics and many more midcentury modern, kitschy casinos, surprisingly casual and friendly, a far cry from their garish counterparts elsewhere in Nevada. There's the Red Bull Chuck Wagon Restaurant, complete with red wagon stencil; the Star Broiler, its pastel, vertical stripes and asterisk-shaped lights wrapping a corner; and unassuming casinos like the Sun Dance, one story and one entrance, a rodeo mural and movie-theater style marquee: Bar. Slots. Snack Bar.

One block off the main drag, I check into the quiet, quaint Town House Motel, L-shaped, crisply whitewashed with sharp green trim, the proprietors' home the rooms behind the office. Sheep statues occupy a patch of grass set in the motel sidewalk outside my door. My room is immaculate and cozy, the double layer of window draperies a welcome bulwark against winter.

I wash up and layer on woolens before Lani pulls up and drives us to the Martin Hotel, which houses a Basque restaurant. Opened sometime between 1898 and 1908, it has catered to sheepherders and stockmen ever since, their home when they weren't living in tents in the hills, sheep and a dog for company. It's a pointy-roofed, white stucco house on a corner, opposite the railroad stop. A second-story porch with a widow's walk railing forms a sidewalk colonnade, and holds flagpoles bearing the Basque, United States, and Nevada state flags, flapping and cracking in the wind. The Martin's luminous windows make the whole place look as warm as a woodstove.

Lani and I take a seat at the bar. "You've got to get Picon punch," she says, and orders two from the bartender. I have no idea what that is, but I will drink it. "It has its own glass," Lani adds, as our drinks—looking like oil-slicked, iced black coffees with orange twists—slide across the bar. The glass, an inverted hand bell with three cut ovals around its low stem, looks too delicate for this bar and all of Nevada. "There's real Picon and there's the other stuff," Lani explains. "Picon punch is made with a liqueur, Amaro, and a brandy splash on top. The real picon, Amer Picon, is made in France and nearly impossible to get in the United States."

I sip my blissfully stiff drink among photos of sheepherding scenes and rodeos, and admire wall-mounted saddles, all an homage to the immigrant Basque labor that made the sheep industry in Nevada and California and, of course, The Martin as well.[1] At least two million sheep grazed the Nevada Sierras in the hundred years between the gold rush and the end of World War II, the heyday of migrant Basque sheepherding. Young Basque men came to work Nevada's gold, silver, iron, and opal mines, but found better lives raising sheep and selling the meat to the mines. They trailed flocks long distances between lowland winter and high-ground summer pastures, a journey Lani's sheep still make with herders, ninety miles out and back every year.

Lani and I move to the dining room, where several long community tables bear carafes filled with red wine. I am stuffed from family-style dishes, including an unexpectedly delicious favorite, warm beans on salad, before our lamb dinners even arrive. Lani reports exciting textile developments. In the fall, in time for peak Christmas shopping season, The North Face will release the Cali Beanie, a 100 percent domestically made ski hat knit from Lani's climate-beneficial wool. Significantly, The North Face will feature her land practices as the product story, the hang tag and website using this language:

> This premium wool was sourced in partnership with Fibershed from Bare Ranch, which raises sheep using carbon farming practices that not only sequester more carbon dioxide than the ranch emits but also improve soil health. Bare Ranch's carbon farming practices are expected to sequester 4,000 metric tons of carbon dioxide each year. This amount of sequestered carbon dioxide is equivalent to offsetting the emissions from about 850 passenger vehicles a year. We believe that a hyper-local, climate conscious approach to sheep ranching can reshape our relationship with our land.[2]

It's a tremendous accomplishment for Lani and her family's work, and a fresh, welcome move from a major clothing manufacturer, not only in terms of sourcing but of how we think and speak about our clothes. Mainstream retailers don't often wish to call attention to a product's true origins or trace finished garments back to the land. The North Face Cali Beanie shows there is a chance to do things differently even at mainstream levels, and boosts my hopes for other choices the textile industry can make.

The next morning, a few inches of fresh snow on the ground, I find the Gilberts parked beneath the shelter of a pole barn at Cole's. Sarah boils water for coffee on a two-burner camp stove, the truck bed a countertop, the kids piled in blankets in the back seat, groggy. I head for the slightly warmer barn and hear small, steady bleats. In a side pen beneath a heat lamp, I find two tiny lambs, hours old, Cole's first of the year. I reach down and scratch their foreheads, and one nuzzles my palm.

Gaps between barn boards split winter sunlight into pale beams across the shearing floor and, in one of them, something glimmers, like dewdrops on a spider web. I walk closer to find a threaded, curved veterinary needle dangling from unwaxed dental floss, draped over the beam above Cole's shearing station. The needle is clean. Cole has not needed it, but has threaded and hung it anyway, responsible. In the worst case, he will not fumble for first aid while trying to keep hold of a sheep. It is so sweet, sincere, considerate, a shepherd's love and care embodied.

For the next two days, our crew of eighteen or so shears, runs, throws, skirts, grades, labels, and bales fleeces. The sheep seem to multiply as collective exhaustion mounts. Every day, Lani cooks and serves lunch for all of us. We fill Cole's kitchen and living room, sprawl on his floor with soaked paper plates of lamb roast, salad, bread, and mugs of hot coffee.

Thursday's work is longer by about two hours, but the sheep started on Monday are finished. Back at The Martin for dinner that night, the Gilberts and I decide to head home the next morning, immediately after breakfast. The forecast predicts a brief window between snowstorms and, if we don't take it, we will not get home until early the next week. We plan to caravan the whole way so that, if anything happens to either party, everyone has help and no one is stuck.

The Martin's wood-paneled walls reflect soft light from frosted glass chandeliers and double wall sconces, and the red table wine is rich and bright. Outside, the opaque, black night is lit only by downcast lamplights beside the railroad track, the moon a barely visible, waning crescent. Cole mentioned bringing in more sheep and is out there working, still, on horseback in 20 degrees Fahrenheit, wind whipping coarse snow across the flatlands. He won't enter his own warm house for another hour or two, after 9 p.m. And, to my shame, I am glad it's not me, so deeply do I not want to be out in the merciless winter night. It's not rodeo that makes Cole a cowboy as much as the fact that he is out there and we are in here and relieved for it, hot food coming. People often ask when I will get my own sheep. When I am willing to work half as hard for them as Cole, I think.

Friday breaks sunny, clear, and dry, and I meet the Gilberts at their hotel. It is Felicity's birthday, and she wishes for snow. "Don't you want to wish for anything else? Anything?" I ask. Felicity laughs and shakes her head. As we head into the Sierra foothills, passage appears clear: no signs alert us to chain check, no AM radio notices flash. Minutes later, though, we see snow, bumper-to-bumper cars, and my car has zero traction, smoothly sliding up an incline, right toward the line of stopped cars. There's no place to go, only a partial shoulder, not recently plowed. Reflexively, I tap the brakes and steer, over and over, until I stop, beached on a low snowbank.

I exit, stand, and look around. In the three days since I passed through, the plowed snow walls have grown to over two stories tall. The hotels that hawked chains are buried, utterly, nary a tall sign or chimney sticking out. The impromptu chain-check service areas have vanished.

In eight hours we move forty-one miles. The Gilberts' truck needs a jump and we repair my breaking snow chains three times, using my hoof trimmers to cut baling wire that holds my used shearing cutters, then pinching the baling wire to tie the chains together. After eleven hours on the road, we recover at the Black Bear Diner in Auburn with coffee and dinner, singing happy birthday to Felicity over dessert, who is completely unfazed at having spent it this way. Three hours later, I'm home.

Mid-October, eastbound on Interstate 80, I pull over to watch the raging Atlas Fire from a McDonald's parking lot atop a low hill. I watch which way the wind blows and evaluate whether it is wise to keep driving. One hour ago, a glowing, golden ember landed in our San Francisco street as I opened the garage door to drive to Robin's. Highways 37 and 12 evidenced evacuation during the Monday morning commute.

The fire's speed and behavior are staggering. It must be moving at one hundred miles per hour: the cars on I-80, where eighty miles per hour is standard, appear in slow motion by comparison. The flames themselves are twenty feet high, parallel with the ground but seemingly not on it, blown west in a horizontal stripe clear up in the air. If the wind shifts, the fire will cross the ridgeline and tear down into the eastern valley, toward Robin's farm and Mr. Wether's flock.

I continue east. The radio news is bad and getting worse; the announcer cannot keep up. Fires are everywhere, many simultaneous starts already spread over one hundred miles, driven by Diablo winds clocking in at over sixty miles per hour. Hundreds of acres burn in minutes. I cannot wrap my head around this: One acre is, roughly, the size of one football field, or two and a half city blocks. The equivalent of fifty city blocks incinerated in minutes, over and over? For how many days?

My phone explodes with messages. The Sears Point Raceway surrounds are burning. Don, who owns and shepherds the flock that Robert Irwin and I sheared there, reports, "The road heading up to the yards is blocked by at least six downed trees and, on the other side (Stephany's bathroom), the fire crew has been cutting the trees down for safety." No eucalyptus grove for me, then.

Ralph McWilliams writes: "How are things going down there? Looks tougher than hell. Hopefully you're out of the fire zone. Have you heard anything about Robert Irwin? Don't want to bother him, probably busier than a one-legged man in an ass-kicking contest." Even in this situation, especially in this situation, Ralph's words make me smile. It is Jaime Irwin, however, eight months pregnant with her second baby, who is evacuating hundreds of ewes from vineyards they graze, the same we've sheared in.

The radio reporter speaks the word "Partrick" and I bang the steering wheel in frustration, fear, and grief: a whole fire is named for the road Mary's ranch is on, where the mushroom dye class was held, where I've since done shearing demonstrations for interested knitters. You do not want a fire named for your road when there are not many places on that road, and your ranch is much of what is there. I hope that her cattle and sheep grazing will help, that her decades of pasture management and shepherding work will somehow be able to stand up to this. I think of the dry forest around her pastures, of singed owl wings and horses seeking creek beds.

Unfortunately, the next fire announced is also named for a too-familiar road: Tubbs Lane, practically the backyard of one shearing customer and one mile from Tim's house, the backyard where Ian and I were married, where his mother's ashes are buried. Cal Fire is trying to keep the fire in the hills above town and out of the valley, so Mount Saint Helena is burning. Ian's father and his wife, Leslie, have packed the car, and we feel lucky for that: the fires are burning so fast that many people did not get this chance, had to drive for their lives, taking nothing.

How can almost every flock and place I have ever sheared be threatened at the same time when they are thirty, sixty, one hundred miles away from each other? How can an entire region burn in hours?

The reporter says Potter Valley is "an inferno" and "a war zone," and I call Marie. Two months ago, Marie, her husband, and her flock of Ouessant moved to their own home on two acres in Potter Valley. They and the sheep are evacuating to her in-laws' in Red Bluff, 153 miles away, because every other place folks might go is also burning. Where do you go when everywhere is burning and the roads are closed? Where can you get to?

The names of fires change as they grow in size and geography: the Potter Valley and Redwood Valley fires spread and merge, become the Mendocino and Lake Complex fires, named for whole counties. I mentally walk the valleys and count Matt Gilbert's many customers, the Gilberts' many neighbors, and the monastery where they worship, all uncomfortably close to Hopland and shearing school.

A dozen fires storm for weeks, until the end of October. The Redwood Valley fire takes 36,523 acres, the Nuns Fire 56,556. The Atlas, the nascent fire I watched from the parking lot, takes 51,624 acres, the Tubbs Fire 36,807, including a huge swath of Santa Rosa, mile after mile and 2,800 homes, gone. But the scale does not hit until we can visit Tim and Leslie, add drive time to geographic area, and comprehend the devastation in experiential terms. Ian and I drive for forty-five minutes, in fire wreckage the entire time, disoriented. Solitary brick chimneys, burnt and melted trucks, cement slab footprints behind the occasional subdivision sign that signifies a magnitude of loss. Churches and homes burnt but vegetable gardens spared, the collards, kale, and brussels sprout stalks tall. Green leaves push out above blackened bark, and Ian wonders aloud how many trees will live, in the end.

In mid-November, the sixth annual Fibershed Wool Symposium is held in Point Reyes Station; it's the first time many of us see each other since the fires. The Gilberts' pickup truck pulls up, towing a small livestock trailer with four sheep from a local fairground evacuation site, wildfire rescues for Matt's shearing demonstration. The sheep are not the only thing in the trailer: Sarah pulls out two plastic, lidded bins, and Matt sets two tall, bright red cylinders on the ground, their ends capped with garbage bags.

"Wait," I say, as it dawns on me. "Those are mill canisters." Matt removes the garbage bags to reveal neat, even coils of roving, smooth and constant as can be. "You lied!" I say, wiping away tears. "So much for 'The machines are not working!'"

"Gotcha!" Matt grins, and points to a white coil. "This one is from Cole's," he says. He lifts that coil away and points to another: "And this one is from the Irwins' flock."

Sarah and Matt Gilbert show the roving they've made at their mill, Mendocino Wool & Fiber, at the Fibershed Wool Symposium in Point Reyes Station, California.

Marie joins us as we admire the coils of roving and reports she, her husband Christian, and the Ouessant are back home in Potter Valley. The ewes move between their own two acres in Potter Valley and a couple of hundred acres at the Oak Granary, while ten wethers are sheep for hire who will make a spring grazing tour through Mark West Springs, Healdsburg, Sebastopol, and maybe Petaluma. The rams mostly stay at home or at the Oak Granary, or sometimes mow grass as a favor to Marie and Christian's neighbors. And, happily, Marie is having yarn made from some of those delectable Ouessant fleeces.

The symposium is an emotional one, full of long hugs, choked-up voices, and stories of how grazing helped save ranches and pastures. Vendors apologize for not having much (or any) yarn to sell this year, because it smells too strongly of smoke. "I'd buy it," comes the usual response. "I'll wash it later, anyway." I want yarn that smells of smoke. Smoke is our terroir this year, the story and taste of our place, of people wrapping bandanas over their faces and running into burning vineyards to fill livestock trailers, of our beloved Cal Fire and first responders saving town after town without rest or relief. The grapes and their wine will taste of smoke, and so should our sweaters, relics of collective loss, fight, and survival, a testament to the supply chain still gathered today. All the pieces to create the regional wardrobe Rebecca Burgess sought out years ago are here, charred, shocked, and grieving though they may be.

A few weeks later, Ian and I head up to the Gilberts' with three fleeces for test processing at the mill: a Merino fleece that Matt sheared at Sally Fox's; a Jacob fleece of Robin Lynde's that John Sanchez sheared; and a fleece I sheared from one of the Irwin's Corriedales.

We find the mill's Western façade painted rich butter yellow, with deep red trim and bright white doors. It has a smooth, clean concrete floor; long, narrow, windows high off the ground for light and ventilation; and ample canned lights overhead. A center wall divides the mill into two rooms: the main carding and spinning room we enter through the front door and, to its right, a smaller room with a computer, loom, and roving and woven scarves stacked on a table. A door at the back leads into a small drying room, where clean fleeces dry on a cleverly constructed drying rack. Sarah and Matt have slid wire shelves into a large, wardrobe style cabinet, like stacks of baking sheets on restaurant racks, and inserted a small ceiling fan in its top.

The drying room leads into the scouring room, with an industrial, stainless-steel sink below a long window that looks onto the Gilberts' backyard and trees. One side door leads from the scouring room to the outside yard and the other back to the main room, past the ADA bathroom my father-in-law whipped up, and to the carding machine. The carder is secured in a wire mesh cage to prevent injury from its sharp, grinding metal teeth. A metal feed table passes wool into the carder and, at its rear, the carder feeds into the pin drafter, which makes carded wool into roving of even width. A large skirting table sits between the carder and the yarn spinner, the only piece of equipment not yet operable.

The equipment needs retooling and tweaking: the carder does not always process wool evenly or thickly enough, sometimes leaves noils, which look like pills on a sweater. It's disappointing and frustrating for the Gilberts, but nuanced processes take time to get right, especially when you're learning from scratch and the equipment sold to you isn't exactly what the broker promised.

Sarah and I shake my fleeces from their bags and onto the skirting table. Each fleece gets a notecard, with my name, the date, and the sheep breed, farm origin, and fleece condition, as if it were the most normal thing in the world. It might be, if not for the grins on our faces.

Five days into 2018, rain streams steadily through fog as I push north on Highway 101. I meet Jordan at a Sonoma County dairy, our second time shearing on this site, to open another shearing season. He and his partner moved to Grants Pass, Oregon, a little over a year ago, to acreage on the Rogue River with some sheep and cows of their own. Happily for me, Jordan often returns to California to shear sheep and hunt rats.

Two friendly guardian dogs push their heads under my hands and escort me between ceiling-high hay bales to the rear of the barn, where I find Jordan smiling, squirting oil into his handpiece beside a pen of brown and white spotted ewes, due to lamb in a month from the looks of them. "How do you do, Miss Steph?" he asks. "Good to see you. We got 132 or so, plus a few lambs and meat sheep, mostly Friesian ewes."

"I'm all right. Good to see you, too. You ready?" I ask.

"You know me, I was born ready. You?"

I lean on the pen gate to peruse the huddled, wary ewes, and smile. "The only thing better than the last sheep is the first sheep."

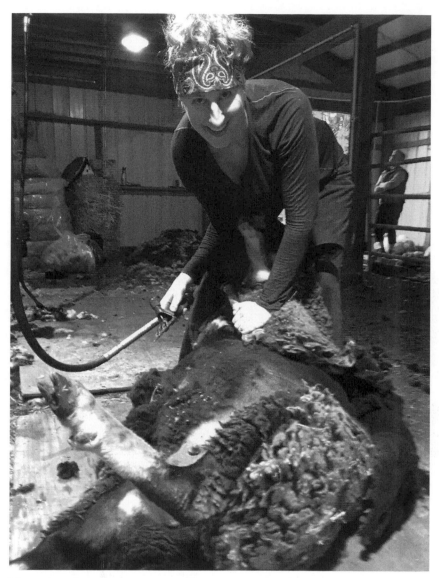

The author shears a very pregnant Friesian ewe in Petaluma, California, January 2018. Mary Pettis-Sarley in background. Photo by Jordan Reed.

Notes

Epigraph
* Accessed January 2016, https://archive.org/stream/
  americanwoolinteoolawrrich#page/2/mode/2up.

Chapter 1
1 National Agricultural Statistics Service, USDA, Sheep and Goats, January
   31, 2014, http://usda.mannlib.cornell.edu/usda/nass/SheeGoat//2010s/2014/
   SheeGoat-01-31-2014.pdf.
2 Michaela D. Platzer. "U.S. Textile Manufacturing and the Trans-Pacific
   Partnership Negotiations." October 5, 2012. Page 7. http://fpc.state.gov/docu-
   ments/organization/199399.pdf.
3 This figure was arrived at as follows: 2,600,000 pounds divided by 450 pounds
   (which is the average weight of a standard wool bale in the United States) is
   5,777 bales. Bale dimensions are 70cm (27.6 in.) × 70cm (27.6 in.) x 98 cm (38.6
   in.) long. Each bale is approximately 12 cubic feet. The volume of a 45-foot
   semi-trailer would be the product of V=(45)(8.5)(9) and expressed in cubic
   feet, so (45)(8.5)(9)=3,442.5 cubic feet of usable area for a 45-foot trailer. For a
   53-foot trailer, the volume would be the product of V=(53)(8.5)(9), so (53)(8.5)
   (9)=4,054.5 cubic feet of usable area. This means that 5,777 bales x 12 cubic feet
   per bale = 69,324/3,442.5 = 20 semi-trailer loads of the 45-foot size.
4 Amber Bieg et al., *Fibershed Feasibility Study for a California Wool Mill* (San
   Geronimo, CA: Fibershed, 2014) http://www.fibershed.com/wp-content/
   uploads/2014/01/Wool-Mill-Feasibility-Study-Feb2014.pdf.
5 Rebecca Burgess, accessed January 16, 2015, www.fibershed.com/about.
6 E. J. W. Barber, *Prehistoric Textiles: The Development of Cloth in the Neolithic
   and Bronze Ages with Special Reference to the Aegean* (Princeton, NJ: Princeton
   University Press, 1993).
7 Juliet Clutton-Brock, *A Natural History of Domesticated Mammals* (Cambridge:
   Cambridge University Press, 1999), 75.
8 Ibid.
9 "Lanolin," Wikipedia, accessed January 16, 2015, https://en.wikipedia.org/wiki/
   Lanolin.

Chapter 2

1 Nonpopulation Census Schedules for California, 1850-1880. Microfilm. The Bancroft Library, University of California, Berkeley.

Chapter 3

1 National Agricultural Statistics Service, USDA, Overview of the United States Sheep and Goat Industry, August 9, 2011, https://usda.mannlib.cornell.edu/ MannUsda/viewDocumentInfo.do?documentID=1760.

2 Phil Mercer, "The Decline of the Aussie Sheep Shearer," BBC News Online, July 28, 2004, http://news.bbc.co.uk/2/hi/asia-pacific/3932999.stm.

3 "Synthetic Fiber," Wikipedia, accessed January 26, 2015, https://en.wikipedia. org/wiki/Synthetic_fiber.

4 Edwin C. Voorhies and Robert W. Rudd, *Circular 399: Sheep and Wool Situation in California, 1950*. California Agricultural Experiment Station, The College of Agriculture, University of California, Berkeley.

5 *Changes in the Sheep Industry in the United States: Making the Transition from Tradition* (Washington, DC: The National Academies Press, 2008), 259.

6 "Uruguay Round," Wikipedia, accessed January 27, 2015, https://e.wikipedia. org/wiki/Uruguay_Round.

7 Changes in the Sheep Industry in the United States: Making the Transition from Tradition. (Washington, DC: The National Academies Press, 2008), 259.

8 "Agreement Establishing the World Trade Organization: Agreement on Textiles and Clothing," Organization of the American States (OAS), http:// www.sice.oas.org/Trade/ur_round/UR15AE.asp.

9 *Changes in the Sheep Industry in the United States: Making the Transition from Tradition* (Washington, DC: The National Academies Press, 2008), 260.

10 Jackie Jones. *Shifts in US Merchandise Trade, 2014: Textiles and Apparel.* Investigation No. 332-345, Publication 4536 (June 2015), US International Trade Commission, https://www.usitc.gov/research_and_analysis/trade_shifts_2014/ textiles_and_apparel.htm.

11 Ibid.

12 Judy Malone, "Convention Continues Work to 'Grow Our Flock,'" http:// www.sheepusa.org/NewsMedia_SheepIndustryNews_PastIssues_2012_ March2012_ConventionContinuesWorkTogrowOurFlock.

13 Combed top is clean wool fiber prepared for spinning into yarn. All short fibers, noils, and vegetable matter have been removed, and the wool fibers combed parallel to one another. Most thin yarns that are woven into fabric are spun from combed top.

14 "Microfibers," Beachapedia, accessed April 9, 2016, http://www.beachapedia. org/Microfibers.

Chapter 4

1   Matthew B. Crawford, *Shop Class as Soulcraft: An Inquiry into the Value of Work* (New York: Penguin Books, 2009).

Chapter 5

1   "What Are Heritage Breeds?" Episode #2, Heritage Breeds Podcast, Livestock Conservancy, accessed June 6, 2015, at http://heritagebreeds. org/2-what-are-heritage-breeds/.

Chapter 6

1   "Time to go, Stephanie." Meridian Jacobs, June 15, 2013, http://www.meridian-jacobs.wordpress.com/2013/06/15/time-to-go-stephanie/.
2   Carol Ekarius and Deborah Robson, *The Fleece and Fiber Sourcebook: More Than 200 Fibers, from Animal to Spun Yarn* (North Adams, MA: Storey Publishing, 2011), 271.
3   Ibid.
4   Helen Swartz, "Treatment and Control of Coccidia in Sheep," accessed May 30, 2015, http://www.case-agworld.com/cAw.LUcocc.html.

Chapter 7

1   John Hittell, *The Commerce and Industries of the Pacific Coast of North America* (San Francisco: A.L. Bancroft & Co, 1882).
2   Ibid.
3   "Our Wool Market: The Effects of the Wilson Tariff," *San Francisco Chronicle*. September 14, 1894. Note: The Wilson-Gorman Tariff reduced the wool tariff (on imports) to $0 and established a federal income tax of 2 percent to offset the loss of funds from reducing or stopping certain import tariffs.
4   "Wool Rail Rate Raise Protested," *San Francisco Chronicle*, September 26, 1923.
5   "An Opportunity for San Francisco," *San Francisco Chronicle*, November 22, 1897.
6   Claude Petty, "John S. Hittell and the Gospel of California," *Pacific Historical Review* 24 (1955): 1–16, doi: 10.2307/3635227.
7   John Hittell, *The Commerce and Industries of the Pacific Coast of North America* (San Francisco: A.L. Bancroft & Co, 1882), 440–441. According to Hittell, the Pioneer Mills absorbed the Mission Mills, hence the combined name. Hittell states that the Mission was started in 1859 and maintained as a separate enterprise for fourteen years, until 1873.
8   Ibid., 44.

9   "Woolen Mills Chinatown," Chinese Historical & Cultural Project, accessed April 19, 2016, http://chcp.org/virtual-museum-library/woolen-mills-chinatown/.

10 "What Is Roving?" Craftsy, July 2014, http://www.craftsy.com/blog/2014/07/what-is-roving/. Note: Batts are fibers that have been processed on a drum carder. A drum carder looks like a gigantic, round hairbrush with a handle on its side. The handle is manually or mechanically turned to push fibers through, in order to have them brushed and blended. Wool batts are usually sold by the pound, and are used in spinning, felting, and quilting; to make mattress pads; and to stuff comforters and pillows.

11 This estimate is for a post-skirting, preprocessing weight. The size of a fleece depends on numerous factors, including the size of the sheep (the body area covered by wool); the density of fibers; the breed (some breeds grow more wool, faster); and the staple length (the length of a wool fiber from the sheep's skin to the tip of the fiber, which grows outward from the body). Staple length alone depends on numerous factors, like climate conditions, quantity and quantity of available nutrition, whether the sheep is sick, stressed, or healthy, and so on. For example, a smaller sheep (i.e., with small frame, and around 80 pounds of weight) of a breed that produces shorter (three to four inches in length) and/or less dense wool will produce a smaller fleece than will a large-framed sheep (150–250 pounds) with a longer-staple fleece (five to seven inches in length) and/or denser fleece. Fleece weight can be deceptive: when freshly sheared from the sheep, fleece is full of lanolin (a heavy oil) and vegetable matter (hay, straw, dirt, and so on), so the weight of a washed fleece is quite a bit lighter than a raw, unprocessed one "in the grease." When all's said and done, though, a typical fleece, weighing about eight pounds, produces fifteen skeins of yarn. One skein contains approximately two hundred yards of yarn, on average, so that's three thousand yards of yarn, or the equivalent of 1.7 miles of knitting yarn from one fleece.

12 Roving is wool that has been run through a carding machine. A carding machine, called a carder, has many teeth that brush the wool fibers into roughly the same direction. Unlike combed top, however, roving fibers do not lay smoothly in the same direction, giving yarn spun from roving a fuzzier texture. When hand spinners spin roving into yarn, the yarn is said to have been spun "woolen style," and is called "woolen spun yarn."

Chapter 10

1   C. Taylor, "Navajo-Churro: America's First Sheep," Navajo-Churro Sheep Association, accessed Feb. 4, 2016, http://www.navajo-churrosheep.com/sheep.html.

2   Ibid.

3 General Orders No. 15; Head Quarters, Dept. of New Mexico, Santa Fe, N.M., June 15th, 1863. In *Lawrence Kelly, Navajo Roundup: Selected Correspondence of Kit Carson's Expedition against the Navajo, 1863–1865,* (Boulder, C): Pruett, 1970).

4 C. Taylor, "Navajo-Churro: America's First Sheep," Navajo-Churro Sheep Association, accessed Feb. 4, 2016, http://www.navajo-churrosheep.com/sheep.html.

5 Ibid.

Chapter 11

1 "About Marin Carbon Project," Marin Carbon Project, accessed November 12, 2015, http://www.marincarbonproject.org/about.

2 *Green Wool Facts: The Wool Industry & The Environment* (Brussels: International Wool Textile Organization, 2014), 18.

3 Ibid., 3. Note: Carbon remains sequestered in our sweaters for as long as we wear them, and until we compost them, at which point it enters the soil. Pure organic carbon makes up 50 percent of the weight of wool, higher than cotton (40 percent) or a wood pulp–derived, regenerated cellulosic fiber, such as viscose. Converted into CO_2 equivalents (CO_2-e), then, 1 kg of clean wool equates to 1.8 kilograms of CO_2-e stored in a durable, wearable form. Extending this concept, the global wool clip (the amount of wool sheared off of sheep each year) represents around 1.05 million tons of clean wool, equivalent to 1.9 million tons of CO_2-e, or 525,000 T of pure, atmosphere-derived carbon.

4 Ibid., 3.

5 Fibershed, "Carbon Farming: Increasing Fertility and Water Holding Capacity, Providing Solutions for Climate Change" (pamphlet from wool symposium, November 2014).

6 Jeffrey Creque, email message to author, October 8, 2016.

7 Full disclosure: I love my Birkenstocks, have numerous pairs, and practically live in them.

8 At the time of this writing, established carbon farm methods by USDA NRCS include converting land from conventional tillage to no till and reduced till methods; soil nutrient management via improved nitrogen fertilizer management, and/or replacing nitrogen fertilizer with soil amendments like manure and compost; conservation crop rotation; cover crops; stripcropping; mulching; combustion system improvement (improved fuel efficiency of farm equipment); herbaceous cover on cropland, including conservation cover when retiring marginal soils; full and partial conversion of cropland to forage and biomass plantings; herbaceous and/or vegetative wind barriers; riparian herbaceous cover; contour buffer strips, field borders, and filter strips; grassed waterways; woody cover on cropland and riparian forest buffer via tree and

shrub windbreak and shelterbelt establishment; hedgerow, multistory, and alley cropping; and, on grazing lands, range planting, silvopasture establishment on grazed grassland; restoring degraded rangeland with compost addition; prescribed grazing; land reclamation of abandoned and/or currently mined land; landslide treatment, and more.

9   "What Is Carbon?" *The Guardian*, February 3, 2011, http://www.theguardian.com/environment/2011/feb/03/carbon.

10   "Overview of Greenhouse Gases," US Environmental Protection Agency (EPA), accessed October 10, 2015, http://www3.epa.gov/climatechange/ghgemissions/gases.html.

11   *Green Wool Facts: The Wool Industry & The Environment* (Brussels: International Wool Textile Organization, 2014).

12   Jeffrey Creque, "Bare Ranch Carbon Farm Plan" (report prepared for Bare Ranch, Cedarville, California, Spring 2016), 1–62.

13   "Frequently Asked Questions," Carbon Cycle Institute, accessed October 10, 2015, http://www.carboncycle.org/faq/.

14   "Carbon Cycle," NASA Science, accessed October 10, 2015, http://science.nasa.gov/earth-science/oceanography/ocean-earth-system/ocean-carbon-cycle.

15   Fibershed, "Carbon Farming: Increasing Fertility and Water Holding Capacity, Providing Solutions for Climate Change" (pamphlet from wool symposium, November 2014).

16   Adam Chambers, Rattan Lal, and Keith Paustian, "Soil Carbon Sequestration Potential of US Croplands and Grasslands: Implementing the 4 per Thousand Initiative," *Journal of Soil and Water Conservation* 71 (2016): 3, 68A–74A, doi:10.2489/jswc.71.3.68A.

17   "Greenhouse Gas Equivalencies Calculator," US Environmental Protection Agency, accessed October 11, 2015, https://www.epa.gov/energy/greenhouse-gas-equivalencies-calculator.

18   Soil organic matter (SOM) in topsoil is approximately 50 percent carbon up to one foot in depth. According to John Wick of the Carbon Cycle Institute, increasing that 50 percent SOM number by just 1.6 percent across global agricultural lands would be sufficient to solve the problem of global warming. Other soil scientists offer more conservative predictions but believe strongly in the potential of soil carbon sequestration to reduce the threats and effects of global warming.

The central idea of carbon farming—also embodied in grazing practices like Allan Savory's Holistic Management—is to recreate natural grazing conditions, to not just mitigate but reverse the effects of climate change and desertification. Grazing animals move frequently, just as wild herds once did when forced to move on by predators. Wild, native Plains bison, for example, could not eat grasses beyond their point of natural recovery and plant cover remains to fertilize the land and sequester carbon. They ate, trampled manure and grass into the soil, and moved on. After their departure, new grass sprouted and the process repeated itself, absorbing ever more carbon in the process.

19 Jeffrey Creque, "Bare Ranch Carbon Farm Plan" (report prepared for Bare Ranch, Cedarville, California, Spring 2016), 1–62.

20 Richard Arnold, "Soil Survey: Past, Present, and Future," US National Resource Conservation Service, accessed October 7, 2016, http://www.nrcs.usda.gov/wps/portal/nrcs/detailfull/soils/survey/?cid=nrcs142p2_053369.

21 Jeffrey Creque, email message to author, October 8, 2016.

22 "Oregon Rancher Gary Bedortha Removes Juniper Trees to Create a Safe Haven for Sage Grouse," Sage Grouse Initiative, accessed October 7, 2016, http://www.sagegrouseinitiative.com/oregon-rancher-gary-bedortha-creates-safe-haven-sage-grouse-removing-juniper-trees/.

23 Conservation planners who want to incorporate greenhouse gas (GHG) impacts in their planning can use COMET-Farm, a qualitative ranking of conservation practices for carbon sequestration and GHG emission reduction developed by the US National Resource Conservation Service (NRCS).

24 "Healthy Soils Program," California Department of Food and Agriculture, accessed March 3, 2017, https://www.cdfa.ca.gov/oefi/healthysoils/.

25 *IPCC, 2014: Climate Change 2014: Synthesis Report.* Contribution of Working Groups I, II and III to the Fifth Assessment Report of the Intergovernmental Panel on Climate Change [Core Writing Team, R.K. Pachauri and L.A. Meyer (eds.)]. Geneva, Switzerland: IPCC.

Chapter 12

1 Peter Castagnetti, "The Kaos Sheep Outfit," accessed on October 17, 2016, https://vimeo.com/132899345.

2 Ibid.

3 Ibid.

4 Ann Thrupp, "'Green' Wine Market Trends: From Green Roots to Great Wines" (presentation prepared for Fetzer & Bonterra Vineyards Ecowinegrowing Symposium, July 2011).

5 Ibid.

6 Ibid.

7 Linda M. Wilson and Linda H. Hardesty, "Targeted Grazing with Sheep and Goats in Orchard Settings," in *Targeted Grazing: A Natural Approach to Vegetation Management and Landscape Enhancement*, ed. Karen Launchbaugh, John Walker, and Ron Daines (Englewood, CO: American Sheep Industry Association, 2006), 99–106.

8 Peter Castagnetti, "The Kaos Sheep Outfit," https://vimeo.com/132899345.

9 Linda M. Wilson and Linda H. Hardestry, "Targeted Grazing with Sheep and Goats in Orchard Settings," in *Targeted Grazing: A Natural Approach to Vegetation Management and Landscape Enhancement*, ed. Karen Launchbaugh, John Walker, and Ron Daines (Englewood, CO: American Sheep Industry Association, 2006), 99–106.

10 Ibid.

11 Ibid.

12 Ibid.

13 Ibid.

14 Peter Castagnetti, "The Kaos Sheep Outfit," https://vimeo.com/132899345.

Chapter 13

1 Michael Ryder, *Sheep & Man* (London: Duckworth, 1983), 406.

2 "Status and Threats," California's Coastal Prairies, SSU Center for Environmental Inquiry, accessed December 7, 2016, http://www.sonoma.edu/cei/prairie/management/threats.shtml.

3 Ibid.

4 Ibid.

5 At the time of this writing, a twenty-seven-year embargo on the import of live sheep and sheep embryos from the United Kingdom to the United States was still in place, but had the potential to change. The ban was originally put in place in 1989 in response to a crisis in transmissible spongiform encephalopathies (TSE), a group of rare, degenerative brain disorders characterized by tiny holes that give the brain a "spongy" appearance. The TSE variants that affect livestock are bovine spongiform encephalopathy (BSE), also known as mad cow disease, and scrapie, which affects sheep and goats.
Scrapie can persist in barns and soil for years and spread across farms. Entire flocks must be culled, and possibly all flocks in a given geographic area. Because of its persistence and risk of reinfection, sheep keepers may not be allowed to have sheep on their property for years. Both BSE and scrapie have the potential to affect humans, though there are no documented incidents of scrapie affecting humans.
For more information, please refer to the following sources: "Importation of Sheep, Goats, and Certain Other Ruminants," Federal Register, https://www.federalregister.gov/documents/2016/07/18/2016-16816/importation-of-sheep-goats-and-certain-other-ruminants;
H. Cassard et al. "Evidence for zoonotic potential of ovine scrapie prions." *Nature Communications* 5:5821(2014), doi: 10.1038/ncomms6821.

6   Peter Costa, "Small Is Beautiful to Lincoln Sheep Breeders," Wicked
    Local, August 19, 2010, http://www.wickedlocal.com/article/20100819/
    NEWS/308199246.

Chapter 15

1 Rebecca Burgess, *Harvesting Color: How to Find Plants and Make Natural Dyes*
    (New York: Artisan, 2011).
2   Liz Bowley, "Removal of Toxic Dyes from Wastewater," Environmental
    Science: Nano Blog, March 10, 2014, http://blogs.rsc.org/en/2014/03/10/
    removal-of-toxic-dyes-from-wastewater/?doing_wp_cron=1498345668.54347610
    47363281250000.
3   D. Ravi et al., "Effect of Textile Dye Effluent on Soybean Crop," *Journal of
    Pharmaceutical, Chemical and Biological Sciences* 2:2 (June–August 2014), 111–117.
4   "Industry Wastewater," in *Environmental Deterioration and Human Health*,
    edited by Abdul Malik, E. Grohmann E., and R. Akhtar (The Netherlands:
    Springer, 2014).
5   Rebecca Burgess, *Harvesting Color: How to Find Plants and Make Natural Dyes*
    (New York: Artisan, 2011).
6   Alissa Allen, "Regional Palettes: A Closer Look at
    Northern California Dye Mushrooms," Fibershed,
    January 12, 2014, http://www.fibershed.com/2014/01/12/
    regional-palettes-a-closer-look-at-northern-california-dye-mushrooms/.
7   Rebecca Burgess, *Harvesting Color: How to Find Plants and Make Natural Dyes*
    (New York: Artisan, 2011).
8   James Bitler, "Indigo," New Georgia Encyclopedia, accessed October 11, 2016,
    http://www.georgiaencyclopedia.org/articles/history-archaeology/indigo.
9   Deborah Netburn, "6,000-Year-Old Fabric Reveals Peruvians Were Dyeing
    Textiles with Indigo Long Before Egyptians," *Los Angeles Times*, September 16,
    2016.
10 Kristine Vejar, *The Modern Natural Dyer: A Comprehensive Guide to Dyeing Silk,
    Wool, Linen and Cotton at Home* (New York: Stewart, Tabori & Chang, 2015).
11 Amy DuFault, "On Makers Row: 8 Frequently Asked
    Questions about Natural Colors and Dyes," Botanical
    Colors, May 5, 2016, http://botanicalcolors.com/2016/05/05/
    on-makers-row-8-frequently-asked-questions-about-natural-colors-and-dyes/.
12 Ibid.
13 Nicholas Wenner and Matthew Forkin, "Indigo: Sources, Processes, and
    Possibilities for Bioregional Blue," Fibershed, June 2017, http://www.fiber-
    shed.com/wp-content/uploads/2017/08/indigo-sources-processes-possibili-
    ties-june2017.pdf.

14 Ibid., 10.

15 "Indigo," Fibershed, accessed January 16, 2018, http://www.fibershed.com/
    programs/fiber-systems-research/indigo/.

16 "Building a Compost Floor for the Japanese Indigo Process: Part 1," *A Verb for
    Keeping Warm,* January 13, 2012, https://www.averbforkeepingwarm.com/blogs/
    news/5182952-building-a-compost-floor-for-the-japanese-indigo-process-
    part-1.

17 Nicholas Wenner, "The Production of Indigo Dye from Plants," Fibershed,
    December 2017, http://www.fibershed.com/wp-content/uploads/2017/12/pro-
    duction-of-indigo-dye-dec2017.pdf.

Chapter 16

1 "Title 17: Commodity and Securities Exchanges," Electronic Code of
   Federal Regulations, accessed July 17, 2016, https://www.ecfr.gov/cgi-bin/
   ECFR?page=browse.

2 "What Is a DPO?," Economic Development and Financing Corporation
   (EDFC), accessed July 6, 2016, http://edfc.org/what-is-a-dpo/.

3 "Frequently Asked Questions: Direct Public Offering," Economic
   Development and Financing Corporation (EDFC), accessed July 6, 2016,
   http://edfc.org/faq/.

4 "Title 17," The Electronic Code of Federal Regulations, accessed July 6, 2016,
   https://www.ecfr.gov/cgi-bin/ECFR?page=browse.

5 "What Is a DPO?" Economic Development and Financing Corporation
   (EDFC), accessed July 6, 2016, http://edfc.org/what-is-a-dpo/.

Chapter 17

1   C.V. Ross, *Sheep Production and Management* (Upper Saddle River, NJ:
    Prentice Hall, 1989), 26–27.

Epilogue

1   Clare O'Toole, *The Roots of Basque Character and the First Diaspora to the
    United States,* accessed December 7, 2017, https://studentdev.jour.unr.edu/
    nevadabasque/who-are-the-basques/.

2   Cali Wool Beanie, The North Face, accessed December 17, 2017, https://www.
    thenorthface.com/shop/cali-wool-beanie-nf0a3586.

Index